D1256697

WRITINGS FOR A LIBERATION PSYCHOLOGY

Writings for a Liberation Psychology

Ignacio Martín-Baró

EDITED BY ADRIANNE ARON

AND SHAWN CORNE

Harvard University Press
Cambridge, Massachusetts
London, England
1994

This book is printed on acid-free paper, and its binding materials
have been chosen for strength and durability.

Library of Congress Cataloging-in-Publication Data
Martín-Baró, Ignacio.
Writings for a liberation psychology / Ignacio Martín-Baró ;
edited by Adrianne Aron and Shawn Corne.
p.   cm.
Translated from the Spanish.
Includes bibliographical references.
ISBN 0-674-96246-X (alk. paper)
1. Social psychology—Latin America.   2. Social psychology—
Central America.   3. Social Psychology.   I. Aron, Adrianne.
II. Corne, Shawn.   III. Title.
HM251.M2864   1994
302'.098—dc20
94-20987
CIP

Contents

Foreword by Elliot G. Mishler   *vii*

Note on the Translation   *xiii*

Introduction   *1*

I   *The Psychology of Politics and the Politics of Psychology*   *13*

1   Toward a Liberation Psychology   *17*
Translated by Adrianne Aron

2   The Role of the Psychologist   *33*
Translated by Adrianne Aron

3   Power, Politics, and Personality   *47*
Translated by Phillip Berryman

4   Political Socialization: Two Critical Themes   *68*
Translated by Adrianne Aron

5   The Political Psychology of Work   *84*
Translated by Cindy Forster

II   *War and Trauma*   *103*

6   War and Mental Health   *108*
Translated by Anne Wallace

7   War and the Psychosocial Trauma of Salvadoran Children   *122*
Translated by Anne Wallace

8   Religion as an Instrument of Psychological Warfare   *136*
Translated by Tod Sloan

9   The Psychological Value of Violent Political Repression   *151*
Translated by Anne Wallace

III   *De-ideologizing Reality*   *169*

10   "The People": Toward a Definition of a Concept   *173*
       Translated by Adrianne Aron

11   Public Opinion Research as a De-ideologizing Instrument   *186*
       Translated by Jean Carroll and Adrianne Aron

12   The Lazy Latino: The Ideological Nature of Latin   *198*
       American Fatalism
       Translated by Phillip Berryman

       Bibliography   *221*
       Complete Works of Ignacio Martín-Baró   *221*
       Works by Other Authors   *226*

       Acknowledgments   *241*

Foreword

ELLIOT G. MISHLER

Ignacio Martín-Baró dared speak truth to falsehood. His steadfast affirmation of fundamental human rights was a dangerous position in the "limit situation" of war and state-sponsored terror in El Salvador. He was in the end searched out by violence and assassinated by government soldiers in November 1989.

His "crime" was to align himself with the Salvadoran people in their collective resistance to oppression and their struggle for peace and justice. He had embraced the "preferential option for the poor," a central tenet of Liberation Theology. This was his stance as Jesuit, parish priest, and theologian. It was also the centerpoint of his work as a psychologist.

Adrianne Aron and Shawn Corne, the editors of this collection of his papers in psychology, tell us he was at work just moments before he was killed, "putting finishing touches on a manuscript." Although his work remains unfinished, it stands as a significant statement of how psychological theory and research might be transformed so as to realize their liberatory potential. With a deep sense of urgency, he calls upon us to develop a new praxis for psychology. We have much to learn from him. This book is part of his legacy, a resource for the living to continue with this task.

I met him less than a year before his death. I learned from him, was inspired by his example, and mourn him. In assessing his contribution to psychology, I cannot put aside my sense of personal loss. Nor can I respond to his work as if it were separate and insulated from the rest of his life— and his death. He would, I believe, view my difficulties with some satisfaction, and perhaps amusement. They acknowledge his criticism and suspicion of decontextualized, abstract, neutral analyses. He was stubbornly resistant to efforts to understand his work by fragmenting and compartmentalizing his different spheres of activity. A praxis of commitment lay at the core and gave unity to the multiplicity of his endeavors. Well aware of differences—in assumptions, aims, practices—between, for example, serving as a priest and doing research as a psychologist, he nonetheless viewed them as alternative opportunities to act on his basic convictions. His self-assigned task was to discover how each could be transformed and redirected to serve the fundamental aims of freedom and liberation.

The clarity, integrity, and unity of his sense of personal identity and his seriousness of purpose are among the strongest impressions I retain from our conversations in early 1989. By then, Martín-Baró's contributions to psychological theory and research were well known and influential in Central and South America. Although fluent in English, he wrote in Spanish, and his work was less accessible to U.S. psychologists and mental health professionals. A small but growing number, concerned about the mental health consequences of violence and war in Latin America and opposed to the U.S. government's support of oppressive regimes, had been learning about his work from his presentations at U.S. and international conferences in psychology.

Searching for ways to integrate our professional work and our political commitments, several of us in the Boston-Cambridge and San Francisco Bay areas—mental health workers, teachers, researchers—organized sister mental health subcommittees within our respective local chapters of the Committee for Health Rights in Central America (CHRICA). Our aim was to show solidarity with, provide help to, and develop collaborative projects with our colleagues in violence-torn countries of Latin America.

We invited Martín-Baró to visit us—the Boston-Cambridge committee—during one of his trips to the United States. There was much we wished to learn firsthand about what was happening in El Salvador and the psychological impact of the devastating, deadly war in his country. We also hoped to gain some understanding of how he was able to continue with his work in conditions where he was constantly at risk. He did not act like a man whose life had been threatened repeatedly and whose office had been bombed several times. Radiating energy and vitality, he expressed hope for the future within a realistically pessimistic view of the situation in El Salvador. He deflected our questions about his personal risks—they were no more, he implied, and perhaps less than those faced by all Salvadorans. Showing an unbounded and attentive interest in our lives and our work, he was eager to hear about the current state of U.S. psychology, about the latest developments in theory and research, and about our own projects.

The deep gravity of his interest was reflected in the seriousness of his fundamental question, to which he always returned: What could he learn that would be helpful to his own task of creating and applying a "psychology" in the service of the Salvadoran people's struggle for freedom and justice? This is not among the standard questions U.S. psychologists address to one another. The "liberatory" potential of our studies is not the typical criterion of grant review committees or journal editors. This does not mean he was uninterested in theories and methods—they were precisely what he wanted to hear about. But dialogue about them was not an abstract, academic exercise. Rather, it had to do with their broader and deeper meaning, that is, with their potential value for those resisting oppression and trying to transform the conditions of their lives.

Our discussions reflected—as do the opening chapters of this book—dissatisfaction with the current state of psychological theory and research. Martín-Baró's critical perspective, his view of the biases and limitations of standard models, grew out of his efforts to understand the subjective experience of the oppressed and traumatized people of El Salvador. Typically, the motives, behaviors, and personal characteristics of oppressed and marginalized people are studied, analyzed, and interpreted from the position of a presumably neutral, external observer. Their own voices are rarely heard, the particularities of their lives and circumstances are not examined, and they are pathologized and objectified. And it became clear to him that characterizations and interpretations based on such an approach serve the interests of the dominant class.

But critique was only the first step. Martín-Baró was always oriented toward possibilities, open to what could be, rather than constrained by what was. His firm belief in the possibility of a "liberatory psychology" pressed us to think about how we might transform our practices so that our work would be more relevant to that goal. He had already grappled with this problem, finding ways to pursue this task by reframing standard methods, such as public opinion surveys, and standard concepts in social psychology, such as attitude, identity, ideology, community. Grounding his approach in a critique of the field's "scientistic" framework—as ahistorical, individualistic, and universalistic—he gave these concepts new meaning by re-embedding them within the actual historical and social contexts of the Salvadoran people. Psychology had been constructed from the top down, reflecting the interests of those in power. His intent was to build a psychology from the bottom up, one in which central place would be given to the needs, aims, and experiences of the oppressed.

The papers selected by Adrianne Aron and Shawn Corne show us Martín-Baró at work. Living among the Salvadoran people, sharing their risks, entering into their collective discourse of resistance—he realized that the traumas of war and violence could not be fully understood by a theory rooted in the individual psyche, such as the medical model of post-traumatic stress disorder. Rather, he argued, we must begin with a recognition of this trauma as a pervasive and collective experience, rooted in the distortions of social relations and the disruptions of community life that are the products of an oppressive, terror-ridden society.

He applied this perspective in his studies of the impact on children of war and violence, one of his deepest and most pervasive concerns at the time of his death (Chapter 7). He proposed the concept of "psychosocial trauma" to replace the usual term, "psychic trauma." The latter emphasizes the acute, unexpected, individual nature of trauma and is inapplicable to the chronic, foreseeable, and collective nature of trauma experienced by Salvadoran children. His analysis focuses on problems of identity development within a system of social relations that are aberrant, alienating, and dehumanizing.

Children are faced with several "existential" dilemmas about how to position themselves with respect to war: action-flight, identity-alienation, polarization-tearing apart. There are no "creative" solutions to these dilemmas. Each choice—and choices must be made—marks the individual and is expressed in particular modes of psychological functioning. The task for psychologists, he concludes, is to do more than treat "post-traumatic stress disorder" as an individual mental health problem. More adequate resolutions to problems of identity development require efforts directed to restoring stable and trusting social relations and the strengthening of the community's capacity for collective action.

His analyses of political attitudes and ideologies, and of cultural stereotypes, follow a similar course. Their sources, he argues, are not to be found through examination of personality traits or individual motives. Rather, as in the stereotype of the "Lazy Latino" (Chapter 12) or the growth of evangelical religions (Chapter 8), their function must be understood in terms of how they serve the needs of people to survive as communities as they try to defend themselves and cope with situations of intolerable oppression. But their full understanding requires a further stage of analysis: We must also examine how, at the same time, these ideological positions serve the political and economic interests of dominant classes. From this perspective, progressive change is not an individual psychological task but a collective one requiring the restoration to the community of a "historical memory" as well as the development of popular forms of political organization and action.

He was clear about the implications of his partisanship, of grounding his psychological theorizing and research in an explicit choice of the "option for the poor." He viewed the reliance on neutrality and objectivity, the shibboleths of mainstream psychology, as reflecting the "scientistic" assumptions of the discipline. Are we any more "objective," he asked, if we implicitly accept the inequities in our society by refusing to acknowledge how they pervade and penetrate our concepts, theories, and methods? Unexamined, they slip insidiously into our analyses and interpretations. His proposed alternative is a psychology that is historical, does not abstract its "subjects" from their social and political contexts, is "nonindividualistic," and locates the sources of values, motives, and behaviors in the dialectical relations among persons, community, and society.

I have been trying, in this brief space, to convey a sense of what can be learned from Martín-Baró's work. Although his papers reawaken the pain of loss, they also evoke his presence. His clarity of thought, his commitment to humane values, his anger and sorrow about El Salvador are here. The title of the book resonates with the more familiar phrase "Liberation Theology." As I suggested earlier, this is not accidental, since the aims of that movement motivated his work as a psychologist as well as a Jesuit priest.

"Writings for," the other phrase in the title, captures the open-ended and unfinished nature of his work as well as its explicit directionality. His papers are meditations about the impact on individuals and communities of widespread, destructive, anti-human forces—economic exploitation, social injustice, political oppression, terror, war, violence. But they are meditations with a purpose; they are "for." First, they are for the Salvadoran people—the "pueblo," the community of oppressed campesinos with whose sufferings he identified and to whom he dedicated his life. His ideas are embedded in and elaborated through the detailed particulars of their lives and the impact on them of a history of state-sponsored violence.

Second, they are also "for" psychology. Without ever letting go of the specific Salvadoran context, he proposes a general conceptual framework for psychological theory and research, a new praxis for psychologists. He believed the development of a "liberatory psychology" was necessary if the field were to fulfill its promise of serving human needs, of providing tools with which people could transform their lives and rehumanize the world.

His "writings" invite us to continue the unfinished work, to take up the task—the dual and inseparable task of transforming our practices and our society. They also challenge us to align ourselves, as he did in El Salvador, with those struggling for equality and justice in our own country.

Note on the Translation

A collection of twelve essays written over a period of fifteen years by a single author, then converted into English by a half dozen translators, is a formidable editorial challenge. We have tried to respond to this challenge by striving not only for clarity, but for consistency in the prose, and for phrasing that captures Martín-Baró's sensitivity to language and style.

Regrettably, the English language offers no graceful translation for terms such as the Portuguese *conscientização* or the Spanish *desideologizar* or *de-salienación*. We have used the Spanish *concientización* because its seven syllables do at least have the virtue of being phonetically friendly. And we have used the terms *de-ideologize* and *de-alienate* in spite of their clumsiness, for the clarity of meaning they manage to convey. The mechanics of language have forced us to anglicize some terms, such as *conscienticizing*, while flight from the problematic "American" has driven us to the still problematic *North American*, when what is really meant is "person who lives in the United States," or *estadounidense*. We ask forbearance for these choices. Certain other terms, like the Spanish *campesino*, that do not have an exact translation, we have welcomed into English parlance in acknowledgment of their natural richness.

In most cases, when meanings may be in question, Martín-Baró provides clarification along the way, as for instance with *concientización*, which is fully elucidated in Chapter 2. The term *common sense*, however, warrants some introduction, lest it be confused with the common wisdom we receive uncritically from our predecessors, or equated with the dependable common sense that allows us to deduce the meaning of things based on our prior experience and knowledge of the world. What Martín-Baró finds in El Salvador (and we must be watchful for elsewhere) is a common sense that cannot be trusted because it has been infiltrated by ideology. Based on personal experience and therefore seemingly valid as a tool for interpreting the world, it is in fact a cruel deception, leading us to misconstrue our own reality and to see ourselves through a distorted "ideologically correct" internal lens. When ideology has penetrated our thought structures, we can neither trust nor learn from our own experience. Thus, not until common sense has been de-ideologized can it be a beneficial guide for action. Absent a de-ideologizing process, we may be condemned to interpret the world through the eyes of the oppressor.

Introduction

Ignacio Martín-Baró never ceased speaking out against injustice. His last words, heard above the din of the high-powered rifles firing at Ignacio Ellacuría, Rector of the Universidad Centroamericana José Simeón Cañas (UCA), were "This is an injustice!" It was the middle of the night, November 16, 1989. It had been quiet on the UCA campus. Until the soldiers stormed into the Jesuit residence, only Martín-Baró had been awake, putting some finishing touches on a manuscript. Forced out to a courtyard, the scholar was to be left there as a crumpled corpse, together with Ellacuría, four of their Jesuit brothers, and their housekeeper and her teenage daughter, who had come to stay with the priests thinking they would be safe there. The U.S.-trained troops of the elite Atlacatl Battalion had aimed their weapons at the Jesuits' heads and blown their brains out. This was more than a mass murder, it was an attempted sophiacide.

Until the massacre of the Jesuits, North America had taken little notice of Martín-Baró, though he was well known elsewhere in the Americas. Of the dozens of essays, books, articles, and reviews listed in the bibliography at the back of this book, only three short pieces had appeared in English. As can already be seen from the scant works translated into English since his death, most notably the several selections in the excellent book edited by John Hassett and Hugh Lacey, *Towards a Society that Serves Its People: The Intellectual Contribution of El Salvador's Murdered Jesuits* (1991), Martín-Baró's writings constitute a major force in the field of social theory. His analysis of contemporary social problems, including the problem of the failure of the social sciences to address those problems, permits us to understand not only the substance of his contribution to social thought but also his life and, lamentably, his death. His analysis helps us to see why it took an act of such "lavish barbarity"—as the Jesuit Provincial for Central America called the assassination—to bring Martín-Baró to the attention of North American centers of higher learning. It also helps us to see why this, the first collection in English devoted exclusively to his work, was produced not by academics but by psychologists of the Committee for Health Rights in Central America, a group that labored throughout the 1980s to expose the realities of El Salvador during the time Martín-Baró was writing.

"In your country," Martín-Baró once quipped to a North American colleague, "it's publish or perish. In ours, it's publish *and* perish." The prologue of his widely used social psychology text tells us the book's chapters "were written in the heat of events, and in fear of the police breaking into the house; following the assassination of a colleague, and under the physical and moral impact of the bomb that destroyed the office where they were being composed" (1983a). All through the decade, colleagues, students, friends, and parishioners were being murdered, "disappeared," imprisoned, tortured, and raped. Many had to renounce or hide their convictions in order to survive the campaigns of state terrorism. The Church was particularly targeted for persecution; not only priests and nuns, but the archbishop himself had been assassinated. "Be a patriot, kill a priest," read flyers posted by the right wing. With a certain melancholy that outrage kept from turning into despair, Martín-Baró elected to remain in that "limit situation" and fulfill his commitment to the people of El Salvador.

We who read him in English translation may find it remarkable that he decided to stay in El Salvador instead of returning to Valladolid, where he was born, or to Chicago, where he earned his Ph.D., or Frankfurt or Bogotá, where he had studied and taught—or for that matter, to any randomly chosen Jesuit institution beyond the reach of the forces of repression. Isn't it interesting, Martín-Baró would have asked, that the unschooled campesinos of El Salvador understood his decision perfectly, while to the educated people of North America it seems a riddle?

Martín-Baró craved to understand the realities of the Salvadoran people, seeing them as paradigmatic of the whole of Latin America, and more generally, of oppressed peoples everywhere. If by living inside that world and grasping those realities he could interpret them for others, he would accomplish, by that very act, an important contribution to human knowledge. Amid the Salvadoran government's ongoing attacks, and as a specific target some six times before the final attempt on his life, he saw an opportunity to achieve a praxis consistent with his ideals.

But how does one even stay alive under such conditions, let alone think, analyze, write, and do creative work? Martín-Baró solved this dilemma by immersing himself in the situation in El Salvador, which afforded him a superb vantage point for understanding the psychological dimensions of political repression. Like Bruno Bettelheim, who preserved his own mental health in the death camps of Nazi Germany by assigning himself the task of observing and analyzing the psychological effects of the extreme situation, Martín-Baró kept himself whole by converting every atrocity and every loss, but also every act of heroism and sacrifice, into an object lesson in the study of human behavior.

In this sense, psychology was his anchor, holding him fast in a storm of repression. He took psychology very seriously: dignifying it, scolding it, praising and challenging it, having no illusions about its devotion to trivial pursuits, but no doubt about its potential to grow up and make a serious contribution to human knowledge.

Martín-Baró looked upon the "young science" as one might behold a problem child, and to understand it he approached it as he did all problems, with an eye to history, so that it could be examined vis-à-vis the matrix of social structures in which it is embedded. He noted that psychology had from its earliest moments modeled itself after the natural sciences, dressing up in lab coats and collecting instruments, to play the part of a discipline investigating truth. In this respect it was similar to the ruling elites of Latin America, who covet goods and styles produced in the United States and think that by importing designer labels—whether from a boutique or a university—they can prove they are "developed." Psychology had become infatuated with methods and measurements, he observed, and blind to many of the structural determinants of individual and group life, including its own allegiances to the privileged and powerful. With its historical mission to guide people toward a critical understanding of themselves, psychology had endeavored to help people enjoy a "normal" life. But it had cared little for the fact that self-knowledge requires a comprehension of social experience, and it had ignored the fact that for large segments of the human family "normal" is not always so normal.

The proper role of psychology, Martín-Baró thought, was to assist people in understanding their own realities through a reflection of their own social experience. He noted that in El Salvador what was broadcast and printed in the government-controlled media had almost nothing to do with everyday life. The vast majority of the population lived in abject poverty and were suffering some of the worst human rights violations known in the modern world, but the television was playing soap operas from South America and the papers carried stories about the beloved armed forces, who were working to wipe out communist subversion. The people's lack of information about the world they were inhabiting, and their inability to see the truth of that world reflected back to them by the communications media, had not been defined as a problem by psychology's established societies and organizations.

By Martín-Baró's criteria, it would have been a very useful project for psychologists to have documented the effects on the mental health of the Salvadoran people of the news reports engineered by the Salvadoran government on November 16, 1989, after the army finished its massacre at the UCA. These reports explained how government forces were looking for the "communist guerrillas of the FMLN" (the Farabundo Martí National Liberation Front) who had killed six Jesuits and two of their helpers earlier that day in an attempt to "destabilize democracy." Statements appeared in the newspaper by the National Association of Private Enterprise, which congratulated the armed forces for their professionalism and their success in avoiding greater loss of life. The private enterprise people beseeched the press to be objective and avoid confusion, because the enemies of the homeland "take advantage" of such things (Instituto de Estudios Centroamericanos, 1990, p. 35).

No study was launched to find out how these reports affected the Salvadoran psyche, just as studies are not conducted on the effects of press censorship and disinformation on the North American collective psyche, though surely these practices have an impact and would warrant investigation. Psychologists in the United States have not taken such matters as high-priority concerns. The American Psychological Association, it is true, had a symposium in its 1990 convention program honoring its member who was slain in El Salvador, and APA does seek accurate press coverage for topics considered important to psychology. But what topics are these, and by what criteria are they judged to be significant? At the 1990 APA convention, new research on the kind of men women find attractive was featured as an important item for the press. Noam Chomsky's presentation on the sociopolitical meaning of the assassination of Ignacio Martín-Baró was not.

Martín-Baró argued that psychology has created a fictionalized and ideologized image of what it means to be human, based on its own ahistoricism and bias toward individualism. This false image presents the individual as bereft of history, community, political commitment, and social loyalties. A still shot, it captures a moment and calls that Us, making it seem that what we are during some frozen, circumscribed moment is all that we can or will ever be. In this distorted picture, he asserted, we cannot hope to comprehend ourselves and our realities, but what is perhaps worse, we are likely to accept what it says about us as right and immutable, for once the existing stereotypical order is consecrated as natural, what you see is what you get: women are weak, campesinos are fatalistic, men attract women or they do not; North Americans are rich and can eat, Central Americans are poor and cannot.

Psychology, he thought, erases the very real things of life that make up what we are as human beings. It acknowledges no fundamental differences between a student at MIT and a Nicaraguan campesino, between John Smith from Peoria, Illinois, and Leonor Gonzales from Cuisnahuat, El Salvador. With that denial as its working hypothesis, it simply ignores the social and economic conditions that shape the daily lives of these individuals and their communities; structural problems are reduced to personal problems and factored out as individual differences. So long as all remain equal before the psychologist, there is no need to examine the disparate historical factors that account for people's differing subjective and objective experiences of reality. Thus, the final destination of psychology's mission, a mission that set out with such good intentions toward self-discovery and a normal life, is a place where people are befuddled, belittled, homogenized, and left on their own to deal with their social oppression.

Martín-Baró could see from his special vantage point of the limit situation unquantifiable realities—things such as commitment, solidarity, hope, courage, collective virtues—that are only visible, only possible, when people act in reference to *others,* a reference point that psychology has seldom adopted. If he could see such amazing human characteristics, he knew, so could other psychologists, by expanding their discipline's horizon to look beyond the individual in isolation.

Even on its own side of the frontier, he claimed, psychology sees only part of what is there. It focuses so intensely on the individual, and yet it misses what has been obvious at least since Aristotle: that human beings are political animals. Martín-Baró's reflections on the inhibition of the formation of political identity in a climate of fear show very clearly the limitations of a perception that excludes the political dimension of human life from the list of things worthy of investigation. He was able to demonstrate that a critical piece of the self suffers damage when political expression is suppressed or forced into narrow, ego-dystonic channels. His attention was at all times on both sides of the frontier.

A psychology that could understand truth in a historical context, and could push out its horizons to encompass previously unseen phenomena, would already be well on the way to a new destination. It would have begun a revision of some of the most basic assumptions in psychological thought and moved its perspective beyond its previous borders. Still, this would not be enough. It would also need a new praxis, committed to the people who have hitherto been ignored—the popular majorities as they are called in Latin America, the poor and disenfranchised as we might call them in the United States. A praxis such as that could furnish psychology with a new way of thinking that conceives of truth not as a simple reflection of data but as a task at hand: "not an account of what *has been done,* but of what *needs to be done.*" Moreover, psychologists would discover in the popular majorities truths of human potential unimaginable to an Abraham Maslow.

Drawing on Paulo Freire's concept of *concientización,* the awakening of critical consciousness, Martín-Baró argued that if psychologists do not develop a critical consciousness that will move them toward a new praxis, they will never be able to make a meaningful contribution to the real problems of the day, which are the problems of human liberation. At the UCA, the Jesuit faculty sought elucidation of the national reality through the principles of liberation theology, and concepts of liberation were integrated into the curricula of all the various disciplines. Hence Martín-Baró's efforts to infuse psychology as a theoretical and practical endeavor with the spirit of liberation both fed and drew nourishment from work being carried on in other fields. When he described himself as living in a limit situation, he was borrowing the concept from Ignacio Ellacuría, the rector of the university. Ellacuría, a theologian, had himself borrowed it from the German philosopher Karl Jaspers, though he found it necessary to transpose Jaspers's individualistic concept into a social key to tune it to the

Salvadoran reality. Ellacuría recognized in 1969 that lawful procedures for maintaining the country's structural injustice could no longer work, and that, inevitably, the power elites would resort to illegal violence and repression to protect their interests. At this critical juncture, he saw basic problems, which people had sought to ignore, emerging in high relief, precipitating a mobilization of the forces of evil, but giving impulse also to positive forces not previously evident. Those positive forces, springing forth vigorously, were challenging the meaning of people's whole existence, and flooding that existence with light, "so much so that it is in these situations and only in them that we grasp our true being" (Ellacuría, 1969, p. 97).

In speaking of himself as living in a limit situation, Martín-Baró meant that he stood, alongside the people of El Salvador, at an important boundary that marked the limits of human possibility: limits not in the sense of an end of possibility; limits rather as markers of the place where all possibilities begin. This is not the division line between being and nothingness; it is the frontier which separates *being* from *being more*.

What was so impressive to him about the Salvadoran popular majorities in their struggle—an impression available to him only because he was with them in that struggle—was their steadfast belief in a future of peace and justice, and their certainty that they themselves could bring it about. The Co-Madres whose children were disappeared and killed and whose offices were repeatedly bombed, but who kept denouncing the crimes; the campesinos whose crops and houses were burned and who were driven into exile, but who returned to repopulate destroyed villages (one of which now carries the name of Ignacio Martín-Baró); the workers in the human rights offices and the leaders of labor unions and student organizations, who buried their martyred colleagues and then took over their jobs so that the work could continue; the refugees who fled to the United States with the death squads at their heels, to live below the poverty line in urban barrios, but from their meager incomes continued to support relatives at home; the young woman, gang raped by government soldiers but willing to risk death to denounce her attackers on national television; the clandestine bands of psychologists and physicians who attended to the tortured although it was strictly forbidden to do so—all these heroic people and their popular virtues showed Martín-Baró the Salvadoran people's "tremendous faith in the human capacity to change the world, and their hope for a tomorrow that keeps being violently denied to them." He was shown the kinds of things that unfold in "limit situations," but cannot be explained by the prevailing scientism of psychology.

He saw the transformative character of such actions and dared to immerse both himself and his chosen profession in the process of *posibilitar,* making possible. With every resource he could muster, he applied his energies to the task of liberation.

Like any of us with a praxis committed to the people, Martín-Baró had to find ways within his particular context to apply his professional skills. Unlike most of us, though, he faced a Byzantinely complex and dangerous context. In situations like that it helps to have a genius for devising creative solutions.

El Salvador presented a formidable challenge to psychology. Martín-Baró rose to meet it. Psychology teaches that people have to be able to draw accurate conclusions about themselves and their world, but the objective Salvadoran reality was that the government projected false images, thus confusing people and clouding the issues. Further, since most people had so internalized the terror of the terrorist state that they were afraid to seek information from one another, and since many, having been told for so long that they were too ignorant to understand anything, had lost confidence in themselves, the information had to come from the people, themselves. The challenge, then, was to reflect back to people their own knowledge and experience, their history and their suffering. With spies everywhere, this would have to be undertaken very carefully, for any inquiry that smacked of discontent could lead to arrest, torture, and death.

Psychology's conventional praxis could hardly grasp, let alone combat, the problem. It would see the whole structure of repression as irrelevant, for if John Smith in Peoria could keep in touch with reality, why not Leonor Gonzales? A praxis of commitment taught that the Salvadorans' difficulty in figuring out what was real was not an individual problem or one wrought by nature, but rather a social problem with a human signature on the blueprints of its design. But it was not enough to understand that. The point, Martín-Baró wrote, echoing a familiar line, "is not simply to understand the world, but to change it."

The task at hand was to take what was impossible—the ability of the people to trust their knowledge of what is real—and, in the midst of the distortions, the closed communications, and the repression, convert that impossibility into a *possibility*. It could be done; the Leonor Gonzaleses had proved that the boundaries were passable. How could existing knowledge be critically revised so as to be adapted to the needs of the people? How to put knowledge into the service of human liberation?

In a limit situation a curious logic can emerge. Given that psychology has always been partial to figures and measurement because those are the trademarks of science, and given that Latin America has always followed the fashions of the United States, believing that this could vanquish, or at least disguise, backwardness, and given that Salvadorans are in desperate need of information about themselves, because what is available to them is inaccurate and debilitating—is it not an embarrassment that in all the history of El Salvador there has never been a public opinion poll, when such surveys are *de rigueur* in North America? And is it not fitting that the chair of the UCA's psychology department—a professor educated at the University of Chicago—develop such polls?

The government was delighted with Ignacio Martín-Baró's proposal for a University Institute of Public Opinion, which he, the only doctoral-level psychologist in the country, would head. It suited the vanities of the ruling powers, giving them something progressive and scientific to show off to their fellow Latin Americans. And it would please their sponsors in Washington as well, who were getting restless about human rights violations and needed a sweetener to keep the money flowing. The only stipulation was that the military high command be shown the contents of each survey before it was conducted—a demand that Martín-Baró simply ignored.

People were of course afraid to answer some of the questions in the Institute's polls. But Martín-Baró the social psychologist knew how to make a statistical analysis of the refusals, and could report that whereas 40 percent of the rich feel free to express their opinions in public, the figure drops to under 20 percent for the poor. When the government claimed that the people were opposed to a dialogue with the FMLN, the Institute's polls proved otherwise. If anyone was so misguided as to think that television novellas of middle class life had anything to do with the Salvadoran reality, they could learn from the Institute's publications that 38.4 percent of the country's urban population in 1987 had a monthly family income of less than 45 U.S. dollars, with more than half of that group having no income whatsoever. And, in direct contradiction to claims of improvements in human rights, the polls gathered clear evidence that government soldiers practiced systematic sexual abuse of women in the countryside. Martín-Baró found in survey research a powerful tool for de-ideologizing reality.

Using the techniques and skills of his profession, and a little imagination, Martín-Baró found ways to put psychology in the service of human liberation. He challenged the Official Lie and disclosed to the Salvadoran people, and to anyone else who would listen, the realities of Salvadoran life, at a time when the absence of that information represented a powerful form of oppression. He could not be certain when he embarked on a project that it would indeed serve the purpose for which it was intended— no one could. But he could be sure that it was consistent with that purpose, and he could look for results. When he sent to press a 130-page book consisting entirely of charts and statistics (1987a) and it became a best-seller overnight, he knew!

Martín-Baró's forte was not statistics but words; his best form was the essay in which he brought theoretical reflections to bear on empirical data or vice versa. The works collected here follow that representative format, and the selection attempts to convey the breadth of his prolific writings. His interests were wide-ranging but disciplined; everything he wrote inquired into matters that directly touched people's lives. He looked at the effects of the civil war on the country's children, the effects of unemployment on the adults, the effects of female stereotypes on women, the effects of liberation theology on religious practice, the effects of solidarity on morale. He was thoroughly eclectic, and in this sense completely non-ideological. He borrowed as freely from Marx as from Jesus, as easily from Freire as from Freud, as confidently from Leonor Gonzales as from Harold Lasswell. Perhaps this was the characteristic that explains why people trusted him, even in the 1980s in El Salvador, where people sometimes complained that their own shadows were traitorous, frightening them on the street.

Martín-Baró's time was the time of cold war in global politics and hot war in El Salvador. But his analysis is cogent to more than a particular situation, place, or historical period. His insight that thought must be rooted in history enabled him to understand phenomena that for some people did not become evident until after the dissolution of the Soviet Union, which he did not live to see. He knew, for example, that the doctrine of national security, used by the United States to justify intervention in Central America, was not simply a piece of the East-West struggle being played out in the cold war, but was also a replaceable cover for the more stable motive of the United States, of hegemony in the hemisphere at any price. He was able to understand also that so long as conditions of structural injustice obtained, as they would if the United States persisted with its agenda, political violence would continue, and escalate, with the repression becoming ever more severe. The lesson in Martín-Baró's analysis is that wherever and whenever structural conditions are such that people are denied the minimal necessities for a human life, those conditions will beget resistance, which will be countered by repression, and this, when it becomes excessive, begets the psychological damage of trauma and fear. From his critical watchtower of the limit situation he was able not only to see and describe but to sound a warning.

Martín-Baró appreciated very well the separate historical and structural circumstances that make it difficult for John Smith of Peoria to comprehend the realities of state terrorism, but he also understood that John Smith and others in the United States know, or have the capacity to know, and certainly the responsibility to demand to know, the part their own government has played in fostering state terrorism in the world. Furthermore, they have the capacity to explore the realities of the disenfranchised of their own country, and to identify the structural features of their society that explain why the disenfranchised must exist. They have the duty to ask, What are the predictable consequences of this injustice? They have the opportunity to reframe the questions being posed in their classrooms, academic departments, and communities, and to dare to insist on addressing what they really know needs attention. They have the security of doing all that without fear of the military breaking into their bedrooms in the middle of the night. But that security does not come with a lifetime guarantee; the forces working on behalf of human liberation know that, and that is why they—working nearly alone—labor to safeguard it.

What Martín-Baró urges is that we consider whether our work is a true ordering of our own priorities, as compared with the default order of the status quo. If it contains truth, he reminds us, it has permission to be more than a simple reflection of data; it can become an account of what *needs to be done*. It can seek to make a real contribution to human liberation. It may even define our own version of a limit situation, marking the place where all possibilities begin and being starts to transform into being more.

I

The Psychology of Politics and the Politics of Psychology

Between 1985 and 1989, when the essays of this section were written, Martín-Baró was deeply immersed in the theory and practice of the liberation psychology he espoused. He was based at the UCA, administering the university as academic vice-rector and chair of the psychology department, as well as teaching, writing, directing the National Institute for Public Opinion Research (which he founded in 1986), and serving as vice president of SIP, the Interamerican Psychological Society. As village priest of Jayaque, he was making frequent trips to the *campo*, offering the sacraments and sharing intimately in the lives and struggles of his parishioners, who sometimes came to see him in San Salvador, where they were ushered into his office ahead of the many others who sought his attention. At the Jesuit residence he relaxed with his brothers, playing the Spanish guitar he loved and scolding the housekeeper for working too hard. When he could, he traveled, not only for the intellectual exchange with students and teachers in Latin America (where he was in demand as a speaker), but because he thought that high international visibility of the UCA faculty would "make it harder for them to kill us."

He was also editing a journal, the *Revista de Psicología*, a successor to the *Boletín de Psicología* he had founded in 1982. Four of the five essays in this section were published in the *Revista*, which, under his direction, addressed topics pertinent to the problems of Latin America and strove to influence Latin American psychologists to attend more earnestly to those problems. Those psychologists were his principal audience, but when we read his work it becomes clear that his message applies equally well to psychologists and social scientists elsewhere. The myopic view described in Chapter 2 as characterizing our perception of the Third World could as easily describe social scientists' view of their own society in the United States. Martín-Baró hoped to correct that nearsightedness by introducing a new lens, a new vision.

What would psychosocial processes look like, he asks in Chapter 1, as seen from the point of view of the dominated instead of that of the dominator? He mentions the unemployed, the illiterate, the marginalized, the people selling odds and ends in the marketplace, the people living in the town dump, in cardboard huts on haciendas—drawing for us a picture of conditions in El Salvador. If we shift the map just a bit, it is not hard to visualize men pushing supermarket carts on city streets, women eating out of dumpsters, families sleeping in doorways, or people walking with bags collecting aluminum cans, hoping to make a dollar. Following Martín-Baró we might wonder, What do such things as mental health, human development, motivation, and power relationships look like through their eyes? Can we understand, if our perspective comes from a well-supplied classroom or a handsome private office? Are we motivated to understand? Would it help if more Third World work in psychology and the social sciences were available in English translation?

"Power, Politics, and Personality" (Chapter 3) was never published in Spanish, possibly because it was not considered finished. In a discussion of political psychology Martín-Baró opens the theme to be developed at length in Chapter 4: what constitutes political behavior. He argues that it has less to do with the character of a specific *act* or *person,* and more to do with a complex constellation of power relations, often very subtle. Without denying the importance of idiosyncratic characteristics of the players in a political situation (the aspect favored by psychology, with its individualist bias), he expands the picture to look at unequal resources and conflicting class interests. Lest psychologists be left wondering what relevance this has to them or their discipline, he states clearly that psychology in Latin America (but again the map can tilt without harm of distortion) is tied too tightly to the ruling classes.

This attachment to the ruling classes is further elaborated in Chapter 5, where Martín-Baró proposes a radical solution to the sorry predicament of organizational psychologists, who promote the alienation of labor by serving the interests of industry. Pointing out that where we stand determines what we see and what we define as a problem, he suggests that if these psychologists were to observe production from the stance of the motivated but unemployed worker—if they were to see labor and unemployment historically and socially as exploitative processes, they would then be able to take empowerment as one of their goals and the active and organized participation of workers as one of their principles. In other words, psychology has no necessary mandate to serve the ruling classes; it can also be put to work for human liberation.

Martín-Baró's ideas for industry have obvious relevance to the more advanced societies, where unemployment and alienation are perennial problems. But in the advanced societies, proposed applications that threaten a scientific stance can encounter a particularly fierce opponent, for "scientistic mimicry" in an "advanced" society involves the imitation of an advanced science—which today happens to be the science of genetics. In genetics, using Martín-Baró's cautionary approach, we may detect the warning signs of new justifications for ignoring the social and historical circumstances that affect human conduct and people's location in the social order. If such phenomena as criminal behavior, aggression, and mental illness can be found to have a genetic basis, the reasoning might go, then they are not *social* problems after all, and no energy need be spent on social interventions to forestall them. (Recall the dismantling of Head Start programs in the 1970s after scientific studies claimed to have found that blacks are born with low IQ.) With language that refers to individuals as "chronically unemployed" or "unfit" for anything but entry-level jobs, we can expect to find a science that has no place on its agenda for such things as empowerment and participation. Such a science is more likely to seek validations of the same kinds of stereotypes that Martín-Baró exposed as spurious.

In recommending new horizons and a new praxis for the discipline of psychology, Martín-Baró hoped to shift both the point of view and the concrete consequences of social research, to place them in the service of humankind; his motive for attacking the ivory tower was to liberate the minds imprisoned in it. In Chapter 4, the most academic of the essays in this section, he shows how careful study of empirical and theoretical work can allow us not only to critique that work and discover its embedded thought structures but also to reflect on our own lives vis-à-vis those structures and possibly arrive at novel ways of thinking about the topics we are analyzing. His critique of socialization theory concedes, for instance, that there is some value in looking at political socialization through acts of flag-waving and voting, as is customarily done, but it occurs to him that we might learn more about the system to which people have been socialized (and by extension, do more with that knowledge) by observing their standard of living, noting how they spend their time, and finding out what kinds of things they enjoy doing.

This deceptively simple observation invites thought about the political socialization of the analysts themselves, and how it might resemble or differ from that of their subjects. It invites thought about matters not directly addressed in the essay: the deep divisions between the genders, between whites and people of color, between North Americans and people of other nationalities—in short, the experiences and outlooks that promote or impede understanding, trust, and common purpose, and that have to be considered when we look at people's lives, at social problems, and at relationships between individuals, groups, and societies. In particular, it invites thought about how power is distributed and exercised (the topic of Chapter 3), and what we ourselves can do about it (the theme of Chapter 2).

What becomes clear when we begin to apply Martín-Baró's ideas on liberation psychology to a U.S. context is that there are in fact deep fissures in our own social structure, carrying profound consequences for individual and social psychology but receiving very little attention from psychologists or other social scientists. As people trying to understand the world, it behooves us to acknowledge those divides. Toward the end of understanding human behavior and promoting humanizing institutions, we must try to understand ourselves and others in history, as social beings subject to social forces. If these are our ambitions, Martín-Baró argues, we must acquire a consciousness that will permit us to go beyond the limits imposed by our socialization and the boundaries set by our professional fields. The articles of Part I propel these ambitions into action.

1

Toward a Liberation Psychology

TRANSLATED BY ADRIANNE ARON

Psychology's Social Contribution in Latin America

Taken as a whole, psychology's contribution as science and as praxis to the history of the peoples of Latin America is extremely weak. To be sure, psychologists have not failed to concern themselves with the great problems of underdevelopment, dependency, and oppression that burden our peoples, but when it comes down to application, these concerns have often had to be channeled through a personal political commitment at the edges of the discipline, for the schemata of psychology break down when we try to use them to respond to the needs of the people.

I am not referring only to social psychology, whose crisis of meaning has been a much discussed theme in the past decade. I am referring to psychology as a whole: theoretical and applied, individual and social, clinical and educational. My thesis is that Latin American psychology, save for a few exceptions, has not only remained servilely dependent when it has needed to lay out problems and seek solutions, but has stayed on the sidelines of the great movements and away from the distresses of the peoples of Latin America.

When one tries to name some Latin American contribution to the fund of universal psychology, the "social technology" of Jacobo Varela (1971) bears mentioning, as does the psychoanalytical thought of Enrique Pichon-Rivière of Argentina. Both deserve all our respect, and I would not want to minimize their contribution. Nevertheless, it is noteworthy that Varela's work was published originally in English and follows the line of North American attitude studies—as if a universal contribution by a Latin American required a surrender of the writer's origins and identity. And Pichon-

Rivière's works, it is sad to note, are still scarcely known outside of Argentina.

Possibly, Latin American contributions with the most vigor and social impact can be found where psychology has given a hand to other areas of social science. What seems to me without doubt the most significant of such cases is Paulo Freire's conscienticized literacy method, growing out of the fertile mix of education with psychology, philosophy, and sociology. The now well accepted concept of the awakening of critical consciousness (concientización) joins the psychological dimension of personal consciousness with its social and political dimension, and makes manifest the historical dialectic between knowing and doing, between individual growth and community organization, between personal liberation and social transformation (Freire, 1971, 1978). But, above all, the awakening of critical consciousness constitutes a historical response to Latin America's lack of the word—both the personal and the social word. It involves more than the possibility of people reading and writing the alphabet; it opens the possibility of their being able to read about themselves and write their own history. Sadly, despite the magnitude of Freire's contribution, little critical study is devoted to his work, especially when compared with the time and energy devoted to contributions as trivial as some of the so-called learning theories or some of the cognitive models so much in fashion today.

The paucity of the contribution of Latin American psychology is best appreciated when compared with other branches of intellectual endeavor. In sociology, for example, the theory of dependency has been an original effort to explain underdevelopment without recourse to the "Protestant Ethic" that casts our Latin American cultures in a derogatory light. The rich contribution of our novelists is another example. It would not be an exaggeration to say that one learns considerably more about the psychology of the peoples of Latin America by reading a novel by García Márquez or Vargas Llosa than by reading our technical works on character and personality. And, with a force much greater than our analysis and psychological prescriptions for modernization and social change, liberation theology has been able both to reflect and to stimulate the recent historical struggles of the marginalized masses.

In contrast to Saxon culture, Latin culture tends to place great importance on personal characteristics and interpersonal relations. In a country like El Salvador, almost all problems, from the biggest to the smallest, are taken to the president of the republic, and he bears the responsibility for their resolution. He is called upon to deal with matters of war as well as quarrels between neighbors, to stimulate economic recovery in the country as well as to shut down an indiscreet brothel located next to a school (see Martín-Baró, 1973c). In this cultural context that tends to personalize and even psychologize all processes, psychology has a vast field for exerting its influence. Yet, instead of helping tear down the edifice of common sense that in our culture both obscures and justifies the interests of the powerful by representing their techniques of control as character traits, Latin American psychology subscribes to the reigning psychologism either by action or by omission. It has even taken the principal categories of Freire's conscienticized literacy and put them in the service of the system, by divesting them of their essential political dimension and turning them into purely psychological categories. Now, with the increasing subjectification of its main foci, psychology continues to feed the cultural psychologism, offering it as a true "ideology of exchange" (Deleule, 1972). In our case, psychologizing has served, directly or indirectly, to strengthen the oppressive structures, by drawing attention away from them and toward individual and subjective factors.

Our effort here is not to establish a balance in Latin American psychology, in part because it still remains for it to develop beyond its partiality to quantitative data (see, for example, Ardila, 1982, 1983; Díaz-Guerrero, 1984; Whitford, 1985). Given what psychology deals with, we must ask ourselves whether, with the tools at our disposal today, we can say, or more important, do something that will make a significant contribution to solving the crucial problems of our communities. In our case more than anyone else's, the principle holds that the concern of the social scientist should not be so much to explain the world as to transform it.

The Slavery of Latin American Psychology

One of the justifications that can be given for the poverty of the historical contribution of Latin American psychology is its relative youth. As confirmation for this point of view, people point to the original proposals beginning to emerge from all over (Martín-Baró, 1985k). The argument is valid, although insufficient, and it becomes dangerous if used as a shield against activists who would move now to correct the deficiencies that have led us (and in many cases, continue leading us) to scientific marginalization and social breakdown.

In my opinion the roots of the misery of Latin American psychology are sunk in a history of colonial dependence—not the history of Ibero-American colonization, but rather the neocolonialist "carrot and stick" imposed upon us a century ago. The "cultural stick" that continually prods our people finds in psychology yet another tool with which to mold minds. It also finds in psychology a valuable ally for soothing consciences when explaining the indisputable advantages of the modern technological carrot.

The historical misery of Latin American psychology derives from three principal interrelated causes: its scientistic mimicry, its lack of an adequate epistemology, and its provincial dogmatism. We will examine each of these separately.

Scientistic Mimicry

What has happened to Latin American psychology is similar to what happened to North American psychology at the beginning of the twentieth century, when it ran so fast after scientific recognition and social status that it stumbled. North American psychology looked to the natural sciences for a method and concepts that would legitimate it as a science. And in order to get social position and rank, it negotiated how it would contribute to the needs of the established power structure. Latin American psychology looked to its already scientifically and socially respectable "Big Brother," and, borrowing his methodological and practical conceptual tools, hoped to gain from the power structure in each country a social status equivalent to that attained by the North Americans.

It is debatable whether the profession of psychology has gained the social recognition it sought in Latin America. What is clear is that nearly all its theoretical and practical ideas have been imported from the United States. Hence, from the psychoanalytic and organicist focus that held sway from early on owing to psychology's dependence on the schools of psychiatry, there arose a strong wave of orthodox behaviorism, with its heavy weight of extreme positivism and methodological individualism.

Today many Latin American psychologists have discarded behaviorism and taken up one or another form of cognitive psychology, not so much because they were won over by the critics of the psychoanalytic or behavioral perspective as because that is the new focus among academics in North America. The problem is not rooted so much in the virtues or defects of behaviorism or cognitive theories, but rather in the mimicry that leads us to accept successive models coming out of the United States, as if an apprentice could become a doctor by hanging onto the stethoscope, or a child could become an adult by putting on its father's clothes.

Uncritical acceptance of theories and models is precisely the negation of science's own fundamental principles. And the ahistorical importing of ideas leads to ideological thinking, with mindsets whose meaning and validity, as the sociology of knowledge reminds us, excuse some social circumstances and foreclose inquiry into certain concrete questions.

Lack of an Adequate Epistemology

The dominant models in psychology are founded on a series of assumptions that are rarely discussed, and even more rarely are alternatives to them proposed. I will mention five of these assumptions that, in my opinion, have held back the development of Latin American psychology: positivism, individualism, hedonism, the homeostatic vision, and ahistoricism.

Positivism. Positivism, as its name indicates, is that scientific conception which holds that knowledge should be limited to positive facts, to events, and to their empirically verifiable relations. Discarding everything that could be characterized as metaphysical, positivism underlines the *how* of phenomena, but tends to put aside the *what,* the *because,* and the *why.* Dividing things up in this way, positivism becomes blind to the most important meanings of human existence. Not surprisingly, positivism is very much at home in the laboratory, where it can "control" all the variables, and where it ends up reduced to the examination of true trivialities that say little or nothing about everyday problems.

The most serious problem of positivism is rooted precisely in its essence; that is, in its blindness toward the negative. Recognizing nothing beyond the given, it necessarily ignores everything prohibited by the existing reality; that is, everything that does not exist but would, under other conditions, be historically possible. No doubt, a positivist analysis of the Salvadoran campesino would lead one to the conclusion that this is a *machista* and fatalistic person, similar to the way the study of the intelligence of blacks in the United States leads to the conclusion that the IQ of blacks is on the average a standard deviation below that of whites. To consider reality as no more than the given—that the Salvadoran campesino is just fatalistic, or the black less intelligent—constitutes an ideologization of reality that winds up consecrating the existing order as natural. Obviously, from such a perspective the horizon drawn for Latin Americans is low, and the future that psychology can offer is poor.

Paradoxically, this positivism is combined in psychological research with a methodological idealism. It is an idealistic scheme that puts a theoretical framework first, ahead of its analysis of reality, and goes no further in its exploration of things than what is indicated by the hypotheses it has formulated. Considering that the theories were pulled out of very different positive situations from our own, this idealism can end up blinding us not only to the negativity of our human circumstances but also to what is positive in them; that is, to what they in fact are.

Individualism. A second assumption of the prevailing psychology is contained in individualism, which proposes the individual as an entity with its own meaning as the final subject of psychology. The problem with individualism is rooted in its insistence on seeing as an *individual* characteristic that which oftentimes is not found except within the collectivity, or in attributing to individuality the things produced only in the dialectic of interpersonal relations. Through this, individualism ends up reinforcing the existing structures, because it ignores the reality of social structures and reduces all structural problems to personal problems.

Hedonism. Much has been said of the reigning hedonism in psychology, although perhaps the degree to which it is embedded, even within the most divergent models, has not been sufficiently stressed—how psychoanalysis is as hedonistic as behaviorism, conditioning as much as Gestalt. I am led to wonder, though, whether hedonism can adequately explain the acts of solidarity of Salvadoran refugees who no sooner learned about the earthquake that devastated the center of San Salvador than they gathered up all their extra food and sent it to the victims in the hardest-hit zone. The belief that behind all behavior there is always a quest for pleasure or satisfaction—does this not blind us to a different way of being human, or at least to a different, but equally real, facet of being human? To integrate hedonism into our theoretical framework as an assumption—is this not in fact a concession to the profit motive that underlies the capitalist system, and as such, an attribution to human nature of something that has to do with the functioning of a particular socioeconomic system (Martín-Baró, 1983a)?

The homeostatic vision. The homeostatic vision leads us to distrust everything that is change and disequilibrium, to think badly of all that represents rupture, conflict, and crisis. From this perspective, it becomes hard, more or less implicitly, for the disequilibrium inherent in social struggle not to be interpreted as a form of personal disorder (do we not speak of people who have "lost their balance"?), and for the conflicts generated by over-throwing the social order not to be considered as pathological.

Ahistoricism. The last assumption of the prevailing psychology that I want to mention is perhaps the most serious: its ahistoricism. The prevailing scientism leads us to consider human nature as universal, and to believe, therefore, that there are no fundamental differences between, say, a student at MIT and a Nicaraguan campesino, between John Smith from Peoria, Illinois, and Leonor Gonzales from Cuisnahuat, El Salvador. Thus, we accept Maslow's Needs Scale as a universal hierarchy, and we assume that with just a little adaptation and modification the Stanford-Binet will be able to measure the intelligence of our populations. A conception of humanness that would see universality in a historical context; that is to say, in terms of natural history, would acknowledge that needs, as much as intelligence, are in good measure a social construction. Once that is granted, it is clear that models created in different circumstances from our own, and assumed to be cross-cultural and transhistorical, can lead to a serious distortion of what our peoples are really about.

What is needed is the revision, from the bottom up, of our most basic assumptions in psychological thought. But this revision cannot be made from our offices; it has to come from a praxis that is committed to the people. Only through such a praxis of commitment will we be able to get a new perspective on the people of our communities, with a view not only of what they positively are but of the negativity as well—of all they could be, but have been kept by historical conditions from becoming. This done, truth will not have to be a simple reflection of data, but can become a task at hand: not an account of what *has been done*, but of what *needs to be done*.

Provincial Dogmatism: False Dilemmas

The dependence of Latin American psychology has led it to debate false dilemmas, false not so much because they fail to represent theoretical dilemmas on paper as because they do not respond to the questions of our reality. Three characteristic dilemmas still raising eyebrows in some quarters are scientific psychology vs. a psychology "with soul," humanistic psychology vs. materialistic psychology, and reactionary psychology vs. progressive psychology.

Psychology vs. Christian anthropology. The first dilemma, perhaps the one dealt with most successfully by academics, was a supposed opposition between psychology and a Christian anthropology. "Rat psychology" was pitted against a "psychology with soul," while psychologists and priests fought over who would get to play the one role to be performed for the bourgeoisie or middle classes. Surely the dogmatism of many members of the clergy made them suspicious of psychology, whose theories they perceived as dangerous to religious faith and whose explanations they saw as a negation of the transcendent dimension of the human being. But neither did the Latin American psychologists, with their "Made in U.S.A." schemata, know how to escape the dilemma, perhaps because they did not have a good enough understanding of their own ideas, let alone what they supposed the clergy were proposing.

Humanistic vs. materialistic psychology. A second dilemma, more present today than the first, opposes a humanistic psychology to a materialistic or dehumanizing psychology. At the personal level this dilemma is disconcerting to me, because I think that a psychological theory or model is either valid or not, useful in practice or not, and in any case, able to work more or less, better or worse, as a psychological theory or model. But I fail to see how Carl Rogers might be more humanistic than Sigmund Freud, or how Abraham Maslow might be more humanistic than Henri Wallon. Rather, I think that if Freud has a better understanding of the person than Rogers has, or Wallon than Maslow, their theories make for a more adequate psychological enterprise and, in consequence, make a better contribution toward humanization.

Reactionary vs. progressive psychology. The third dilemma opposes a reactionary psychology to a progressive psychology. The dilemma, again, is valid, although it is badly expressed. A reactionary psychology is one whose application lends support to an unjust social order; a progressive psychology is one that helps people to progress, to find the road to their personal and collective historical fulfillment. Thus, a psychological theory is no more reactionary for having come from the United States than one with origins in the Soviet Union is automatically progressive or revolutionary. What makes a theory reactionary or progressive is not so much its place of origin as its ability to explain or uncover reality and, above all, to strengthen or transform the social order. Regrettably, there is a great deal of confusion over this, and I know of academic centers and teachers who accept conditioning owing to Pavlov's nationality, and who are more attentive to political orthodoxy than to the historical verification of their ideas.

These three dilemmas denote a lack of independence in setting forth the most glaring problems of the communities of Latin America. They indicate an inability to freely use those theories and models which praxis shows to be the most valid and useful, or the inability to devise new ones as needed. Behind the three dilemmas are hidden dogmatic postures that belong more to a spirit of provincial dependency than to a scientific commitment to find, and more important, do, what is true for our Latin American peoples.

Toward a Liberation Psychology

From the preceding reflections there clearly follows a conclusion: if we want psychology to make a significant contribution to the history of our peoples—if, as psychologists, we wish to contribute to the social development of the countries of Latin America—we have to redesign our theoretical and practical tools, but redesign them from the standpoint of the lives of our own people: from their sufferings, their aspirations, and their struggles. If I may be permitted to formulate this proposal in Latin American terms, we must affirm that any effort at developing a psychology that will contribute to the liberation of our people has to mean the creation of a liberation psychology; but to create a liberation psychology is not simply a theoretical task; first and fundamentally it is a practical task. Therefore, if Latin American psychology wants to get started on the road to liberation, it must break out of its own enslavement. In other words, to achieve a psychology of liberation demands first that psychology be liberated.

Elements for a Liberation Psychology

Recently I asked one of the most renowned liberation theologians what he would say are the three most important intuitive truths of that theology. Without much hesitation my good friend pointed to the following:

1. Affirmation that the object of Christian faith is a God of life and, therefore, that a Christian must accept the promotion of life as his or her
   primordial religious task. From this Christian perspective, what is
   opposed to faith in God is not atheism but rather idolatry; that is, the

belief in false gods, gods which produce death. The Christian faith in a God of life must search, consequently, for all those historical conditions that give life to people, and in the particular case of Latin America, this search for life demands a first step of liberating the structures—the social structures first, and next the personal ones—that maintain a situation of sin; that is, of the mortal oppression of the majority of the people.

2. True practice has primacy over true theory, orthopraxis over orthodoxy. Actions are more important than affirmations in liberation theology, and what one does is more expressive of faith than what one says. Therefore, the truth of faith must be shown in historical achievements that give evidence of and make credible the existence of a God of life. In this context, everything becomes meaningful that mediates the possibility of people's liberation from the structures that oppress and impede their life and human development.

3. Christian faith calls for a preferential option for the poor. The theology of liberation affirms that one has to look for God among the poor and marginalized, and with them and from them live the life of faith. There are multiple reasons for this option. In the first place, that was, concretely, the option of Jesus. Second, the poor constitute the majority of our peoples. But third, it is only the poor who offer the objective and subjective conditions for opening up to the other, and above all, to the radically other. The option for the poor is not opposed to universal salvation, but it recognizes that the community of the poor is the theological place *par excellence* for achieving the task of salvation, the construction of the Kingdom of God.

From the inspiration of liberation theology, we can propose three essential elements for the building of a liberation psychology for the peoples of Latin America: a new horizon, a new epistemology, and a new praxis.

A new horizon. Latin American psychology must stop focusing attention on itself, stop worrying about its scientific and social status, and instead propose an effective service to the needs of the majority of the population. It is the real problems of our own peoples that ought to constitute the fundamental object of our work, not the problems that concern people elsewhere. And at the present time the most important problem faced by the vast majority of Latin Americans is their situation of oppressive misery, their condition of marginalized dependency that is forcing upon them an inhuman existence and snatching away their ability to define their own lives. It stands to reason, then, that if the most incontrovertible objective need of the majority of the people of Latin America consists in their historical liberation from the social structures that continue to oppress them, it is toward that need that psychology must focus its concern and energy.

Psychology has always been clear about the necessity for personal liberation; that is, people's need to gain control over their own existence. Psychology has believed that, were it not for unconscious mechanisms or conscious experiences holding them back from their existential goals and personal happiness, people would turn their lives toward a pursuit of those objectives which they consider worthwhile. Nevertheless, psychology has for the most part not been very clear about the intimate relationship between an unalienated personal existence and unalienated social existence, between individual control and collective power, between the liberation of each person and the liberation of a whole people. Moreover, psychology has often contributed to obscuring the relationship between personal estrangement and social oppression, presenting the pathology of persons as if it were something removed from history and society, and behavioral disorders as if they played themselves out entirely in the individual plane (see Chapter 6).

Psychology must work for the liberation of the peoples of Latin America. As the conscienticizing literacy of Paulo Freire has demonstrated, this involves breaking the chains of personal oppression as much as the chains of social oppression. The recent history of the Salvadoran people provides a case in point. Overcoming their existential fatalism (which some psychologists modestly or ideologically prefer to call "external control" or "learned helplessness," as if it were a purely intra-individual problem) entails for the Salvadoran people a direct confrontation with the structural forces that oppress them, deprive them of control over their own existence, and force them to learn submission and expect nothing from life.

A new epistemology. If our objective is to serve the liberation needs of the people of Latin America, this requires a new way of seeking knowledge, for the truth of the Latin American peoples is not in their present oppression but rather in the tomorrow of their liberty. The truth of the popular majority is not to be found, but made. That supposes, at the very least, two aspects: a new perspective and a new praxis.

The new perspective has to be from below, from the same oppressed majorities whose truth is to be created. Have we ever seriously asked what psychosocial processes look like from the point of view of the dominated instead of from that of the dominator? Have we thought of looking at educational psychology from where the illiterate stands, or industrial psychology from the place of the unemployed, or clinical psychology from the standpoint of the marginalized? What would mental health look like from the place of a tenant farmer on a hacienda, or personal maturity from someone who lives in the town dump, or motivation from a woman who sells goods in the market? Note that we say "from" the illiterate and the unemployed, "from" the tenant farmer and the woman in the market, not "for" them. This is not a matter of thinking for them or bringing them our ideas or solving their problems for them; it has to do with thinking and theorizing with them and from them. Here, too, the pioneering insight of Paulo Freire asserts itself. He put forth a pedagogy "of" the oppressed, and not "for" the oppressed; it was the very person, the very same community, that constituted the subject of its own conscienticizing literacy, that in community dialogue with the educator had to learn to read its reality and write its historical word. And just as liberation theology has underlined the fact that only from the poor is it possible to find the God of life enunciated by Jesus, a psychology of liberation has to learn that only from the oppressed will it be possible to discover and build the existential truth of the Latin American peoples.

To take on a new perspective obviously does not mean throwing out all of our knowledge; what it supposes, rather, is that we will relativize that knowledge and critically revise it from the perspective of the popular majorities. Only then will the theories and models show their validity or deficiency, their utility or lack thereof, their universality or provincialism. Only then will the techniques we have learned display their liberating potential or their seeds of subjugation.

A new praxis. All human knowledge is subject to limitations imposed by reality itself. In many respects that reality is opaque, and only by acting upon it, by transforming it, can a human being get information about it. What we see and how we see is of course determined by our perspective, by the place from which we begin our examination of history; but it is determined also by reality itself. Thus, to acquire new psychological knowledge it is not enough to place ourselves in the perspective of the people; it is necessary to involve ourselves in a new praxis, an activity of transforming reality that will let us know not only about what is but also about what is not, and by which we may try to orient ourselves toward what ought to be. As Fals Borda (1988, p. 88) says, speaking of participatory research, only through participation do we get the voluntary and living rupture of the "asymmetrical relationship of submission and dependence implicit in the subject/object binomial."

Generally, psychologists have tried to enter into the social process by way of the powers that be. The attempt at scientific purity has meant in practice taking the perspective of those in power and acting from a position of dominance. As educational psychologists we have worked from the base of the school, not of the community. As industrial psychologists we have selected or trained personnel according to the demands of the owners and bosses, not according to those of the workers or their unions. And even as community psychologists we have often come into the community mounted on the carriage of our plans and projects, bringing our own know-how and money. It is not easy to figure out how to place ourselves within the process alongside the dominated rather than alongside the dominator. It is not even easy to leave our role of technocratic or professional superiority and to work hand in hand with community groups. But if we do not embark upon this new type of praxis that transforms ourselves as well as transforming reality, it will be hard indeed to develop a Latin American psychology that will contribute to the liberation of our peoples.

The problem of a new praxis brings up the problem of power, and, therefore, the problem of the politicization of psychology. This is a touchy subject for many, but no less important for that. To be sure, to adopt a perspective, to put oneself inside a popular praxis, is to take sides. There is an assumption that taking a stand represents an abdication of scientific objectivity, but this assumption confuses bias with objectivity. The fact that something is biased does not necessarily mean it is subjective; bias can be the consequence of interests, more or less conscious, but it can also be the result of an ethical choice. And while we are all affected by the class interests that bias our knowledge, not everybody makes conscious ethical choices consonant with those values. For example, although a position has to be taken with respect to torture or assassination, this does not mean that one cannot be objective in understanding the criminal act or the actor, the torturer or assassin. If we were not able to take an ethical stand while still maintaining objectivity, we might easily condemn as murder a death caused by a guerrilla, but condone and even exalt as an act of heroism a death produced by a soldier or the police. Thus, I agree with Fals Borda, who maintains that practical knowledge acquired through participatory research should lead toward the people gaining power, a power that allows them to become the protagonists of their own history and to effect those changes which would make Latin American societies more just and more humane.

Three Urgent Tasks

The tasks, both theoretical and practical, that present themselves to a Latin American liberation psychology are many. I will present here three that seem to me of special and urgent importance: recovering historical memory, de-ideologizing common sense and everyday experience, and utilizing the virtues of the people.

The recovery of historical memory. The hard struggle to satisfy everyday basic needs forces the popular majorities to stay in a here and now without a before or after—in a permanent psychological present. Furthermore, the prevailing discourse puts forth an apparently natural and ahistorical reality, structuring it in such a way as to cause it to be accepted without question. This makes it impossible to derive lessons from experience and, more important, makes it impossible to find the roots of one's own identity, which is as much needed for interpreting one's sense of the present as for glimpsing possible alternatives that might exist. The predominantly negative image that the average Latin American has of himself or herself when compared with other people (see Montero, 1984) indicates the internalization of oppression, its incorporation into the spirit itself; fertile soil for conformist fatalism, and so very convenient for the established order.

To recover historical memory would mean "to discover selectively, through collective memory, those elements of the past which have proved useful in the defense of the interests of exploited classes and which may be applied to the present struggles to increase [*concientización*]" (Fals Borda, 1988, p. 95). It has to do with recovering not only the sense of one's own identity and the pride of belonging to a people but also a reliance on a tradition and a culture, and above all, with rescuing those aspects of identity which served yesterday, and will serve today, for liberation. Thus, the recovery of a historical memory supposes the reconstruction of models of identification that, instead of chaining and caging the people, open up the horizon for them, toward their liberation and fulfillment.

De-ideologizing everyday experience. Second, a contribution to the de-ideologization of everyday experience is indispensable. We know that knowledge is a social construction. Our countries live burdened by the lie of a prevailing discourse that denies, ignores, or disguises essential aspects of reality. The same "cultural stranglehold" that day after day is imposed upon the people of Latin America by the mass media constitutes a reference point that has little bearing on the everyday experience of the majority of people, and even less on the poorer people. It goes along, deceptive and alienated, conforming to a fictional common sense that nurtures the structures of exploitation and conformist attitudes. To de-ideologize means to retrieve the original experience of groups and persons and return it to them as objective data. People can then use the data to formally articulate a consciousness of their own reality, and by so doing, verify the validity of acquired knowledge (see Chapters 2 and 11). This process of de-ideologizing common sense must be realized as much as possible through critical participation in the life of the poorer people, a participation that represents a certain departure from the predominant forms of research and analysis.

Utilizing the people's virtues. Finally, we must work to utilize the virtues of our peoples. Going no further than my own people, the people of El Salvador, current history confirms, day by day, their uncompromising solidarity with the suffering, their ability to deliver and to sacrifice for the collective good, their tremendous faith in the human capacity to change the world, their hope for a tomorrow that keeps being violently denied to them. These virtues are alive in the popular traditions, in popular religious practices, in those social structures which have allowed the Salvadoran people to survive through history in conditions of inhuman oppression and repression—virtues that enable them today to keep alive faith in their destiny and hope for their future, in spite of a dreadful civil war that already [in 1986] has gone on more than six years.

Oscar Romero, the assassinated Archbishop of San Salvador, once said, referring to the virtues of the Salvadoran people, "With this people it is not hard to be a good pastor." How is it possible that we, Latin American psychologists, have not been able to discover all that rich potential in the virtues of our peoples, and, consciously or unconsciously, have turned our eyes to other countries and other cultures when pressed to define objectives and ideals?

There is a big task ahead if we hope for Latin American psychology to make a significant contribution to universal psychology, and above all, to the history of our peoples. In light of the current situation of oppression and faith, of repression and solidarity, of fatalism and struggle that characterizes our peoples, that task must be one of a liberation psychology. But a psychology of liberation requires a prior liberation of psychology, and that liberation can only come from a praxis committed to the sufferings and hopes of the peoples of Latin America.

2

The Role of the Psychologist

TRANSLATED BY ADRIANNE ARON

The Central American Context

There is a growing consciousness among Latin American psychologists that, with respect to defining our professional identity and the role we ought to be playing in our societies, it is much more important to examine the histories and needs of our peoples than to define ourselves in terms of psychology's parameters as a science or activity. We note with increasing clarity that generic definitions that come to us from other places only hinder our understanding of self and others, because they do not see far enough to fathom our peoples' realities, and do not reach far enough to grasp our social and cultural uniqueness. When we ask, then, what role the psychologist ought to play in the Central American context, we should turn our eyes to the context before looking at the parameters, and we must not presume that because we are part of that context we therefore know enough about it, or that because we live in it, it automatically becomes our professional point of reference.

In a superficial characterization, passing over important differences, three major features can be named that seem to characterize the peoples of Central America at this time: structural injustice, revolutionary struggle, and the accelerated conversion of the nation states into satellites of the United States.

Structural Injustice

To begin, in light of biased diagnoses that ascribe the ills of Central America to the recent East-West confrontation or the rise of the Sandinistas to power [in Nicaragua], it is necessary to insist that the fundamental problems of Central America are rooted in an unjust structuring of the social systems (Torres Rivas, 1981; Rosenthal, 1982). Sitting on top of poor and underdeveloped societies are regimes that subject the majority of the population to miserable conditions, allocating goods unequally so that small minorities can enjoy all manner of comforts and luxuries (for a paradigmatic case see Sevilla, 1984). In Central America the majority of the population has never been able to satisfy its most basic needs for food, housing, health, and education, and the contrast between this miserable situation and the superabundance enjoyed by the small oligarchic minorities constitutes the first and most basic violation of human rights in our countries. The secular maintenance of this situation has been possible only by the application of violent mechanisms of control and social repression, which through history have hindered or frustrated all efforts to change, and even to reform, the most oppressive and unjust of social structures (for the case of Guatemala see Aguilera et al., 1981).

There is no question that notable differences exist between, for example, the situation in Costa Rica, where considerable gains have been made in the areas of education and sanitation, and that in Honduras, where schooling and health services barely reach the population. Still, among the Costa Ricans abysmal differences can be observed: large marginalized sectors alongside oligarchic minorities, with vast segments of the population sunk in exploitation and misery. These conditions make Costa Rica a sister and partner in the common destiny of the Central American nations.

Revolutionary Struggle

A second characteristic is the situation of war or quasi-war in which all the countries of the region are immersed. There is a bloody civil war in El Salvador, which has already [in 1985] claimed more than 60,000 victims and has displaced some 20 percent of the civilian population. There is a no less bloody war on the borders of Nicaragua, financed and directed by the United States. There is a diffuse guerrilla war in Guatemala, resisted by an awesome counterinsurgency campaign. And in Honduras there is a pre-war psychosis, for that country (and to a lesser extent Costa Rica as well) has been forced by the U.S. government to serve as an aircraft carrier in its warring counterinsurgency policy for the region.

The consequences of this generalized state of war can be fully appreciated only when added to the situation of structural misery, which is already catastrophic. In recent years, economic development in Central America has not only stagnated but positively regressed. In the case of El Salvador, optimistic estimates figure that the national economy has been set back by at least twenty years, and that, in the best of cases and the most favorable of projections, the country might be able by the end of the century to recover to the point at which it stood when the war started (see Instituto de Investigaciones Económicas, 1983; Argueta, 1985; Ibisate, 1985). Economies like those of El Salvador or Nicaragua, which are already weak, are forced to direct the better part of their reserves to the war effort, that is, to the destruction of their own people and their own country. Where factories ought to stand, military barracks are built; and when money should be invested in seeds and tractors, it is used for bombs and artillery helicopters.

The militarization of Central America is one of the most serious processes we confront (Bermúdez, 1985; Bermúdez and Córdova, 1985). If El Salvador has for more than fifty years been faced with an oppressive, exploitative regime under the administration of armed forces that in 1979 consisted of 15,000 men and some 300 officers, what can we expect in the future, with an army that at the present time numbers 50,000 men, plus 15,000 members of the so-called security forces and some 2,300 officers, and that hopes to grow to 100,000 men in the very near future? Add to these figures the number of guerrillas, probably no fewer than 10,000, as much or more militarized than the government army, and the paramilitary groups armed by the government or by sectors of the extreme right, and you get a pathetic perspective on the situation in El Salvador. Nor is the situation much better in Nicaragua or Guatemala. Honduras, it is well known, has been converted into a military camp of the United States, with gigantic military maneuvers, one after another, and with the cancer of the anti-Sandinista Contra, which for obvious logistical reasons cannot remain on the Nicaraguan border. And Costa Rica? Well, Costa Rica is also besieged by the economic crisis and its share of Contras, and is the object of an accelerated militarization by the Reaganite warriors. One day, very soon I fear, Costa Rica will awake from its anti-Sandinista stupor and find that without ever knowing it or wanting it, it has obtained a real army, to feed and keep content and busy.

Nation States as U.S. Satellites

The third characteristic of the current situation in Central America is the increasing tendency for nations to become satellites of the United States. This is an obvious consequence of the "national security" doctrine, according to which the countries' whole existence must submit to the logic of total confrontation against communism (see Mattelart, 1978; Insulza, 1982). Clearly, Central America during the present century has been part of the backyard of the United States, and at no time has it been an irony to assert, with the Salvadoran poet Roque Dalton, that "The President of the United States is more the president of my country than the President of my country." Nevertheless, the avatars of U.S. policy have allowed moments for the countries of the area to enjoy a certain autonomy, at least in their internal politics (see Maira, 1982). Those "degrees of freedom" (if I may use the expression) are being rapidly eliminated. The Central American governments are repeating today what Admiral Costelo Blanco expressed with great clarity twenty years ago, about the Brazilian coup that installed one of the most repressive military regimes in the history of the South American continent: "The critical character of the moment demands the sacrifice of a part of our national sovereignty" (quoted in Mattelart and Mattelart, 1978, p. 56).

The case of El Salvador is paradigmatic, but not exceptional. As the vicissitudes of the Contadora process show, Costa Rica, El Salvador, and Honduras can only interpret the song composed in Washington, using instruments made in Washington, and satisfying the tastes of Washington. Accepting that the poverty of our countries is rooted in a certain dependency on those who can help us deal with our problems is not so terrible; what is hard is that we are mortgaging our identity and independence without getting anything in return: our problems are not being solved, and we are closing off the very possibility of a future for our peoples. The great political decisions for our countries are made according to the needs of the national security of the United States, not the needs of our peoples, with the justification that San Salvador and Managua are closer to San Francisco than are New York and Boston. This same demand for the "national security" of the United States intensifies the polarization that already exists in our countries, where the world is automatically divided into good and bad, friend and enemy, with nobody able to escape this Manichean dichotomy (see Martín-Baró, 1983c). But have we stopped to ask ourselves what would happen if the United States were to achieve its "national security" objectives in the area? Would it begin to devote some of its attention to solving the most serious problems of our peoples? Would it help us bring justice to our societies, lending a hand as we dismantle unnecessary military structures? Or would it suspend the flow of dollars, satisfied with the abolition of the revolutionary movements, but requiring that we maintain the whole counterinsurgency apparatus so as to avoid future problems for its national security?

The structural injustice, the revolutionary wars, and the turning of our countries into satellites help us characterize the present Central American situation, thus offering a historical context for defining the role psychologists can properly perform.

The Role of the Psychologist

Some years ago, in 1968, a French psychologist, Marc Richelle, asked, "Why psychologists?" The reason for this query lay in what he called the sudden and "disquieting proliferation of a new species" (1968, p. 7). At about the same time another Frenchman, Didier Deleule, offered a very radical reply: the proliferation of psychologists is explained by the fact that contemporary society requires an ideology of exchange, and psychology provides it. Psychology offers an alternative solution to social conflicts: it tries to change the individual while preserving the social order, or, in the best of cases, generating the illusion that, perhaps, as the individual changes, so will the social order—as if society were a summation of individuals (Deleule, 1972; see also Bricht et al., 1973).

Truly, when looking dispassionately at the place some psychological concepts occupy in the dominant political and cultural discourse, or when pondering the role played by the majority of psychologists in our countries, one has to concede that Deleule makes a lot of sense. Obviously, the problem does not have to be seen in terms of the subjective intentions of the professionals in the field, or even, I dare say, in terms of their politics; the problem lies in psychology's own qualities as a theoretical-practical endeavor. The question, then, is not what this or that subfield of the discipline is trying to do, but first and fundamentally, in what direction psychology is being propelled by the weight of its own activities. What objective effect does the activity of psychology produce in a particular society?

Among the criticisms most often made of psychologists in Central American countries is that the majority devote most, if not all, of their attention to the well-to-do social sectors, and as such, their work tends to center on the personal roots of problems—a focus that causes them to ignore social factors (see Zúñiga, 1976). The social context is thus converted into a kind of natural phenomenon, an unquestioned assumption, before whose "objective" demands the individual must seek, individually and even "subjectively," the solutions to his or her problems. With this focus and with this clientele, it is no surprise that psychology is serving the interests of the established social order, as a useful instrument for reproducing the system (see Braunstein et al., 1979).

One could say, and rightly so, that all the professions in our societies are at the service of the established order, and that our profession is no exception. One could also take note of all those psychologists who have served, and continue to serve, popular and even revolutionary causes. But all this points to the fact that, if we take as a point of departure what psychologists have done or are doing, we cannot get beyond a positivist idea of our role—one that may show a more or less satisfactory factual image but will leave out all the historical possibilities that were dropped by the wayside. Our imperative is to examine not only what we are but also what we might have been and, above all, what we ought to be, given the needs of our peoples—whether or not we have pre-existing models. It needs to be asked, for instance, if Nicaraguan psychologists continue today [under the Sandinista revolutionary government] using the same work arrangements that they used in Somoza's time, or if the change in clientele, the need to attend to the poorer sectors of the population, has led also to a modification of their conceptual models and practices (see Whitford, 1985).

A good way to approach a critical examination of the role of the psychologist is to return to the historical roots of psychology itself. To do this, we would have to revert back to the movement that restricted psychological analysis to behavior—observable behavior—and turn our eyes and thoughts again to the "black box" of human consciousness. Consciousness is not simply the private, subjective knowledge and feelings of individuals. More than anything, it represents the confines within which each person encounters the reflexive impact of his or her being and actions in society, where people take on and work out a knowledge about the self and about reality that permits them to be somebody, to have a personal and social identity. Consciousness is the knowing or not knowing of self, through the world and through others, with praxis coming before mental knowledge. Before it becomes thought, knowledge as praxis is inscribed in the appropriateness of all behaviors to objective realities, becoming reflexive only conditionally, and only in part (see Gibson, 1966; Baron, 1980).

Understood in this way, consciousness is a psychosocial reality, related to what Durkheim called the "collective consciousness." Consciousness includes, first and foremost, the image people have of themselves, an image that is the product of the history of each individual, which, obviously, is not a private matter. But consciousness includes also social representations (Banchs, 1982; Deconchy, 1984; Farr, 1984; Jodelet, 1984; Lane, 1985), and therefore, all the social and everyday knowledge we call common sense, which is the privileged domain of ideology (Martín-Baró, 1984f).

To the degree that psychology takes as its specific objective understanding the processes of human consciousness, it has to attend to the knowledge people have of themselves as individuals and as members of a collectivity. From a psychological point of view, the knowledge that counts most is not explicit and formalized knowledge, but rather the knowledge inherent in everyday praxis, usually implicit, structurally unconscious, and ideologically natural. This knowledge is important insofar as it works (or fails to work) for dealing with objective realities, contributes or not to the humanization of people, and assists or obstructs the efforts of groups or peoples to take command of their own existence.

It is important to underline that this vision of psychology does not throw out the analysis of behavior. It does insist, however, that behavior be seen in light of its personal and social meaning; that it be analyzed in terms of the knowledge it makes manifest and the sense it acquires from a historical perspective. We may take learning as an example. Learning is not only a matter of elaborating and reinforcing a sequence of stimuli and responses; more significantly, it structures the way a person relates to his or her environment, shaping a world where the individual occupies a place and social interests take on concrete forms. Or take work. To work is not only to apply a series of thoughts and abilities so as to satisfy one's own needs; to work is first and foremost to make oneself through the act of transforming reality. In the web of interpersonal and intergroupal relations that work introduces, one encounters oneself or becomes alienated from oneself. In either instance, the formal meaning of the activity is pierced by a sense that is not decipherable from the measurable surface—yet absent a comprehension of this intangible substance, little or nothing can be understood about human existence.

In light of what has been said, we can assert that the fundamental horizon for psychology as a field of knowledge is *concientización*. To some, this assertion may seem somewhat escapist, while others may consider it too much of a commitment; some may think that it sees psychology too narrowly, while others may feel perhaps that it tries to take psychology to a place where it doesn't belong. But let us examine this proposal in greater detail, since some misunderstanding may arise over the term *concientización*, which is so evocative of contemporary history in Latin America.

As is well known, *concientización* is a term coined by Paulo Freire to characterize the process of personal and social transformation experienced by the oppressed of Latin America when they become literate in dialectic with their world (Freire, 1971, 1973, 1978; INODEP, 1973). For Freire literacy does not consist simply in learning to write on paper or to read the written word; literacy is above all learning to read the surrounding reality and to write one's own history. What counts is not so much knowing how to code and decode strange words, but rather learning to say the word of one's own existence, which is personal but, more significantly, collective. And to pronounce that personal and collective word, people must take hold of their fate, take the reins of their lives, a move that demands overcoming false consciousness and achieving a critical understanding of themselves as well as of their world and where they stand in it.

There are three aspects to the process of concientización:

1. The human being is transformed through changing his or her reality. It follows that this has to do with a dialectical process, an active process that cannot be taught by imposition but only through dialogue.
2. Through the gradual decoding of their world, people grasp the mechanisms of oppression and dehumanization. This crumbles the consciousness that mythifies that situation as natural, and opens up the horizon to new possibilities for action. This critical consciousness of others and of the surrounding reality brings with it the possibility of a new praxis, which at the same time makes possible new forms of consciousness.
3. People's new knowledge of their surrounding reality carries them to a new understanding of themselves and, most important, of their social identity. They begin to discover themselves in their mastery of nature, in their actions that transform things, in their active role in relation to others. All this allows them to discover not only the roots of what they are but also the horizon, what they can become. Thus the recovery of their historical memory offers a base for a more autonomous determination of their future.

Hence, concientización does not consist in a simple change of opinion about reality, a change of individual subjectivity that leaves the objective situation intact; concientización supposes that persons change in the process of changing their relations with the surrounding environment and, above all, with other people. No knowledge can be true if it has not attached itself to the task of transforming reality, but the transformative process requires an involvement in the process of transforming human relationships.

In asserting that concientización ought to be the principal feature in psychology's horizon, we are proposing that the task of the psychologist must be to achieve the de-alienation of groups and persons by helping them attain a critical understanding of themselves and their reality. Psychology has taken it as given that individual consciousness should be de-alienated, that is, that those mechanisms which block consciousness of personal identity and lead a person to act as an estranged or alienated being, "a crazy," should be eliminated or controlled. But, significantly, it has cast aside the work of de-alienating social consciousness: psychology has not addressed the question of the mechanisms that block consciousness of an individual's social identity, causing him or her to act like a dominated being or a dominator, an oppressive exploiter or a person who is marginalized and oppressed. If, as even the *DSM-III* (American Psychiatric Association, 1980) has recognized, all behavior involves a social dimension, then the work of psychology cannot limit itself to the abstract plane of the individual but must also confront social factors, which form the arena for the expression of all human individuality.

Taking concientización as the horizon for psychology's work preserves the focus on the personal that psychology finds necessary, but not the personal as opposed to or foreign to the social. The personal here is the dialectical correlate of the social and, as such, incomprehensible if its constitutive referent is omitted. There is no person without family, no learning without culture, no madness without social order; and therefore neither can there be an I without a We, a knowing without a symbolic system, a disorder that does not have reference to moral and social norms.

In reference to a social situation and a concrete historical condition, concientización requires the psychologist—in our case, in Central America—to produce an answer to the great problems of structural injustice, of war and national alienation, that overwhelm our peoples. One cannot do psychology today in Central America without taking on a serious historical responsibility; that is, without trying to make a contribution toward changing all those conditions that dehumanize the majority of the population, alienating their consciousness and blocking the development of their historical identity. But this must be done *qua* psychologist—from the specific place of psychology as a scientific and practical endeavor.

In the first place, concientización responds to the situation of injustice by promoting a critical consciousness of the objective and subjective roots of social alienation. It is not supposed that a simple consciousness of reality in itself can change that reality; but it would be difficult indeed to struggle for that necessary change while a veil of justifications, rationalizations, and myths covers up the basic determinants of the situation of the Central American peoples. Concientización not only makes possible, but can go so far as to unleash, the change by breaking up the fatalistic thought processes that give ideological sustenance to the alienation of the popular majorities.

In the second place, the same process of concientización assumes an escape from the reproductive machinery of the relationships of dominance and submission, for it can be realized only through dialogue. The dialectical process that allows individual self-knowledge and self-acceptance presupposes a radical change in social relations, to a condition where there would be neither oppressors nor oppressed, and this change applies whether we are talking about psychotherapy or formal schooling, production in a factory or everyday work in a service institution.

Finally, the seizing of consciousness points directly to both personal and social identity, as well as to group and national identity. Concientización leads people to recover historical memory, to get back what is most authentic in their past, to purify what is most genuine in their present, and to project all that into a personal and national plan. No learning process, vocational guidance, or therapeutic counseling can hope to see the development or realization of persons if it does not cast the individual in his or her social and national context, thereby setting forth the problem of one's authenticity as member of a group, part of a culture, citizen of a country.

Possibly the difficulty for the majority of psychologists is not so much in accepting this horizon for their endeavor as in visualizing their job in practice. What does concientización mean in and for the activity of psychology? Does it have to do with applying some particular technique? Must it include in its processes some form of political reflection? Does it mean changing the types of tests that are used, or the topics of those now in use? Should we be abandoning individual therapy and doing something like collective ergotherapies? Let us try to flesh out the thesis with two examples of how concientización can be sought in psychological activity.

Clearly, one of the most serious problems we face today in Central America is the problem of victims of war: wounded and permanently disabled soldiers and guerrillas, people who have been traumatized, perhaps by battle experiences; whole populations terrorized by bombings, counterinsurgency operations, or "sanitary" massacres, or by witnessing repressive cruelties; victims of terrorism or torture; orphaned children who have had to flee for prolonged periods in fear of the violence of war. These are the people who make up the population of displaced persons and refugees, the children of repression and war, whose number grows apace and already includes no fewer than two million Central Americans (see, for example, Lawyers' Committee for International Human Rights, 1984; Instituto de Investigaciones de la Universidad Centroamericana, 1985). Undoubtedly, this population is in extreme need of food, shelter, health, and work; but it has other needs as well—less pressing, though equally serious—for personal development and humanizing relationships, for love and hope in life, for identity and social standing (Peña, 1984). That is why a fundamental objective of Central American psychology at the present time and in the near future must be to pay special attention to the victims of war, whoever they may be. For that attention to be provided, clinics must be made accessible to the groups that make up the majority of the population, for they are the ones who are suffering most from the impact of war.

Is it possible to confront this most serious problem of the victims of war simply by extending the reach of clinical psychology as it is now practiced, to cover more people? Would this not merely represent an effort to reestablish the terms of a social reality that is at the very root of the conflict we are living through? Clinical attention to the victims of the Central American wars has to involve a process of concientización, a process that returns the word to these human beings, not only as individuals, but as part of a people. This means that psychotherapy must aim directly at the social identity worked out through the prototypes of oppressor and oppressed, and at shaping a new identity for people as members of a human community, in charge of a history (see Chapter 6). Overcoming the traumas of war has to include seizing consciousness of all those realities, both collective and individual, which are at the root of the war. Thus, a conscienticizing psychotherapy must construct a process that will enable the individual to assert his or her personal and social identity as part of a movement of collective and national affirmation.

A great many Central American psychologists are employed as educational psychologists. Sometimes this work is reduced to a more or less systematic administering of test batteries, to try to determine the academic grade level and developmental progress of each student, to detect possible problems and decide on an educational plan consistent with the student's abilities and interests. The implicit assumption in this work is that within the confines of the existing society each and every individual will find a productive and satisfying place to suit his or her characteristics and personal ideals. The effort, therefore, is to achieve an adjustment, a good fit between each individual and the society, that would never for a moment put into question the basic schemata by which we live, nor, therefore, how social roles are determined for people. That is how educational psychology contributes to the reproduction of the established system, with its schemata for passivity and lack of creativity, its domination and submission.

An educational psychology with concientización presupposes an effort to construct alternative social schemata: the critical and creative ability of students, as opposed to what school and society offer them; a different style of confronting social and occupational life. It would have to do not only with students learning pre-designed academic curricula but, above all, with learning to confront the reality of their existence through critical thinking. So, just as there is a junior Chamber of Commerce which initiates adolescents into small business administration, there might be something like national reality laboratories, where young people could directly confront the social conditions of the majority of the population and reflect critically on those conditions.

There is no doubt that for clinical practice as much as for educational psychology the horizon of concientización assumes an important change in the profession's way of conducting its work. It does not entail giving up the technical role the psychologist now performs, but it does involve scrapping theoretical assumptions about adaptation and interventions made from a position of power. For this, what is needed is the elaboration of a different conceptual vision, and perhaps also new methods of diagnosis and intervention. Some of the gains made by the anti-psychiatry movement can be illuminating for clinical psychology in this regard, considering the changes psychiatry needed to make as a result of a different conception of the reality of psychiatric disorders, and therefore of therapeutic practice (see Basaglia, 1972; Cooper, 1967; Heyward and Varigas, 1973; Jervis, 1981; for Latin American experiences, see Grimson, 1972; Moffat, 1975). In educational psychology the experience of concientización itself, and especially the way it parallels and differs from de-schooling (see Illich, 1971; Reimer, 1970) will allow a glimpse of new orientations.

Of what does this new theoretical and practical idea for a psychology with concientización consist? In my opinion, it is not something that some exclusive area of psychology has to come to grips with; rather, the whole of the professional purpose must fix on it, whatever might be the specific area of work. Because that is so, the critical questions that psychology must formulate with regard to its activity, and, it follows, with regard to the role it is carrying out in society, should not be centered on *where* the work is done, but rather on *by whom;* nor should it be looking at *how* something is done, so much as *for whose benefit.* Thus, what is at stake is not so much the kind of activity that is practiced (clinical, educational, industrial, community, or other), as *what are the concrete historical consequences* this activity is producing?

Conclusion: A Historical Choice

It is clear that it is not the psychologist who must be called on to solve the basic problems faced by the peoples of Central America today. To think otherwise would be to fool oneself about both psychology and the problems in Central America, and it would also be an act of psychologizing, and this has rightly been denounced as an ideology of exchange. It is not in the hands of the psychologist, *qua* psychologist, to change the structural socioeconomic injustices in our countries, to resolve the armed conflicts, or to rescue the national sovereignty which has been servilely mortgaged to the United States.

Nevertheless, there is important work for the psychologist to do. It requires an objective recognition of the main problems burdening our Central American peoples, and equally important, a specific definition of psychology's contribution to their resolution. If it is not the calling of the psychologist to intervene in the socioeconomic mechanisms that cement the structures of injustice, it *is* within the psychologist's purview to intervene in the subjective processes that sustain those structures of injustice and make them viable. If the psychologist is not called upon to make peace for the forces and social interests at war, he or she *is* competent to help find paths for replacing violent habits with more rational ones; and, if the definition of a project for national autonomy does not lie within his or her competence, the psychologist can contribute to the formation of a personal and collective identity that responds to people's most real demands.

There is no doubt that Central American psychologists face a historical challenge for which we probably were not prepared. Nevertheless, instead of looking for justifications for our deficiencies, we should look to how we can discharge our social responsibility (Martín-Baró, 1985j). With regard to this, three points seem necessary:

1. Central American psychologists must rethink their image of themselves as professionals. They cannot go on with the inertia of already known theoretical ideas and customary ways of acting; our psychological knowledge has to be confronted by new problems, the problems of the peoples of Central America, and with the questions that such knowledge brings forth. The case of the war victims is perhaps the most pointed and urgent, but it is not the only case, and maybe not even the most radical one.

2. It is urgent to take on the perspective of the majority of the population. We know from the sociology of knowledge that what is seen of reality, and how it is seen, depends essentially on the social location from which it is viewed. Up to now our psychological knowledge has been nourished basically by an analysis of problems that apply to the dominant sectors of the society. It is not probable, and perhaps not even possible, for us to achieve an adequate understanding of the most profound problems that burden the majority of the population today if we do not place ourselves, hermeneutically, at their historical lookout point.

3. Perhaps the most radical choice Central American psychologists face today concerns the disjunction between an accommodation to a social system that has benefited us personally and a critical confrontation with that system. In more positive terms, the choice is between accompanying and not accompanying the poor and oppressed majorities in their effort to emerge into history, in their struggle to constitute themselves as a new people in a new land. This is not a question of whether to abandon psychology; it is a question of whether psychological knowledge will be placed in the service of constructing a society where the welfare of the few is not built on the wretchedness of the many, where the fulfillment of some does not require that others be deprived, where the interests of the minority do not demand the dehumanization of all.

3

Power, Politics, and Personality

TRANSLATED BY PHILLIP BERRYMAN

Psychology and Politics: Political Psychology

In a country like El Salvador, where the Reagan administration, eager to overcome the Vietnam syndrome, is attempting to make a full-scale application of the idea of so-called low-intensity conflict, it has become rather commonplace to refer to "psychological warfare." Even top military officers like to say that the war is "90 percent psychological" and only 10 percent strictly military. While military warfare seeks to defeat opponents, psychological warfare seeks to win them over, that is, to win the "hearts and minds" of enemies and sympathizers alike.

The dividing line between what is strictly military and what is psychological is often not very clear. For example, the pencils and notebooks that the colonel of a garrison—with photographers and film crews on hand—donated to people of a small settlement in one of the most conflictive areas of the country were confiscated during a major military sweep the following week, as material suspected of serving the purposes of "subversion." It is even much less clear what may be specifically psychological in certain methods of "psychological torture" which consist of unending interrogation over several days without allowing the victim to sleep.

Psychological warfare is a branch of political psychology, namely the part that winds up an "extreme form of politics" pursuing social interests by means of war. But "political psychology" itself is ambiguous, and can be understood in at least two very different senses: as the *psychology of politics* (that is, the analysis and psychological understanding of political behaviors and processes), and as the *politics of psychology,* or the political dimension of psychology (that is, psychology understood as representing particular social interests and therefore serving as an instrument of social power).

We are here using the term in the first meaning, the psychology of politics, and more concretely, the psychology of political life in Latin American countries. The aim is to lay down some theoretical foundations so as to be able to examine political activity from a psychological perspective, and more specifically from the perspective of social psychology. A psychology of politics may take as its object of study everything from the behavior of the president of a country to the unfolding of psychological warfare, including the way a government cabinet is put together, or the factors that lead a person to participate in an electoral process or to join a guerrilla movement.

We would certainly be deceiving ourselves to think it possible to develop a psychology of politics while ignoring the politics of psychology, as though psychological processes could be understood from some presumed scientific limbo untouched by social conflicts. If we seek to focus on the psychology of politics we cannot simply ignore the politics of psychology. Like any other activity, psychology, both theoretical and applied, is conditioned by the social interests that are at stake. The sociology of knowledge has demonstrated that when one examines things or gets involved in activities, the social perspective one adopts essentially limits what one knows and how one knows, and therefore what one does and how one does it. It has been accurately pointed out that as it is applied here in Latin America, psychology is tied too tightly to the ruling classes; that is, the class interests of those who wield power. If the political activity of psychologists in areas seemingly as innocuous as school performance or behavioral disturbances tends to serve political interests (conservative in this case), it is all the more necessary to bear in mind the workings and political impact of the politics of psychology in the area of social conflict *par excellence*—political life.

In order to avoid falling into a psychology of politics that would be one more ideological discourse at the service of the established order, we would need to construct a political psychology of political life, one that would be aware of how it was socially conditioned. Such a psychology, instead of adopting a stance of presumed scientific neutrality, would start out with a clear awareness of its own assumptions, of where it sits in society, and therefore of the scope and limitations of its own perspective. In other words, we cannot be content with simply applying certain set psychological theories and models to the realm of politics. We have to examine the psychological dimensions of our societies, conscious of the fact that this examination itself is involved—and has a stake—in the very processes and conflicts it is analyzing.

Let us begin our analysis with some actual events. I will use three political events from the time when the first draft of this paper was being written, presenting them as they were summarized in *El Diario de Caracas,* Saturday, 17 January 1987. In view of what was said above about political psychology, we must keep in mind that, in the very act of arranging the news they provide, the mass media themselves act as an ideological filter. We should also keep in mind that the newspaper I am citing is very conservative, in a country that wants democracy and makes formal claims to having it, even though the facts strongly suggest otherwise. Here are the news items:

1. "OAS [Organization of American States] and UN begin peace efforts (in Central America) . . . The United States is concerned that their mission might lead to settlement out of line with U.S. objectives in Nicaragua."
2. "The President of Ecuador was kidnapped by the Air Force for ten hours. Febres was exchanged for the rebellious general."
3. "Ligia de Gerbasi, president of the Federation of Urban Communities (FACUR) says that in view of growing electoral skepticism in Venezuela, she fears that political parties will begin to put pressure on local community leaders to follow party directions and to channel the votes of neighborhood associations toward one or another party."

Obviously we could multiply such examples, drawing on the same edition of the newspaper, or on the news provided by any of the other mass media. These particular events are not any more significant than others that might have been selected. The only criterion for choosing them was that they exemplify several aspects of everyday political activity at a particular time. The first item is an event in international politics (the efforts of Contadora, the OAS, and the UN to reach peace in Central America), the second is national (the kidnapping of President Febres Cordero in Ecuador), and the third is more local (party pressures on neighborhood associations in Caracas).

The first thing we must ask ourselves here is why psychology ought to study these three events. What does political analysis gain, or how is it enriched through the contribution of psychology? In principle, it is political science that ought to study politics, with the aid of sociology, economics, law, and history. What can psychology, which is considered a science of the individual and the subjective, add to such analysis?

The answer, obvious but no less important for that, is that *psychology ought to study these events because persons or groups carry them out.* These are human events, and the actors in them, when they are engaged in politics, are subjected to the same factors of determinism and conditioning as when they establish a family, educate their children, or work in collaboration with others. Therefore, we must ask to what extent the character and specific shape of these political events depend on their being carried out by one particular person and not another, or by one group rather than another.

It may well be that in some instances political events are influenced not at all, or not significantly, by the way persons or groups behave. It is quite likely that the reaction of the Contadora Group or the UN or OAS did not depend on who served as foreign ministers of the Contadora countries or as Secretary-General of the UN or OAS. In this instance it certainly does not seem that the personalities of those involved played an important role in their visit to Central America as part of the peacemaking efforts. It is clear, however, that in other cases the personalities or psychological idiosyncrasies of the actors in fact play a very important role. The way Febres Cordero's kidnapping was resolved, by his giving in to the demands of rebellious officers and freeing General Vargas Pazzos, probably has a lot to do with his personality, his particular perception of what was happening, and his set of values. What makes the event all the more striking is that President Febres was well known for his macho style, and even bragged that he always packed a pistol. In similar circumstances a Fidel Castro or a Salvador Allende would have acted very differently. Thus we have here an instance in which the psyche of the individual, the fact of it being one actor as opposed to another, is all-important.

Two tentative conclusions follow from this initial observation. First, the personalities of individuals can indeed significantly affect the outcome of certain political events, and therefore psychology has a contribution to make to political analysis. Second, psychology cannot seek to become the hermeneutics of politics or explain everything in the realm of politics, in part because there are many political events whose character is not affected by the involvement of particular actors. Psychology's specific contribution ought to be limited to examining political behavior (behavior insofar as it is a mediation of politics); in other words, to politics insofar as it is played out by persons and groups.

It would be a mistake, however, to think that the mediation of political events by the individual personality has only certain superficial effects, or affects only the way events are carried out. It also affects what is actually done, that is, whether it is one political action or another one that is actually taken. The character of the actor may determine what act is chosen for promoting particular political interests. The air force officers in Ecuador, for example, employed violence and weapons to achieve what members of the Assembly had tried to attain through peaceful and legal arrangements several weeks earlier. Both groups were pursuing the same objective of freeing General Vargas Pazzos, but they did so through completely different kinds of behavior. Similarly, the fact that it was Febres Cordero who was kidnapped probably was the deciding factor in the capitulation to the demands of the officers. Another president, in the mold of Salvador Allende, would probably have chosen to risk death rather than surrender.

The previous example illustrates an important aspect of psychological analysis in politics: that individual and social psychology are necessarily intertwined; the psyche always operates in a social context. As political actors, individuals and groups are bearers of social interests: Febres Cordero, the air force officers, and the members of the Ecuadorian Assembly are not merely isolated individuals, as certain psychologizing kinds of analysis could lead one to think; rather they represent forces in society. However, the fact that they are representatives of certain social interests does not mean that they act simply as instrumental mediators, either. Along these lines, we must likewise reject the simplistic picture presented by a kind of mechanistic pseudosociology or some kinds of orthodox behaviorism. What one side attributes to class-based economic determinism, the other explains through stimuli from the environment: for both, the person is no more than a puppet of external forces. That is simply not the case— at least it is not always the case.

Once it has been accepted that psychology can and even should contribute to political analysis by studying the behavior of political actors, we may then ask what specific object political psychology is to study. In other words, what is it that defines a behavior as political? What gives a human act a political character? In principle, that depends on: (1) who is carrying it out, that is, the character of the actor; (2) what is being done, that is, the nature of the act itself; and (3) the social meaning of what is done, that is, the relationship of actor and act to the social order in which the act takes place. Let us take these up one by one.

The Character of the Actor

The first possibility is that an act becomes political by virtue of the title or position of the person carrying it out. Activities undertaken by people in government positions or working in the state apparatus would accordingly be political. This is like the vision of those who identify politics with the state. No doubt a wide range of behaviors can take on a political character simply because those who engage in them hold a government position or work in some adjunct or connective organization, like the UN or the OAS. You can visit Central America as a simple tourist, or as a business person, or a journalist looking for front-page stories, but when you are the Secretary-General of the UN or the OAS the visit takes on a political character by that very fact. That is why people in high political positions like the president or the foreign minister find it difficult to have a private life. It is hard for them to engage in activities outside their job, such as touring through Central America on vacation, without those activities taking on a political character.

But people with government positions do not have a monopoly on political actions. When the leader of a neighborhood association draws attention to pressures from political parties, she is engaging in a political act. The same may be said of a union strike or demonstration, the activity of a business association, the sermons of a member of the clergy, or the community education of a group of marginalized people in a slum, and yet neither the union nor the business association, the cleric nor the marginalized group, has a position in the government. While some acts take on political significance as a result of those who carry them out, many other acts are political no matter who carries them out. What makes a behavior specifically political does not derive from the author of the act— at least not always or inevitably.

The Character of the Act

A second possibility is that the political nature of an act depends on the kind of behavior itself. In other words, certain specific actions would be political no matter who engaged in them. Voting in a presidential election, for example, or taking part in a party rally would always be political acts. What kinds of actions are those? How are we to determine them to be political, except by identifying them as such after they have taken place?

One possible response, an alternative to what was proposed above, is that political actions are those—and only those—which have to do with the functioning of the state and its various branches. This vision, however, runs into the same difficulties and shortcomings as the one that looks at particular actors, only this time the situation is reversed. Thus, just as some behaviors are political no matter who carries them out (such as the act of voting in a presidential election), some actions, as we have seen, become political because of the actor. Any action, even the most trivial, becomes political if the one involved is the president of a country.

Another possible answer to the question of what constitutes a political act is actions involving power; that is, actions in which some power is exercised. This view has wide acceptance among students of politics, who tend to equate the concepts of politics and power. But such an answer seems to make the area of political action too broad. It is hard to conceive of any human behavior that does not require power or put some kind of power in motion. And yet, except in a very loose sense, it is not obvious that every behavior has a political impact. As we will see, power has to do with a disparity of resources. Power can be found in any human relationship, from a children's game at nursery school, to a young couple falling in love, to the development of an agricultural cooperative, all the way to organized activities in an old age home. Not all these acts and processes ought to be regarded as political. But if the point of identifying politics with power is to assert that any act of wielding political power is political, then we just get further away from identifying what is meant by the political nature of an act.

Whatever the answer to this question, our three examples show that the political character of a behavior does not necessarily derive from the specific nature of the action. Activities as different as a trip, a kidnapping, and a press conference can all be political. Normal everyday actions such as a party meeting or a press release, and abnormal and extraordinary actions such as the violent kidnapping of a president or a civil war, may all be political. If some actions are political, no matter who carries them out or what the circumstances, others derive their political character from the actor responsible for them or the circumstances in which they take place.

We should note that the behavioral unit we are considering is not simply a "response" in the technical "stimulus-response" sense of the term—an isolated behavior of the kind behaviorism postulates. Rather, it is a complex body of behaviors, an activity or series of activities that have a unified personal and/or social meaning. The very analysis of a seemingly simple political behavior such as voting misses something crucial if it is reduced to the moment when the ballot is placed in the box, and especially if it looks at the election results. To understand a vote—the whole broad process that leads to a particular result at the polls—entails taking into account all the circumstances and all the individual and social conditioning that give it meaning. Voting, then, is a whole series of actions. It is an activity, not simply a behavioral response.

The Relationship of Actor and Act to the Social Order

A third possibility for understanding what is specifically political about a behavior is to situate it in terms of the forces and order that exist within a particular social situation. Insofar as an activity promotes the interests of a particular social group, and affects or influences the existing balance of social forces and the social order, that activity has a political character. Using this approach we may consider that an activity is political to the extent that it influences or conditions the established order or affects the processes taking place between social forces. Thus, the kidnapping of Febres Cordero has a greater political impact than statements made by a leader of a neighborhood association or visits to Central America made by the Secretaries-General of the UN and the OAS. To have such a political impact on behalf of social interests, the behavior of the actors must make use of or give rise to some kind of power vis-à-vis other actors. However, power is an instrument of politics, not its foundation.

This approach to the question seems more adequate than the other two. Neither the actors nor the actions alone make an act political. What makes an act political is the relationship of any action by any actor to the established order in a society. To the extent that such an act has a negative or positive influence on either maintaining or changing the existing system, it has a political character. Naturally, when broadly viewed, the fact that any society is a totality leads to the observation that any behavior is political, since in some fashion the behavior contributes to maintaining or changing a social order, even if it does so indirectly. An act may contribute more by what it does *not* do than by what it *does*. Such an extension of the political obviously offers no help for understanding what is specific, for if everything is political, then nothing is specifically political. Hence political behavior should be limited to those acts which have a verifiable and meaningful impact on the shape and functioning of any social order. It does not follow that errors cannot be made in identifying such political activities, or that behaviors seemingly not directly related to the social order, such as a sermon or the workings of family life, may not have greater political impact than other acts more visibly connected to the social order, such as party meetings. The upshot is that we must establish qualitative and quantitative criteria to determine which activities are political and which are not.

In light of these observations, we could define political psychology as the study of the psychological processes through which persons and groups shape, struggle over, and exercise the power needed for satisfying particular interests in a social formation. This involves the social interests within a social formation, the way they are mediated through the individual psyche of the various actors, and the behavior involved in shaping, struggling over, and wielding power.

Social Interests

Latin American countries are societies split into social classes, whose interests are at odds. This does not mean that in all the countries the classes are alike, either in number or in character. Their differences depend on the particular social formation in each country. What they do have in common is the fact that different social classes struggle with one another. It is precisely this class struggle that gives rise to the concrete shapes of different social classes. Therefore, political activity ultimately is tied to class interests.

Why then does our definition not speak of class interests rather than the more generic and perhaps theoretically less precise social interests? Because in the dialectic of history, social classes themselves are organized into other more concrete kinds of groups. Although these groups may be secondary in relation to the basic structural divisions, they are not on that account less influential when class interests come into play. Thus, while the major interests of social classes might enter into politics in a given social situation, so might the interests of sectors, associations, or groups and even families and persons. All these interests mediate class interests, which are their final reference points, but not everything that is political is a reflection of class interests, and sometimes class interests are not at stake.

A behavior is political when it plays a role in the social confrontation of class and group interests. For a deep understanding of its political nature, we must know how a behavior, activity, or process is related to the social interests in a given social situation at a particular moment in history. What interests does Febres Cordero represent? To what extent are these social interests opposed to those of the air force officers who kidnap him? To what extent are the social interests pursued by the military class interests, and to what extent are they specific to the officers' occupation, or to particular individuals or a group within the corps of officers? An answer to that question demands a careful analysis not only of Ecuadorian society's unique features and its social configuration, but also of the particular historical crossroad at which Febres Cordero is kidnapped.

Mediation through Individual Personality

In every situation and circumstance social interests are acted out by specific players, whether they be persons or groups: Febres, military officers, the Contadora foreign ministers, Ligia de Gerbasi. Because they are trying to advance certain social interests though the social confrontation that exists within a particular system, these actors and their actions are political. The behavioral mediation they perform is precisely what political psychology finds interesting. One aspect of political behavior is the process whereby social interests are translated into patterns of knowing and valuing; into principles, values and attitudes; into specific ways of speaking and deciding; into the specific behaviors in which they are embodied.

When Febres Cordero, while still being held by the rebellious officers, signs an amnesty for General Vargas Pazzos, he justifies his action as a way to "safeguard peace and democracy in Ecuador." Obviously, such reasoning entails a very peculiar understanding of what peace and democracy are all about. It is especially revealing of Febres's very odd picture of his own role as president of a democracy, as well as of the ethical scale he uses to decide which values to preserve in a moment of conflict. These mediations by individual personality—by the actor's unique way of perceiving and understanding, reasoning and assessing, thinking and deciding—are the specific focus of political psychology's attention.

Persons and groups represent social interests for different reasons. Sometimes they themselves are part of the class or group whose interests they are defending (for example, the landholder who joins an association in order to block any kind of agrarian reform). Sometimes persons and groups represent interests that are not their own, for other kinds of reasons (for example, the lawyer who works for that same business association, not because his own social circle wants to prevent land reform, but to profit from the legal battle). Finally, in other cases persons and groups may not be clearly aware of the social interests they are promoting, and indeed may promote interests that are opposed to their own personal interests or those of their social class (for example, campesinos who are drafted into a paramilitary group and then harass and attack the defenders of agrarian reform). It follows that although different people or groups may represent the same social interests, this does not necessarily mean that the same psychological motivation should be attributed to all of them.

Furthermore, if we are emphasizing that social interests are articulated by the personality of individual actors, it is because those interests are not reflected mechanically in social life, nor are persons or groups passive mediators of social forces. It is true, as Althusser (1969) observes, that persons and groups experience life in and through ideology; they do so, however, not passively but as agents who can modify this ideological mediation of life to a greater or lesser extent. That is, the behavior of persons is generally not a pure expression of the interests of the bourgeoisie or of the proletariat, or any particular class that might exist in a given social configuration, but rather the peculiar, partial, and complex expression of such class interests. Sometimes it may even be a contradictory expression, that is, a behavior with some aspects that may be politically useful to their adversaries.

Gaining, Wielding, and Struggling over Power

Since behavior that is political or has political features seeks to advance particular social interests within a social milieu, it requires power. That is to say, it needs the capacity to impose those interests over the opposing interests that are present within the same social milieu. We may reflect on the role of psychology as it is played out in the gaining, wielding, and struggling over power, always in relation to other social forces.

Political psychology tries to examine the extent to which the mediation of persons and groups figures positively or negatively in the satisfaction of their social interests. To what extent, for example, did the personality of Febres Cordero and his particular understanding of events in Ecuador become instruments to diminish the power of the interests he was defending, while strengthening the claims and interests represented by the rebellious officers? The president's name became a joke, with people in the street saying he went into the barracks like a "lion" (Leon) and came out like a "lamb" (Cordero). In individual personality lies a power source. When social interests are articulated, psychology is a means of power: people's character, their strengths and weaknesses, the consistency or inconsistency of their attitudes, serve to confer power or to take it away.

Actors seek to advance certain social interests through behaviors that bring into play different forms and amounts of power. The dissident officers in Ecuador used the power of weapons (physically violent behavior) to attain objectives that members of the Assembly had tried to attain through the power of laws (physically nonviolent behavior). From the standpoint of political psychology, it is interesting to observe the extent to which a militaristic disposition led to pressuring President Febres with violence, while a more peaceful attitude sought to convince him to grant General Vargas Pazzos amnesty. The point is not simply that the actors seize whatever resources are available; we need to understand that personality mediates which resources they reach for or try to use when they are advancing the interests they represent.

The effort to satisfy particular social interests entails confrontation with other powers that are trying to advance other social interests. But in this clash of interests, where class struggle is articulated on different levels of social interaction, personality plays a role. When a community leader in Caracas looks to public opinion to defend the interests of neighborhood associations, and invokes the notion that these associations must remain "apolitical" in relation to pressures from political parties, she is opting for a kind of political confrontation. Likewise, before the Secretary-General of the OAS could travel to Central America, he had to overcome opposition, for the United States government strongly objects to other forces interfering with its militaristic policies in what it regards as its own backyard. In this case the United States argued that the Secretary-General was not authorized to engage in such activity—that it was illegal, in other words. Clearly, the mediation of personality plays a more significant role in the case of the community leader wrestling for power than in the case of the OAS. Some other leader might have preferred to engage in private negotiation with the political parties, or to make alliances with other groups, or to act in some other way; whereas if another person were OAS Secretary, it is not clear how much difference that would make in the wrestling with the United States. Values and attitudes, as well as principles and inclinations to particular kinds of behavior, can influence the struggle for power between different social interests, depending on who the actors are, and on the processes, circumstances, and issues.

Our proposed definition of political psychology is an application of the definition of social psychology to the particular sphere of political behavior. If social psychology focuses its attention on the ideological side of behavior, understood as all those elements which refer to historic social factors (Martín-Baró, 1983a, pp. 17ff), political psychology will have to examine what is ideological in political behavior. Doesn't that become redundant? Political behavior is ideological by definition: its objective aim, the end toward which its own behavior tends—and as a rule, even its subjective intentionality, the aim the actor is pursuing—is precisely to satisfy particular social interests, and to do so over opposing interests.

The redundancy is only apparent, however, since political psychology is a subheading of social psychology. In other words, all political psychology is social psychology, but not all social psychology is political. The fact that political psychology is quintessentially ideological means that it is the quintessence of the realm of social psychology. Stated differently, the study of political activity is the most fitting object of social psychology, since by definition it has to do with promoting social interests, that is, it is ideological. Drawing the line between political psychology and the rest of psychology entails taking into account the character of different behaviors vis-à-vis the social system. This means that political psychology will study only those behaviors that have a significant impact on the structure or functioning of the established social order. It will study only those behaviors we have defined as political.

Pablo Fernandez Christlieb (1987) makes a similar proposal. He says that if social psychology studies the workings of a given society, then political psychology, which is a particular dimension of social psychology, studies the possibilities and conditions of possibility of the various social agents in the overall working of society—individuals, groups, collectivities. The "possibilities and conditions of possibility" point to the problem of the power of actors or agents in a given social formation. What is their real potential for asserting themselves and promoting certain interests— their own, or those of their class, or those of other persons, groups, or classes? This potential is not something that can be measured abstractly. It must be measured in the specific relationships between actors within each social order. Therefore we must clarify what constitutes political power from the standpoint of social psychology.

Political Power from the Standpoint of Social Psychology

The Nature and Components of Power

The basic feature that makes behavior political is its objective purpose of advancing particular interests and its use of power for that end within a social system. This reference to the "objective purpose" of political behavior indicates that it is independent of the actors' subjective awareness; in other words, whether or not a particular behavior is political does not depend on the conscious intention of those involved or whether the actors are fully aware of its political purpose. Politics functions by denying its purpose, and by either ideologically claiming to be above the interests of particular sectors or suggesting that power is not being used to satisfy these interests. Such procedures make it all the more necessary to utilize social psychology to study power, especially political power as mediated through behavior. To take the three examples employed earlier and focus them on the aspect of power, they would look something like this:

1. The Ecuadorian air force officers, through the use of weapons, overcome President Febres Cordero and force him to free General Vargas Pazzos, even though the president had personally refused to grant Pazzos amnesty only a short time before.
2. The Contadora Group is able to get the Secretaries-General of the OAS and the UN to endorse its trip through Central American countries, despite the opposition of the U.S. government. Prior to this endorsement, the Contadora has had enough power vis-à-vis the United States to prevent the Nicaraguan war from spreading or reaching a point of more direct U.S. intervention, but has not had enough power to bring about peace in the region, which would involve recognition of the Nicaraguan government, something the Reagan administration finds unacceptable.
3. The battle to put Venezuelan neighborhood organizations at the service of one political party or another is visible through such means as offering help or taking advantage of local leaders. FACUR leaders generally try to fend off such party efforts by parading their own moral strength before the public.

Since these behaviors are expressly political, the power manifested in these behaviors is also political in nature. But not all power is political; that is, not all power is immediately or directly at the service of social interests within an established order. We might note, for example, that the father remains the most decisive element (the one with most power) in most Latin American families, despite the loss of a good deal of power in recent years. In principle, the power of the father in a family is not political in nature, and its exercise does not have a direct impact on the existing order. This is not to deny that the overall hierarchical and male-dominated nature of the Latin American family has a political significance and impact, and that should it change, the consequences for the social order could be enormous.

Power is not something one possesses as one might possess a house or even certain human qualities. In this sense it is important to distinguish it from those resources which might furnish power in a given circumstance or for a given activity and purpose. Power is not something that the Ecuadorian officers had in their armories or that Febres lost when he went into the base where he was kidnapped; nor is power something present in Contadora's filing cabinets or in the FACUR offices, nor is it in the pants pocket of the father of the family. From the standpoint of social psychology, power is a characteristic of social relations among both individuals and groups. The Ecuadorian officers had enough power to force President Febres to free General Vargas, just as President Febres had enough power to bring legal proceedings against them a few days later. However, this does not mean that power arises as something created in the here and now of each relationship. Rather it arises out of the resources the various actors bring to each relationship. This makes it possible, even before the relationship begins, to state that one particular actor has more power than another to meet a particular objective. Hence power is not something extrinsic to relationships but rather is essential to defining the very nature of human relationships. Thus, both relationships and the actors within relationships are constituted on the basis of the exercise of social power. Consequently we can understand power in terms of four components: its relational character, its objective basis, its intentional nature, and its actual effect (see Martín-Baró, 1984f, pp. 103–126).

Power is a feature of relationships between persons or groups. Every relationship is defined largely by the power present in the confluence of the actors and the interests they embody. Hence there is some discussion as to whether power resides in the actors or simply arises in the relationship. I believe it is analytically unsound even to attempt such a distinction, since there can be no relationship without the actors or subjects of the relationship. Power certainly resides in the actors, not, however, as isolated individuals but rather insofar as they enter into relationship. The actors do not shift their power from one relationship to another, but rather their power or lack of it comes into play by the very fact of their entering into relationship with others, and can vary accordingly. The Ecuadorian air force officers do not have power in the abstract; they may in this instance have power over President Febres Cordero or over other individuals and actors, but in other relationships they may not have such power over others. In fact, two days later, the officers and soldiers involved in kidnapping Febres were disarmed and jailed by the Ecuadorian army.

What, then, is this feature of human relationships that we call power? What does this feature of relationships between actors consist of? Power is that condition which makes it possible for one of the actors to make his or her will or objectives prevail—and in the case of political power, to make the interests he or she represents prevail over the aim and objectives or the social interests of other actors. The father has power over the mother, the armed forces officers over President Febres Cordero, the U.S. government over the Contadora Group; and it is not difficult to anticipate that the power that rules in the interests of Venezuelan political parties will prevail over FACUR's wish for independence, at least in the short run.

Power is based on the resources available to the actors in a particular relationship. It must be stressed that resources are not power, but the basis of power. Naturally the more resources available and the greater their variety, the greater the likelihood one will gain power in social relations. To say, however, that the Ecuadorian air force officers have power, is to make an abstract statement. They may have enough power to overcome Febres Cordero (and to do so in a particular circumstance with a given objective) but they do not have enough to defeat the Peruvian army, their traditional rival, much less the U.S. armed forces. An older brother may have resources such as physical strength or knowledge and so prevail over a younger brother, but not over his father, and perhaps not even over his mother. Even more to the point, the father of a family may have resources for prevailing over his own family but not over his boss at work. Gissi Bustos (1976) observes, and rightly so, that the lack of social power or "importance" in the work relations of the Latin American male can lead him to become very authoritarian in his relationships with his spouse at home. Hence it is psychologically consistent that Febres Cordero's normal machismo should break down under violent pressure from military officers.

In social relationships what counts is not so much the number of resources (relevant resources, of course) the actors have at their disposal as the relationship between the resources and the actors; that is, which actor can bring more resources to bear in each case and situation. Hence power arises as the difference established between the various actors' resources that exist in a relationship in a particular circumstance. That is how the military defeat of the United States in Vietnam is to be explained, even though in the abstract its military power was incomparably greater.

Resources encompass a wide spectrum: material, personal, and symbolic. Not all resources are equally useful in all circumstances, nor are all resources interchangeable. Reason or knowledge generally has little influence when up against the immediate power of weapons, as is evident in the lot of Latin American intellectuals under military dictatorships. As the now somewhat trite saying goes, the "force of reason" is of little value when confronting the "reason of force." Certainly some resources are more universal than others and are more easily generalized to different situations. Obviously economic power is important, as is proven by the shape of our societies, which are structurally oriented to serve the interest of oligarchical elites. Thus the statement that "all economics equals political economy" is basically on the mark. Latin American oligarchies may not have moral or intellectual resources, but their money enables them to buy minds and even consciences to further their class interests.

Power is defined in relation to specific objectives; as well as arising within a social relationship, it is structured toward an end. Political power, though, seeks social control in a broader sense, for it aims at subjecting the social order to particular group or class interests. It does this in a variety of ways, and the outcome may be less comprehensive than what was desired, with results that are only partial or only effective in certain sectors. When political actors have power, they apply it toward achieving more specific and concrete ends, imposing their will to make the interests of their program prevail.

Max Weber (1925, p. 180) defined power as the "chance of a [person] or of a number of [persons] to realize their own will in a communal action even against the resistance of others who are participating in the action." Given our previous observations, we can propose a definition from a social-psychological standpoint that amounts to a slight modification of Weber's: power is the disparity of resources that occurs in human relationships and that allows one of the actors to make his or her objectives and social interests prevail over those of others (see Martín-Baró 1984f, p. 110). I agree with Weber that power is more a potential than an act and that this potential occurs in human relationships. My modification lies in specifying that this potential consists of a disparity of resources, and in making it clear that power serves objectives and interests greater than the actor's own "will."

Political Power

All power can be regarded broadly as political and may in any case be put to political use. In a more restricted sense, however, political power is the disparity of resources that arises in social relationships and is used to assure that society's organization and functioning will respond to the social interests of a particular group or social class. To speak of a power struggle or the exercise of power is to point to that situation in which an actor, person, party, group, or class has gained control over the state resources that will enable it to orient the social system toward serving the interests it represents or embodies.

To analyze power that is specifically political requires examining in each case the four constitutive aspects of power: the relationships between actors, the actors' respective resources, the objectives and interests they are pursuing, and the actual effect produced both in the actors and in their relationship.

Political actors. In each political relationship, we must ask who are the main groups or persons involved, and not be content to stop at their apparent identity. In reality, the most relevant fact for political behavior is that actors are embodiments of social interests. We cannot understand who they are except by viewing them in each circumstance in light of the interests they represent or set in motion. Thus, if the kidnapping of President Febres Cordero were regarded simply as a personal clash between him and a group of air force officers in Ecuador, it would be poorly understood. Both Febres and the officers must be analyzed as actors who embody particular social interests in a specific situation within the Ecuadorian social context. This demand for analysis means that political psychology must take into account the overall nature of the social milieu in which political behaviors take place, as well as the relationships the actors establish in each circumstance. These relationships will depend on the alliances, groupings, and secondary contradictions taking place at a given moment in history.

Resources available (and utilized) in the relationships between actors. Understanding the political power of a given actor involves examining the available resources that can be utilized in each relationship and specific circumstance. The distinction between the resources available and those actually mobilized or utilized must be emphasized, since one actor may in principle have available more resources than others and yet for one reason or another not use all of them. And other actors may profit from the resulting disadvantage. In other words, resources need to be looked at in each conjuncture, and not thought of simply as an abstract potential that is ever available. The United States war machine was vastly superior to that of North Vietnam and the Vietcong, and yet the United States could not put it fully to work, and was defeated. Similarly, the U.S. government cannot openly use all its power to impose its will in the Central American conflict, since it is aware that most governments in the world, even Latin American governments, will not consent to such a move. Hence the United States is forced to adopt ambiguous or ambivalent stances toward the Contadora Group, and finds itself in continual contradictions in its political decisions about the region.

It is also important to examine the kinds of resources available to the various actors in each relationship. In labor disputes, for example, the resources that management can draw on, which are economic and legal, are very different from those available to workers and unions, which are mainly human and moral. Febres Cordero and the Ecuadorian officers obviously had very different resources at their disposal (weapons as opposed to the law) making it difficult to determine in advance or in the abstract where the balance of power would be decided in a showdown. Furthermore, although we do know that a good portion of the official political forces sought to obtain amnesty for General Vargas through legal means, we do not know which forces were supporting Febres and which were behind the efforts to free the rebellious general. Often the actors may have equivalent resources, or there may be no disparity clearly tipping the balance. In that case, the relationship may force the actors to come to an agreement or to seek further resources, such as alliances with third forces, in order to shift the balance.

Objectives sought. To understand a political behavior we must ask what is at stake and what the actors are trying to achieve. Are the various actors pursuing the same objectives, or are their goals distinct? Are these objectives compatible? Or are they incompatible, so that if the objectives of one are satisfied, those of others must remain unsatisfied? Naturally we must connect the specific objectives the different actors are pursuing with the social interests they embody. These interests will not always be clearly visible; they may be hidden or even denied, as tends to be the case when power is exercised. However, the true political scope of each objective can be clearly understood only in the light of this connection with social interests; that is, by the fact that it is a concrete instance in which one social class is seeking to advance its own interests. Venezuelan political parties may promise the leaders of a neighborhood association support for their immediate plans for improving city services, but what they are actually trying to do is to co-opt their forces, by taking advantage of the organizing strength of the group for their own interests as parties. The seemingly unconditional support offered at the beginning often ends up the other way around, as they absorb and nullify the neighborhood associations' possibilities for independent action.

As a result of the difference between the objective aim or direction of an action (in light of the social system as a whole) and what the actor seeks or believes is being sought, complex effects may occur. A very wide gap between the objective and the subjective may demonstrate how politically alienated some actors are. It is also important, however, to examine how the subjectivity of the actors and the specific groups they represent may affect underlying class interests and what they may add to those interests. Without ceasing to have a meaning and purpose in terms of their ultimate objectives—class interests—some political behaviors more immediately and more clearly reflect the point of view of functional groups, such as the military, and even family and individual interests. Thus we must keep clearly in mind the different objective and subjective importance of behaviors as well as their distinct significance for underlying class interests. A national election is not the same as a local election, and approving a country's national budget is not the same as exempting a charity benefit celebration from taxes.

Actual effect of power. The way power comes into play in political relationships will basically define the nature of these relationships as well as the nature of the actors involved. Day by day the very existence of power defines the meaning of being the president of a country, or being officers in an army, or the relations between them. A president may, in constitutional terms, be the commander-in-chief of the armed forces of the country, but in practice may not have any real power over these forces and may have to continually submit to their judgment and to the interests embodied in the military. Such is the case, for example, of some Central American governments (El Salvador, Honduras), whose constitutional president has almost no real power over the armed forces, who serve as the primary instrument of U.S. interests in the region.

Political relationships may accordingly be characterized as relationships of collaboration or imposition, pluralism or control, freedom or oppression. When we want to define these relationships and understand the actors who participate in them, we do well to consider that those who obtain power achieve a favorable disparity of resources; they are able to lay down the "rules of the game." They are also able to define the scope of the relationship by controlling what can be done politically. And finally, those who hold the power are those who control the character of the actors, deciding who can engage in politics.

4

Political Socialization: Two Critical Themes

TRANSLATED BY ADRIANNE ARON

Introduction

From the perspectives of both sociology and psychology, socialization tends to be conceived as a series of mediating processes to explain the connection between individual and society (for a fuller discussion of this point see Martín-Baró, 1983a, pp. 113–120). Some writers see it in terms of individuals acquiring the norms and abilities for living in society and getting their needs satisfied; others see it as a molding of the individual to a society's values, demands, and requirements. But whether the emphasis falls on the individual or on society, socialization is understood as a kind of intermediate bridge between the two.

It becomes clearer all the time, though, that the standard conceptions of socialization are too abstract and fall short as explanatory principles. Their flaw lies in having adopted a particular unit for analysis, and then— as often happens—treating the analytic unit as a reality in itself. With individual and society we are dealing with historical entities, not abstract realities, and while it is perfectly all right to speak of individuals and societies, it will not do to think of them as independent realities, as absolute totalities. It goes without saying that individuals do not exist without society, nor society without individuals, but this almost self-evident assertion has important consequences for the subject of socialization.

If society and individual exist as mutually dependent realities, in a dependency running through the backbone of history, then we have to consider socialization dialectically, recognizing that neither society nor the individual is real in itself, but rather, both exist to the extent that they mutually give each other existence. If the individual is a human individual, it is because he or she is shaped by society; if a human society exists, it is because there are individuals who make it up. From a psychosocial perspective, this means that there does not first exist a person, who then goes on to become socialized, but rather that the individual becomes an individual, a human person, by virtue of becoming socialized.

This assertion does not deny that society—for instance, Salvadoran society—exists apart from any particular individual. Nor does it deny that each individual has a genetic endowment which is extremely important for understanding who that person is. Individual and society do not come from nowhere, and clearly they have unique characteristics that cannot be explained solely by mutual reference. But if we want to understand real individuals, Juan and María, we will have to consider their genetic heritage in reference to a social context. What Juan and María become is not simply a function of their genetic endowment, nor a linear function of their genes plus social influence; they are, rather, the living result of a complex process in which the two factors interact and mutually shape each other.

We may consider socialization, then, as those processes through which an individual becomes a person in history. This dialectical understanding has important consequences for the analysis of specific socialization processes, for it means that the variables we study can never be considered as orthogonal, and microprocesses must always be understood as connected in their essence to more fundamental macroprocesses. Berger and Luckman (1966) maintain that when we perform a micro-sociological or social-psychological analysis of the phenomena of internalization, we must always do so with a macro-sociological understanding of their structural aspects. To this we should add that externalization is no simple mechanical consequence of internalization, but rather has to be understood in terms of how a particular individual actively and dynamically works things out.

The present work is an effort to examine two critical themes in political socialization from a dialectical perspective. As can be inferred from the previous reflection, the first theme will be an examination of political socialization itself: What type of processes should political socialization study? The second theme has to do with one of the first matters ever studied in this area, what some writers call the individual's basic political bonds.

The Object of Political Socialization

From its beginnings, the study of political socialization has met with the thorny problem of determining what constitutes the specific area of the political. "The political" is not the same as "politics," and this distinction has important practical consequences. As we know, psychologists have concerned themselves directly with political behavior. But what is a political behavior?

The most common answer has been, those actions which refer to the area of power. Harold Lasswell, one the first social scientists to study the psychology of politics, declares that "when we speak of the science of politics, we mean the science of power" (Lasswell, 1949, p. 8), and he defines power as "decision making" (see also Lasswell, 1948). But using terms such as "power" or "decision making" instead of "politics" does not solve the problem. Explicitly or implicitly, all action presupposes a more or less conscious decision, undertaken to resolve a play of forces. As Freedman and Freedman (1985) point out, very few behaviors exist that do not have some sociopolitical repercussion, and strictly speaking, if we think of behavior not in the confining sense of behaviorism but rather as a unit of significant action, we can see that every act has either direct or indirect political effects.

This assertion introduces yet more confusion into an already confused field. Most psychologists have tried to resolve this confusion by identifying as political action those acts which are oriented toward institutionalized political objects: voting, participating in political meetings, belonging to some political party, flag waving, singing the national anthem, engaging in political debates. But if the perspective that considers all action as politically significant is too vague, this one, which identifies political action with actions oriented toward institutionalized political objects, is too wide.

It is doubly wide. In the first place, even when we accept those units of institutionalized action as constituting "the" political, what are their limits? Where does an act of voting begin and end? Do we reduce this action to the mere act of marking a ballot with a name or party symbol, or should we also include the cognitive and affective processes that surround it, or what this action signifies for the subject who carries it out? Can we omit the frame of reference and the values that determine the personal meaning of an act of voting? Can we consider the votes of two subjects as psychologically equivalent simply because both mark the symbol of ARENA (an ultra-right Salvadoran party), or must we try to understand what this vote means for each of them? Perhaps a sociological focus could ignore the internal meaning of the vote, though that would not seem very appropriate; but surely the social psychologist cannot ignore it (see Moscovici, 1972; Geertz, 1973).

Let us take an interesting example. In surveys carried out before the 1984 presidential election in El Salvador, the great majority of Salvadorans indicated that they had decided to go to the polls; nevertheless, only a small percentage of them trusted that the elections would be clean and honest, as shown in this tabulation:

Date of survey	N	Decided to vote (%)	Think there will be no fraud (%)
March 1984	2,178	85.2	35.6
April 1984	2,113	81.7	21.5

So, what does it mean to have a vote under these conditions? What is the meaning of the vote of those who believe the election is fixed? Simply to assume that every vote has the same meaning is to ignore the multiplicity of causes that may lead a person to vote, and the multiplicity of motives that can be hidden behind a vote for a given party or candidate.

In the second place, to reduce political action to actions that refer exclusively to formal political objects is to eliminate some very important items from the political sphere. We can analyze this claim with an example.

In a study of reference groups, Sherif and Sherif (1964) found that cars represent an important feature of the socialization process of North American adolescents, not only insofar as they reveal what the young people are exposed to (objectivity), but also inasmuch as they constitute desired objects (subjectivity). To have one's own car seemed to be a necessity for a majority of North American adolescents. In El Salvador, a study conducted in 1981 with a representative middle-class sample from metropolitan San Salvador found that 83.5 percent of the subjects felt a need to have their own car (Martín-Baró, 1981d, p. 780). To feel a need to have one's own car is not by any means something explicitly political. Yet, if a particular government consistently frustrates this need, it can produce unease, even serious political conflict. On the other hand, to satisfy this need might require channeling into the production or importing of auto-mobiles a great many material and social resources that could be devoted to other ends—a channeling and organization of social resources that is already political. When poor countries like El Salvador devote a large part of their scarce economic resources to the acquisition of expensive goods for an elite minority to consume, they are satisfying needs that, although not expressly political, have serious political implications.

For the ancient Greeks, the political domain was characterized by liberty and equality, as distinguished from the household, the domain of necessity and inequality. As Hannah Arendt (1958) points out, the emergence of the social in the modern era has erased that distinction and brought necessity into the sphere of the political. For the Greeks, it was taken as a given that human needs would have to be satisfied before political participation could begin. In modern society, by contrast, the political has penetrated every part of human existence, including the family home, and is seen as essential to the satisfaction of all sorts of needs.

The satisfaction of human needs is no longer simply a private or indi-vidual matter; on the contrary, it is a point of reference and a basic objec-tive of all political activity. Accordingly, political socialization cannot be reduced to the process by which we acquire norms and behaviors directly related to formal political objects, though this cannot be excluded. More fundamentally, it involves the social shaping of the human needs of a given population, and specifically, of each individual person within it.

Human needs are not formed and developed in the abstract. They arise initially from biological demands and the organism's adaptation, but they develop, are modified, and are organized according to social patterns. In other words, the particular historical needs psychologists discover in people are not simply biological ("natural") facts, but also social phenomena (see Sève, 1975).

Clearly, society does not determine primary needs: regardless of the type of society in which they live, all human beings have to eat and sleep. Still, what we find in actual human beings is not the simple need for eating and sleeping but the need for eating certain things and sleeping under particular conditions, and both needs are manifested in a very specific reference system. If instead of primary needs we look at what psychologists call secondary needs—needs that are less biological and more specifically human, like the "need to have one's own car"—the argument becomes yet more compelling.

To be sure, the social configuration and historical reality of needs is a psychosocial phenomenon with political meaning. How the needs of a particular population are shaped, what kinds of needs the members of a given group or social class develop, how needs are hierarchically organized in different strata—all these are processes that have to do directly and essentially with a society's political organization. To the extent that a set of needs corresponds to the demands of the established political order, it will benefit the interests of the dominant classes, whose social power will tend to be bolstered by this good match. Likewise, if needs fall outside the bounds of the ruling order's interests, or contradict them, those needs turn into a potential for rebellion and political subversion. Thus, people's political socialization is necessarily tied to the way their needs are formed and organized, both in terms of how their primary needs were historically shaped and in terms of the types of secondary needs they have gone on to elaborate (see Knutson, 1973).

According to Dawson and Prewitt (1969, p. 13 ff), "political socialization processes operate at both the individual and community levels," with the former involving the development of a self, or political subject, and the latter the transmission of culture. The argument is that the self, even when it has no explicit political orientation, is necessarily a political self, for its needs, orientations, and attitudes have direct implications for the political system. The difference between a political self and a nonpolitical self is in the degree to which one is conscious of how one's needs relate to political consequences; or stated differently, the extent to which one's values, principles, and actions are or are not consistent with one's needs.

"The political self," Dawson and Prewitt (1969, p. 19) point out, "is made—not born . . . It is political socialization which molds and shapes the citizen's relationship to the political community. Part of this process can be seen as taking general predispositions of the child and directing them toward political objects." This is an acceptable point of view; however, one would have to add that the molding of a relationship between the citizen and the political community is already implicit in the shaping of needs, values, and lifestyle.

The organization of a frame of reference presupposes an implicit political attitude, whether or not the individual comes to recognize that organization in his or her life or consciously reflects on it. Some predispositions become political by coming into contact with explicitly political objects; but, even when this process does not take place, the standard of living and lifestyle of any given person will incorporate a number of the political order's demands. The need to have one's own car is a political demand, even when it is not made explicit. As Frey (1964) points out, political socialization goes beyond the transmission of information and evaluation of the formal government. It also includes more general attitudes about the use and distribution of power, so that even if a particular family never discusses politics, the children of that family are still undergoing political socialization. They are acquiring some basic attitudes toward authority and toward what kinds of influence and forms of conduct should be accepted as legitimate, and they are gaining a general impression about the distribution of power in a particular system or some of its subsystems. From this perspective we can accept the position of Langton (1969, p. 5), who defines political socialization as "the process by which an individual learns politically relevant attitudinal dispositions and behavior patterns." Thus, not only what is transmitted in socialization but also what is not transmitted has political significance. An intentionally depoliticized socialization is a type of socialization that is very politicized.

Many researchers have pointed out that most families in the United States are not very interested in politics. While this may be true, it does not mean that North American children are lacking in political socialization. The values they receive at home or at school, the lifestyle ("the American Way of Life") to which they are introduced very early, constitute a political posture, or at least directly imply one. It is not by sheer accident that political figures like Nixon tend to appeal to "the silent majority," or that mediocrities like Reagan can achieve a high level of popularity and political success with the North American population.

Frey's observation cited above turns us toward a very important aspect of socialization: the acquisition of a social identity. We have asserted that the individual becomes a person through socialization, that is, by becoming a social being. This means that the personal identity each individual acquires through socialization is conditioned, though not completely determined, by the particular society in which he or she grows up. All personal identity is tied to a social status and a variety of social roles that presuppose a politically sanctioned social structure. Even something as apparently remote from the political as sex has a political meaning, as the contemporary women's liberation movements have shown. To be a woman and identify as such has immediate political significance: note what happens if someone tries to reject certain aspects of what this identity has stood for.

Paulo Freire (1971) has analyzed the way in which Latin Americans acquired as part of their personal identity a host of implicit attitudes that determine individuals' basic relationships with most institutionalized political objects. For example, the needs developed by the "oppressor" demand a political system with built-in structures to maintain inequality in the distribution of wealth. Most people are not conscious of the political implications of their needs; nevertheless, as soon as something comes along to call attention to those implications, their political dimension becomes perfectly clear. Salvadoran women of the bourgeoisie, who had always valued "not mixing in politics," took to the streets in 1979 when a growing popular uprising demanded social reforms that threatened their class interests.

Berger and Luckman (1966) hold that through socialization individuals introject the objective world of the society in which they were born. Identity, objectively defined as location within a particular world, is understood subjectively as something that is appropriated *together with* that world. The world the individual internalizes, the reality that he or she constructs as *the* reality, is not abstract; it is *this* concrete, historical reality, this concrete symbolic universe, congruent with the ruling political system or at odds with it. The reality internalized by the individual, inherent in his or her political identity, involves a distribution of power, a hierarchy of values, an organization of social needs—that serve to a greater or lesser degree the interests of the dominant classes.

What, then, is political socialization? In keeping with what has been said so far, we can define it as *the individual construction of a reality and a personal identity that are or are not consistent with a particular political system*. Let me explain this definition.

Political socialization is, above all, a process of personal formation. Each individual becomes a person through the socialization process, which is to say, through those processes which, in a dialectical interaction between one's genetic heritage and a particular society or social group, narrow down the possibilities of what one will become.

On becoming socialized, the individual internalizes a reality, an objective world, and shapes his or her own personal identity. Basically, to accept an internalized reality is to incorporate a scheme of values, a frame of reference, that will work as a system for decoding objective acts and subjective experiences. Csikszentmihalyi and Beattie (1979) maintain that the pattern of affective and cognitive "coding" one holds comes mainly from the family in which one grows up. Using the available codes, a person is able to perceive the surrounding environment in a consistent way, to interpret events in terms of an underlying causal order, to discriminate between relevant and irrelevant stimuli, and to decide what actions are appropriate in a given situation.

It should be stressed that this cognitive structure is not simply a style of knowing; it also includes contents and values. It has to do with what certain European social psychologists, following Durkheim, have termed *social representations* (see Farr, 1984; Jodelet, 1984). In the case analyzed by Freire (1971) the "oppressors" not only perceive the world from a perspective of domination and superiority, but feel that in the natural order of things everything—both objects and persons—belongs to them. Hence, reality is shaped not simply by the transmission of an objective structure of knowledge but by the acceptance of an evaluative scheme for analyzing that supposedly objective reality. Socialization involves both the formation of people's ways of knowing and the criteria they use for evaluating what is known.

Through socialization, the individual also acquires a personal identity. This identity or personal "I" locates individuals in the world with respect to others, placing them within the matrix of interpersonal relations that characterizes all societies of history. Identity constitutes, at least in part, the human condition Marx perceived so clearly when he defined the essence of humankind as "the ensemble of the social relations" (Marx, 1845, p. 122). This is not to say that the human being is not "more than" that confluence of social relations. What it argues is that the individual's personal identity grows out of the combined social influences of his or her particular historical situation. What an individual comes to be or not be that is "more than" that, I see as a different problem.

Our discussion up to now has not been specifically about political socialization, but applies rather to the whole socialization process. More specific to political socialization is the question of how an individual's personal identity and reality relate to a given political system. Political character comes from the way an individual's identity and world fit the political system of the society in which he or she lives. A successful political socialization from the point of view of the established system would be one in which the individual's thoughts, values, and abilities are congruent with those of the political system—with the interests of the dominant classes and the hierarchy of values the system implicitly or explicitly defends.

This conception of political socialization does not deny the part played by what are usually considered socialization processes; for example, the experience the individual has with authority figures, or people's relations with formal political objects and symbols such as the government, the president, the army, the national flag, or political parties. What it claims is that these types of experiences and relationships are concrete instances through which a more general cognitive structure is actualized or by which more fundamental values become concretized. But those are not the only instances shaped by the cognitive-evaluative schemes, or even the most important ones. The child is learning constantly how to behave according to certain values and to judge life from certain frames of reference. Moreover, day after day the child is learning the theoretical and practical ways of organizing needs and getting them met by means of these cognitive-evaluative structures. And these structures and needs either are or are not congruent with the interests of the dominant classes, with the ruling political system.

In his distinction between a "latent" and a "manifest" political socialization, Almond (1960) sets forth something similar to this, though not identical. His idea of latent political socialization includes personality formation and the learning of basic values that are not necessarily political but have political consequences. Manifest political socialization consists in "the explicit transmission of information, values, or feelings vis-à-vis the roles, inputs, and outputs of other social systems such as the family which affect attitudes toward analogous roles, inputs and outputs of the political system" (Almond, 1960, p. 28).

Time and again, political revolutions have found upon taking power that one of their staunchest enemies is the cognitive-evaluative structure—the personal reference scheme internalized by large sectors of the population during their socialization under the "old regime" (see Le Vine, 1963). That was so in the Cuban revolution, for example, as Oscar Lewis had occasion to confirm personally (see Lewis, Lewis, and Rigdon, 1977a), and as was made manifest by the exodus of the [disaffected] Marielitos from Cuba [in 1980]. Wilhelm Reich (1933) captured the essence of the problem when he held that a political system could survive only if it succeeded in molding the basic character of its citizens to fit its political agenda.

The absence of an explicitly political posture in no way proves "apoliticism." This was shown in the case of Chile during the Popular Unity government [of Salvador Allende, 1970–1973] (Zúñiga, 1975) and in the case of the Salvadoran oligarchy when its government tried to bring about a very timid project of "agrarian transformation" (Martín-Baró, 1977c). In El Salvador, values such as "development," "productivity," "technology," and "Christian faith," apparently innocuous and apolitical, show their political essence and consequences the minute practical measures are introduced that challenge not the values per se but the political system. When the agrarian reform was enacted, the Salvadoran oligarchy in the name of those values demanded a retention of the established political system, and in the name of those values fought all political change, first peacefully, then violently (see also Martín-Baró, 1985j). What we can conclude from this is that the individual socialized in those values has, through the very same socialization process, also been politically socialized, for those internalized values and those cognitive structures were congruent with one particular political system but incongruent with alternative possibilities.

The study of political socialization has to focus on the processes by which individual needs, thoughts, and values are formed with respect to the needs, thoughts, and values demanded by a given sociopolitical system. A congruence or incongruence may be expressed in a child's relationship to explicitly political objects and symbols, but this expression is not the one with the greatest political importance, and surely not the only one that exists. An examination of the standard of living, of the way activities are organized and how much time is devoted to each one, of the kinds of experiences most frequently sought, could supply excellent information on the type of political system to which the individual is being socialized. In the long run, it is this type of congruence or incongruence that will determine most decisively the explicit political actions the individual adopts in his or her adult life.

Basic Political Bonds

One of the most common claims in the literature on political socialization is that people's basic political attachments are developed during early childhood. At first, this seems consistent with the point of view we are taking here, but the claim rests on a number of suppositions that warrant closer inspection.

First, let us look at what is meant by this assertion. Dawson and Prewitt (1969), reviewing a fair number of studies on the subject, see the citizen as acquiring a political orientation from the roots of his or her political self, including political attachments and loyalties; from diverse forms of specific knowledge about and feelings toward political institutions; and from other more transient points of view. These authors hold that the identifications and basic emotional bonds of the first kind, with political symbols or social groups, are acquired in early childhood, and orientations of the second kind later. Hence, "the experiences and developments that contribute most to the acquisition of political orientations are concentrated in the early years. This is especially true of basic political loyalties, identifications, and values" (p. 43).

Given that primary emotional identifications and bonds represent a type of structural framework to accommodate elements acquired later, one would expect that knowledge acquired later in childhood and still later, during adolescence, would be consistent with the primary ties; and indeed, Hess and Torney's study of children's political attitudes reports that "much of the basic socialization of political attitudes has taken place before the end of the elementary school years" (1967, p. 114). Following Berger and Luckman (1966), one might draw a similar conclusion. They hold that secondary socialization passes through the cognitive-evaluative filter established by primary socialization, with primary socialization determining the basic structures of knowledge, telling each individual what reality is and is not.

The problem with basic political bonds begins as soon as the authors try to make the proposition specific and operationalize it. The first confusion comes up when they try to define the object of the bonds. A bond or attachment is always *to* something. What are children bonded to politically during their primary socialization? According to Dawson and Prewitt, the primary attachment has as its object certain political symbols: democracy, the fatherland, the national flag, and so on. Hess and Torney (1967, p. 213) maintain that "The young child's involvement with the political system begins with a strong positive attachment to the country," in a bond that is basic, strong, and stable, showing almost no change during the elementary school years. They see this bond as essentially emotional:

"it apparently grows from complex psychological and social needs and is exceedingly resistant to change or argument." This quotation from Hess and Torney is a very good summary of the characteristics that researchers have found in children's primary political attachments: an identification with a central political symbol (in this case, the nation), with ties that are positive, stable, and basically affective.

More recent research has questioned both the object and some of the characteristics of basic political bonds. Sears (1974) observes, for example, that blacks, because of the way they have been mistreated in the United States, are socialized with attitudes that are more cynical, cold, and mistrustful. Still, he considers that the special hostility of blacks is directed at the "authorities" more than at the regime.

Easton and Dennis (1969) postulate four steps in the development of children's feelings toward political authority: (1) *Politicization:* the child learns that there are authorities. (2) *Personalization:* the child acquires a knowledge of political authority through individual personalities, particularly the figure of the country's president or of the police. (3) *Idealization:* the child tends to consider political authority as benevolent. (4) *Institutionalization:* political authority becomes increasingly depersonalized in the mind of the child. Notwithstanding, as Niemi (1973, p. 122) points out, "As children get older, these images change quickly and dramatically," and furthermore, although these schemes may seem very generalizable, the level of "positive or benevolent views of political authority may often be lower than what was found by earlier researchers."

When one considers that the Salvadoran campesino identifies "authority" with members of the National Guard, and that the behavior expected from them is imposition of arbitrary power and abuse (see Argueta, 1983), we can see how precarious are Easton and Dennis's ideas about developmental schemes and their postulates about basic political bonds, in this case toward authority.

Taking as a case in point the black population of the United States, Sears, too, questions the stability of primary political ties. As he reviews Easton and Dennis's theory, and especially their basic proposition that early idealization and personalization constitute necessary conditions for a later diffuse support of the system, Sears (1974) points out that the concept of "diffuse support of the system" is very ambiguous and does not predict any kind of later political commitment or behavior. He concludes that neither idealization nor personalization seems to be a necessary condition for later support of the system, and that support of the system may vary constantly, depending on how much satisfaction the different groups in the system are getting.

We really do not yet have enough data to resolve this argument, and many aspects of it need further research (see Renshon, 1977). The people of Latin America, finding themselves in political circumstances much more unstable than those which exist in the United States, help us see the need for rethinking the concept of "basic political bonds," in order to view it in terms that are more historical and more relative. Unfortunately, there have not been many studies of political socialization in Latin America, and those that have been done refer to adolescents and youth (Montero, 1985). An exception is the study of Rafael Segovia.

Segovia (1977) surveyed 3,573 Mexican children between 10 and 15 years of age, who were between fifth grade and the third year of secondary school, to examine various aspects of their political opinions and attitudes. He found that "Mexican children who were able to go to school at the end of 1969 . . . were well socialized: they give adequate answers about their expectations; the child-society relationship does not appear overly harsh; they display a differential adaptation, perfectly fulfilling roles corresponding to each social grouping" (p. 3). According to Segovia, children show an almost universal acceptance of nationalist symbols and myths, and although in the child's world the boundaries of elites and masses are not completely defined, they have already taken shape, with the profiles of future leaders and followers clearly differentiated. He comes to the conclusion that "children's nationalism is the strongest legitimizing pedestal on which the Mexican state rests. What cements the blocks of that pedestal is authoritarianism" (p. 152). Segovia's study seems to confirm the idea of the formation of basic attachments (for example, to the fatherland), but it sketches out significant differences in political attitudes according to groups and social levels.

An examination of basic political bonds requires not only empirical data but, above all, a theoretical clarification. Neither the object nor the nature or characteristics of basic political attachments has been well defined theoretically. In this sense, the dialectical focus presented here may be of some help. From this perspective, the political ties a child establishes are not necessarily in connection to some object or particular political symbol, nor even to the nation per se. We should not forget that the conception of country and nationality we know today is quite recent in human history.

Basic political attachment is a function of the hierarchy of needs, of the frame of reference, and the cognitive-evaluative structures the child acquires through socialization. Psychologically, this attachment has to be to some specific object, but what that object will be depends on each particular situation, on the personal experiences of each child.

It is normal for a child of the middle classes to adhere to political objects or symbols like the fatherland, the national flag, or the president of the republic. Nevertheless, these specific attachments are circumstantial, and probably correspond to a type of concrete social situation, not to a general need felt by all children. When children's attachments are to the fatherland, the flag, or the figure of the president, this is in all probability because those political objects and symbols are consistent with the values and needs of middle-class children, with their individual experiences, and ultimately, with the social interests defended by their social class. But the same cannot be said about children of other groups and social classes. If we find in the United States today that the attachment of blacks to their country seems more questionable than before, it may be that a good part of the black population has become conscious of the fact that their needs and values just do not coincide with those of the System, and that this new consciousness has an influence in the socialization of black children. What is said about black children in the United States can with much more reason be said about the indigenous Guatemalan, the Salvadoran campesino, or the Colombian "gamín."

It seems clear that the socialization process necessarily involves the identification of the individual with one or several social groupings: family, friends, neighborhood, race, social class, or any other group. That this social identification with a group transfers to greater or different political units such as a political party, the state, or one's country seems not to be an *a priori* necessity. It is more logical to think that children relate to those political objects and symbols through the experiential and axiological associations they have with those groups during their primary socialization. Thus, we might expect a certain variety in the objects with which children form political attachments, and great diversity in the nature and character of childhood feelings toward institutionalized political objects and symbols. That, I think, is the reason why different researchers have obtained apparently contradictory data (see partial summaries in Niemi, 1973; Sears, 1974; see also Kohn, 1963, 1969). Palestinian children socialized in refugee camps develop political loyalties completely tied to the peculiar situation in which they find themselves (Sayigh, 1977a, 1977b); and similar processes, of a conflictive nature, have been observed in children belonging to groups displaced by the Salvadoran civil war.

Basic political bonds seem to be relatively stable, and the examples mentioned of Cuba, Chile, El Salvador, the United States, and Mexico corroborate this point of view. But these examples also show that the basic political attachments of different social groups are not always the same. In the case of the United States and Mexico, socialization firms up already significant differences in politically relevant attitudes of children belonging to different social classes. In the cases of Cuba, Chile, and El Salvador, while some groups defended the old social order, others adhered to new political projects, according to the greater or lesser congruence of those projects with their own values, ideas, and needs and, ultimately, according to whether the projects were in agreement with the interests of their social class. It has still not been proved that a concrete political object is a universal and necessary requirement for basic political bonds; on the contrary, existing data call for a more complex explanation of political attachment, linking it to class values, needs, and cognitive-evaluative structures, more than to a specific object.

It is possible that in adults basic political bonds and political commitments and actions are directly linked to, though not exclusively conditioned by, the level of their class consciousness. One would expect that a high level of class consciousness would cause individuals' attentions and energies to be channeled toward objects, values, and political activities consistent with their basic needs. By basic needs we mean their objective needs, not so much as individuals per se, but as members of a social class. But that same reasoning would lead us to expect that a low level of class consciousness would permit political attachments to objects and symbols inconsistent with the needs of the individual and the interests of his or her social class—an incongruity between bonds and objective needs. The duration and permanence of this incongruity, of this state of alienation, would depend on the level of consciousness the individual acquires in the course of living a life.

5

The Political Psychology of Work

TRANSLATED BY CINDY FORSTER

Latinos: Lazy or Hard Working?

One of the most common stereotypes floating around is that of the lazy, shiftless Latin American. Several studies carried out in Latin American countries show the extent of this stereotyped image, which people attribute more to their compatriots than to themselves (see Chapter 12 and Salazar, 1983; Santoro, 1975). This same image of the Latin character appears in countries such as the United States, where the Latino is stereotyped as outgoing, superficial, very emotional, little given to work, and loving a good time. Curiously, these attributes also apply to "homo psychologi-cus"—consumed by emotional conflict, completely removed from the world of work, and as Codo (1987) notes, portrayed as soap opera characters who for years have inflamed the hearts of Latin American housewives.

The image of "the shiftless Latino" is simply an international version of "the lazy Indian," harking back to colonial times (Fanon, 1963; Alatas, 1977), when such stereotypes justified one people's dominion over another, or the oppression of the popular majority by an oligarchic elite (see Chapter 3). Raised to the level of theory, this demeaning vision reappears in Weber's classic proposition (1904–1905) that draws a contrast between a North American "Protestant ethic" and a Latin American "Catholic ethic."

Yet in the face of this widespread image of the lazy, shiftless Latin American it comes as something of a surprise to discover that the trait most commonly attributed to the Salvadoran is "hardworking" (Martín-Baró, 1988i). What explains this startling discrepancy between the perception of

El Salvador's natives and the most widespread stereotype of Latin Americans? Does it correspond to a real difference? Or does it maybe suggest that Salvadorans do not consider themselves Latin American?

In Cuba, likewise, one does not find this degrading image of their own compatriots or Latin Americans in general. On the contrary, Monica Sorín shows in her work (1985, 1987) that Cubans hold a very positive image of Latin Americans and locate the origin of negative traits in the nature of social structures or governments, rather than tracing their genesis to individual character.

These striking differences compel us to revise our psychosocial understanding of the "lazy Latin" image. Group stereotypes, it is widely conceded, arise from concrete historical experiences. They are not produced out of thin air but rather emerge as phenomena shaped by specific dilemmas and circumstances facing diverse groups within a given society. Thus "a grain of truth" lies in the oversimplification of every stereotype, insofar as it refers back to some strain in the history of the stereotyped group as well as the other social groups among whom the stereotype holds sway. The contradictions oblige us to ask what part the situation of labor in Latin America has played in shaping the stereotype of the "lazy" versus the "hardworking" Latino. What interplay of social forces do these stereotypes reflect? To what extent do they reveal or obscure the psychosocial realities of the people of Latin America?

Needless to say, it is not the study of stereotypes in and of themselves that is of interest. Rather, what demands our attention is the social reality, both collective and personal, of Latin Americans. As psychologists we cannot countenance the underdevelopment of our peoples, the poverty and backwardness that afflict the overwhelming majority, and the prolongation of their suffering. Our task is to help overcome these historical conditions, and in so doing, to enhance the physical and emotional well-being of our peoples. Carlos Alberto Montaner, a well-known right-wing Puerto Rican journalist, expressed the problem with special clarity in a recent article, where he claimed that "what is absolutely wrong with Latin America is not the economic structure of society, but rather the personal work habits that most of us have. If Latin Americans are not disciplined, serious, rigorous, demanding, punctual, methodical, or studious, is it any wonder that the product of their labor is less than that achieved by Koreans, Taiwanese, Swiss, or Germans?" (Montaner, 1988, p. 73). Is Montaner on target? Could it be true that we Latin Americans are constitutionally inclined toward indolence and incapable of discipline, rigor, or dedication to our labors?

The Situation of Labor in Latin America

Generalization is a hazardous practice, especially in this case where none would question that enormous differences exist in the labor situation from one country to the next, and within each country from region to region, especially if we consider a place as large, for instance, as Brazil. If we wish to fashion a valid, over-arching vision that moves beyond a mere repro-duction of pertinent statistics, we need to mark out broad interpretive parameters with the understanding that these will be more valid for some cases than for others. It seems to me that three salient trends best define the reality for the continent as a whole: (1) the unequal division of labor, (2) massive unemployment and marginalization, and (3) the dynamic of exploitation and repression.

The Unequal Division of Labor

Every social order adheres to its own social division of labor, which the classic functionalist theoreticians maintained was a product of the objective needs of the society on the one hand and individual character traits on the other (see Davis and Moore, 1945). This view holds that the most capable individuals will rise to the tasks and positions of greatest social responsi-bility, and will be rewarded most generously for their labors. As surprising as it may seem, this kind of thinking still thrives in the propositions and techniques applied by psychologists and administrators who work in hiring and training, as though nature spontaneously takes charge of defining work routines and delivers the type of individual best suited to perform each task.

An opposing view sees the social division of labor as the creation of dominant class interests who define the existing order and who, by exten-sion, shape institutions to meet their own needs. Thus a hiring system that is intrinsically linked to class status determines the location of a person at one or another level of production or services. Although it is possible that an individual belonging to the proletariat or the peasantry might ascend the social pyramid over time, the assignment of job classifications obeys a rigid class order.

Even a superficial analysis of the situation of labor in Latin America today demonstrates that the second proposition holds the greater truth. Above and beyond the simple division of tasks necessary to maintain a society, the social division of labor is a primary demarcation that maintains class hierarchy and ensures the reproduction of this unequal model. Three principal boundaries or divisions characterize the hierarchy of labor (though of course others exist as well); we may identify these three as urban-campesino, professional-manual, and male-female.

The urban-campesino divide. Until fairly recently, the countries of Latin America were overwhelmingly rural. As late as 1970, only Argentina, Chile, Uruguay, and Venezuela could say that more than half of their population lived in cities of over 20,000 people (CEPAL, 1987). At present, other countries, including Mexico and Peru, find themselves more urban than rural, while a number of nations such as those in Central America must still be considered fundamentally agricultural, especially since they tend to exaggerate their degree of urbanization by defining as urban all towns with more than 5,000 inhabitants. Further, in a number of countries, the majority of the campesino sector is Indian, which magnifies social divisions even more.

Regardless of the actual percentage breakdown between city and country, no one would doubt that the social division of labor favors the city. Huge urban areas aggressively absorb all the principal social services such as education, health, and housing, not to mention the benefits that accrue from the state apparatus and whatever economic development does takes place. To say this, however, is not to downplay the existence of belts of misery that circle and crisscross every Latin American metropolis, augmented daily by massive migration. Rather, the point is that these shantytowns, and this migration, occur precisely because the countryside offers fewer opportunities for subsistence with each passing day. Thus in countries such as El Salvador it is accepted as fact and enshrined in law that campesinos are paid a lower minimum wage than urban laborers for comparable work.

Allow me to add that psychology contributes, more by omission than design, to this discriminatory state of affairs that is injurious to the campesino. Rarely has psychology placed the reality of the campesino at the center of its inquiry, probably because the social schemata that hold sway among those who dominate the profession are imported from the United States. In industrial/organizational psychology this weakness is even more glaring: psychologists in this field seem to have forgotten that working the land qualifies as a form of labor.

The professional-manual divide. One of the most common errors in the analysis of social stratification is the confusion of occupational strata with social class. By no means is social class equivalent to strata defined by job type. With this caution in mind, it is nevertheless clear from any overview of Latin American societies that a tremendous distance separates professionals, administrators, and businesspeople from employees, workers, and laborers. With each passing year, the socioeconomic gulf between the two groups widens, in spite of the existence of various intermediate sectors that struggle to fill the intervening gaps along the stratification scale. Put simply, it would seem that the so-called middle classes in Latin America are shrinking, while the abyss grows deeper and wider between those who possess a lot and those who possess next to nothing. Living within the narrow confines of the most developed cities one can lose sight of this reality, as happens with most professionals in the field of psychology.

The male-female divide. Without doubt this divide is another of the main boundaries that define labor discrimination. For the majority of Latin American women, nature is destiny. Only in the face of great difficulty can women aspire to positions of greater social responsibility, whether in the public or the private sphere. Crushing and virtually complete domination by men can be confirmed by even the most perfunctory glance at the cabinets of Latin American governments, the composition of assemblies and parliaments, the directorships of large corporations and industries, and the people at the helm of all the most influential institutions. The presence of women in some of these posts is the exception that proves the rule, and serves as the best argument to establish the fact of structural discrimination. In practically every country in Latin America, moreover, the identical work done by a woman and a man receives a different reward, to the woman's disadvantage of course. Thus in El Salvador, for every colón that a woman earns, a man earns one colón and 20 centavos (see Rodriguez, Luzzi, and Vidaurre, 1983).

While one could add other examples to shed light on the basic hierarchical divides that define labor in Latin America, these three establish beyond doubt that the prevailing socioeconomic order is at root discriminatory and harms the most vulnerable sectors, namely campesinos, workers, and women.

Massive Marginalization and Unemployment

To recap the argument thus far, in Latin America, under the existing socioeconomic system, distinct sectors of the population suffer discrimination. For sectors not incorporated into the system, this discrimination is even harsher—in an occasional or periodic way for those who are unemployed, and on a virtually permanent basis for those who are marginalized.

Social scientists first began to occupy themselves with the problem of marginalization in the 1960s, when centers of power in the United States grew alarmed at what they perceived to be the uncontainable revolutionary potential of marginal populations, multiplying like new "Cubas" the length and breadth of the continent. These power centers smothered outbreaks of popular rebellion throughout the Americas using "national security" as their justification. Today, the fear overcome, the theme of marginalization no longer generates serious political, academic, or social debate, in spite of its ever-sharpening severity. Instead, attention now centers almost exclusively on the problem of underemployment and unemployment—a strange switch, considering that unemployment and marginalization overlap in large measure.

While the unemployed are not found only in the marginalized sectors, it is fair to say that the majority of the marginalized—almost by definition—are permanently unemployed or suffer endemic underemployment. The problem rises to terrible proportions owing to the sheer inability of Latin American nations to generate new jobs on the massive scale that would be required for a solution, since they are strangling in the noose of external debt payments (see Wells, 1987). Official statistics in El Salvador, for instance, generally locate unemployment at over 30 percent of the economically active population, and when these figures are joined with underemployment, we find that barely half of Salvadoran workers enjoy the privilege of a paid job. Of course, as a country at war, El Salvador is a place where practically no one risks investing money, and the economy has been severely disrupted by massive displacements of populations. Even so, similarly high levels of underemployment and unemployment grow more apparent every day throughout Latin America. It is a cruel paradox that so many of our countries' men and women spend all their waking hours looking for an occupation that will let them make a living.

How do the marginalized and the permanently unemployed—people who are tied only by chance or a slender thread to the dominant economic order—survive without falling prey to serious mental disorders? Or are we perhaps dealing with entire populations that suffer full-blown pathologies? More than a decade ago the Chilean anthropologist Larissa Adler de Lomnitz answered some of these questions in her study of a marginal shanty-town in Mexico (Lomnitz, 1978). She found that marginalized sectors create their own system of alternative social relations, based on a principle of reciprocal exchange which in turn relies on physical proximity and mutual trust. The marginalized—Oscar Lewis notwithstanding—are not part of a parallel "culture [of poverty]" that translates into a set of char-acteristic behaviors, or worse still, behavioral disorders. Rather, their exclu-sion from the dominant socioeconomic system forces them to seek alter-native ways to survive.

It must be stressed that it is only because of their ingenuity, creativity, and energy that the poor manage to survive the pervasive poverty that goes with marginalization. Outside the stale air of the laboratory no one could really believe that the marginalized populations of Latin America suffer serious mental disturbances. The fact is, the poor show signs of a vitality that is astonishing considering the objective conditions they face (see Chapter 6). What might appear as "laziness" is perhaps better described as economy of strength, and what passes as unreliability might well be a consequence of having to maintain alternate sources of income. In El Sal-vador an expression of this vitality can be seen in a group called the Com-mittee of Laid-off and Unemployed workers of El Salvador [CODYDES in its Spanish acronym], which is taking on government and private employers and dedicating itself to defending the social rights of people who have been temporarily or permanently marginalized by the system of production.

Exploitation and Repression

A third trait of the labor situation in Latin America is the extreme degree of exploitation suffered by large numbers of workers, especially manual laborers, campesinos, and low-level employees. The same system that inflates the capitalists' returns on whatever business they operate in our countries necessarily demands the pauperization of the workers, whose horizon of aspirations stops short at the barest minimum of family repro-duction of the worker's labor power.

The system of course relies on a wealth of diverse mechanisms and institutions to make the worker accept this state of affairs as "natural" and even desirable. In times of crisis, it is able to channel and control ill will (Cable, 1988). The entire ideological apparatus in fact functions to feed the false consciousness of the dominated classes with illusions that promote individual success and vicarious satisfactions such as watching other people's conspicuous consumption, not to mention the dubious satisfactions of conformity.

The moment workers organize unions to struggle for their interests and rights, the regime shows its repressive face. The history of trade unionism in Latin America is bloodied by an interminable chain of beatings, blacklists, imprisonments, tortures, murders, and disappearances suffered not only by the leadership but by rank and file members as well. In El Salvador over the last decade, workers in search of better conditions have had to choose between unions yoked to the dominant interests and those which remain independent and combative and hence are singled out for repression with special ferocity (see Martín-Baró, 1988g).

Although there may be a great deal of difference between the Salvadoran worker and the Brazilian laborer, between Mexican trade unionists and their Uruguayan counterparts, or between the way racism and unemployment are manifested in Venezuela and in the Peruvian Andes, the three broad conditions outlined here nevertheless offer valid points of reference that allow a faithful interpretation of the situation in each country as well as in distinct regions within each country.

Psychology's Approach to Work

How has the field of psychology in Latin America tried to understand this world of work? It has tended, for reasons that need not detain us, to employ the social unit of the family as its primary point of departure, judging the working world as secondary and subordinate, best understood through a prism of family relations that offers the primary schematic framework. Insofar as psychology has in fact explored the world of work, it has done so from the perspective of the boss, the factory owner, or the company executive. More or less explicitly, the worker is held responsible for bending to the needs of production, without any suggestion that production should be tailored to the needs of the worker. Psychologists have tended to see the laborer's well-being as relevant only insofar as it is a function of efficiency, as opposed to viewing labor efficiency as one among many mediating factors that can enhance the growth and humanity of the worker. Furthermore, among all the interpretive models available to psychologists, the most commonly employed is the medical approach. This kind of thinking weighs the mental health consequences of processes in the workplace, assuming all the while that the findings reflect an individual and self-contained condition.

Within these conceptual parameters, one can distinguish two principal currents in the present practice of psychology: an individualist approach and a systems approach.

The Individualist Approach

This approach views work as one of several settings in which an individual finds meaning. Eager to reshape character or mold the subject in order to achieve a happy match with working conditions, it examines personality traits, habits, and skills, and places great importance on the aspirations and motivations of the particular individual. It does not, however, question the fundamental goals of the industry, business, or service institution. Rather, it limits its demands to ways of reorganizing the workplace, changing conditions that directly affect workers, and adjusting the benefits they have already won. Thus, psychology becomes a useful instrument to help individuals adapt to their working conditions and to enhance their productivity by improving their personal satisfaction, but without ever questioning the larger institutional order, much less trying to understand what the labor processes mean in terms of the social system as a whole.

In this vein of psychology, one of the most typical and successful models has been achievement motivation, put forth years ago by David McClelland (1961) and so well known it is unnecessary to elaborate. It is important, though, to draw attention to the kinship between this theory and Weber's conception of the Protestant ethic. Both lay blame for personal success or failure on the specific individual, the particular group, or even an entire society. To this way of thinking, the failures of a worker stem from that person's substandard achievement motivation, and similarly, blame for the underdevelopment of a given country would be assigned to its population for their inability to rouse themselves toward more ambitious goals.

Through the lens of individualist thinking, the discrimination against workers that holds sway across Latin America is best explained by the organizational pattern of hiring according to the personal qualities of each worker. Further, massive unemployment represents the unfortunate outcome of insufficient motivation or collective effort on the part of the workforce, while exploitation is nothing more than a false justification trotted out for political purposes by progressives who malign the system rather than recognizing the workers' personal deficiencies.

This perspective permeates theoretical models that on the face of it seem very different, but that at root are quite similar. Among them it is worth mentioning the model of locus of control (see Rotter, 1966), very much in vogue during the last decade, and invoked by various analysts to distinguish two classes of individuals: those whose personality inclines them to perceive the consequences of their acts as something under their control, and those who believe the consequences are dictated by forces beyond their control. In the first place, this dichotomy assumes that such consequences are always under the control of the person, a suggestion that is really quite insulting when you look at the untiring efforts of Salvadoran campesinos to rise above conditions of exploitation and misery, only to end up in the same situation or worse than that of their forebears. Salvadoran campesinos hardly lack achievement motivation or the willingness to strive for the best possible results from their labor. Yet such progress is denied them, as individuals and as members of a given social class, because the fruit of their labor is privately expropriated and diverted to the advantage of elites through existing class structures and distribution mechanisms. And this, it must be said, is a psychological problem, one that lies in the realm of political rather than individual psychology.

Systems Theory

So-called systems theory has achieved one of its fullest elaborations in the field of organizational psychology. From this vantage point, problems in the workplace are treated not with primary reference to the individual but instead as a pattern of relationships between subjects enacting various roles within the organizational hierarchy. Special emphasis is placed on the nature of institutional leadership, the structuring of tasks or roles, and the design of guidelines for decisionmaking in accordance with the aims of each organization. Interestingly enough, McClelland himself has turned his gaze from achievement motivation to power (see McClelland, 1975, 1985), which entails a more relational and less individualistic theoretical approach (see House and Singh, 1987).

Systems theory holds that each organization operates as a discrete universe of meaning without respect to its location in the larger society, its relationship to the exchange of goods, or changes in the larger environment. The logic of each business enterprise, regardless of the historical moment in which it happens to find itself, is defined by a kind of functional autonomy. The theory applies with particular acuity to the huge multinational corporations that exist simply to take advantage of whatever local resources each country offers, while only peripherally responding to their needs. Neither wage rates, hiring and firing policies, production quotas, nor assembly line changes are designed to meet the needs of the country or region where they operate; on the contrary, they reflect the internal demands of their own global networks. Rather than responding to the needs of the population, their interaction with the host country is reduced to judging available opportunities against the standard of whether conditions elsewhere might allow a more favorable development of the company's objectives.

The case of multinationals is raised here not for its singularity but rather because it shows the characteristic approach of organizational psychology. A steady stream of studies have addressed organizational needs, for instance, with the objective of bringing hiring practices to a point of perfection (see Guion and Gibson, 1988), with reference to training (see Latham, 1988), or in order to explore the institution's leadership and its general ambience (see House and Singh, 1987). Without doubt, all this tends to be very effective within the system of the given organization and the larger corporation. Yet it does not bear any relation to the specific needs of the workers, much less to Latin American countries. As Sloan and Salas (1986) have shown so well, this conception of industrial psychology promotes a variety of development that is insensitive to the social situation of Third World countries, and serves to reinforce their marginalization and structural dependency. Fixated on the goal of hiring, training, and motivating personnel in strict accordance with company policy, this approach never questions the larger economic setting, the primacy of the profit motive as opposed to service, the division of labor, or the inequality in decisionmaking power which lies at the foundation of its workplace organization.

Thus, from the standpoint of systems theory, technological backwardness and poorly conceived organizational systems that are linked to Latin American culture explain discrimination in the workplace, marginalization, massive unemployment, and even exploitation. To this way of thinking, the heart of the problem lies not in the political order but in cultural traits; not in the distribution of power but in the absence of advanced technology.

Political Psychology's Approach to Work

Political psychology would not propose that we toss overboard all the gains of traditional psychology or, in this case, industrial/organizational psychology. The challenge it poses is to overcome the deficiencies of the dominant theories, which too often isolate psychological processes from the concrete sociopolitical context that first produced them and that continues to shape them. In other words, political psychology is making an effort to restore the historical context that psychological analysis lost during its mistaken attempt at scientific universalism. Labor psychology has a particular need to do the same, given the intimate connection between the social division of labor and the political order.

The individualist approach has the great merit of paying attention to the impact of character traits, showing how a certain kind of motivation or skill, when possessed by the people engaged in labor processes, not only enhances efficiency but also produces greater personal satisfaction for the worker. We are dealing here with a thesis that is amply confirmed by empirical evidence, and to ignore this evidence would be foolish.

Having said this, we must insist that the individualist approach suffers from serious limitations and, in the end, offers a dangerously psychologized perspective on labor processes. Perhaps its principal defect, namely the emphasis on the individual, is also its greatest strength. Locating the explanation of labor processes in characteristics peculiar to the individual, it loses sight of the obvious, that people are a product of their circumstances, and that work itself constitutes a social process that transcends the individual. The psychologizing of labor turns the working environment and the world of industry into a supposedly fixed and immutable creation as though it existed outside of history. This type of approach, further, looks to the person of the worker as the source of all solutions for problems that arise in the workplace—a focus that often amounts to blaming the victim. In any case, this approach tends to posit behavior in the workplace as an abstracted activity devoid of historical reference and entirely dependent on the individual's character, understood as innate personality traits.

Beyond question the systems approach is far richer than the individualist approach because, among other things, it integrates the strengths of the latter while rising above its psychologizing bias. Its value lies in the examination of labor processes as a meaningful whole, that is, as constituent parts of a business or institution, making sense only in their entirety. Thus, the workplace behavior of each person is situated within a web of multiple relationships that shape a given system. This invests individual traits with new meaning, for they come to be seen in the context of interpersonal relations and in terms of their fit, or lack of fit, with the demands of the larger system.

The upshot is that systems theory is shackled by a limitation that parallels the individualist approach, though they operate on different levels. Both abstract the system under scrutiny, divorcing it by a technical sleight of hand from the reality of the surrounding society. In theory, the business or institution is conceived as an open system linked with others, yet in practice, this openness is limited to hiring and firing, which hardly affect the analysis of labor processes. Thus, the meaning of workplace behavior is explored without reference to the here and now of the system itself. Owing to this, the systems approach in industrial/organizational psychology falls into technocratic excesses that mirror the ahistoricism of the individualist approach. Its adherents minutely analyze the requirements for each job and the training necessary to carry it out; they determine the most productive forms of supervision, information flow, and decision-making mechanisms; but they never move beyond this supposedly objective technical analysis to consider the basic problems and needs that afflict society at large.

And what exactly does political psychology propose as a way of preserving the strengths of the dominant approach to industrial/organizational psychology, while overcoming its limitations? First, we must clarify that political psychology cannot be reduced to the psychology of the political, which is to say, a psychological analysis of political behaviors and processes. Political psychology takes a much broader sweep to examine the spectrum of behaviors, looking at the social order and observing the manner in which each behavior responds, either directly or indirectly, to particular class interests represented within the social structure (Martín-Baró, 1988g).

Applied to the case of labor, such an approach requires a study of how workplace behaviors are articulated and what forces shape them. Thus, political psychology tries to make the meaning of internal psychological processes explicit without neglecting their deep roots in the wider social context, and to take account of these connections whether they are direct and immediate or indirect and mediated by other forces. In the case at hand, we are trying to understand workplace behavior as a politically mediated phenomenon, and/or in terms of its influence on a country's political order.

Few would deny that the underlying power structure of a society comes into being through economic relations that dictate the social division of labor. If, then, power is rooted in the resources available to groups and people as they carry on in the diverse realms of social life, it is obvious that the world of work constitutes the political sphere *par excellence,* a political gold mine in terms of both groups and individuals. As people act to get their human needs met, social classes take shape, through mutual interrelation within the boundaries defined by the modes of production. In this same process, individuals flourish in their development, or they stagnate; they achieve their hopes, or retreat into alienation: they are humanized, or dehumanized.

The three qualities we have elaborated to describe the world of work in Latin America are historical expressions of a social order based on the domination of one class over others, and as such they respond to the demands of that social order. Discrimination clarifies class differences and reproduces the boundaries separating the dominators from the dominated. Marginalization and unemployment on a massive scale then allow the uninterrupted high margins of profit demanded by the dominant classes or foreign investors. And finally, exploitation and repression cement the stability of a supposedly harmonious system, which in truth is held together by the coercion of the dominant classes to which others must submit by choice, by conviction, or by force.

In its ideological dimension, behavior in the workplace appears as the product, expression, and channeling of the interests of the various forces that make up a society. Only when psychological analysis steps back to view the sociopolitical whole can it recognize the alienating quality of many work situations that, when examined one by one without reference to the larger context, seem innocuous enough and even desirable. The lack of meaning that plagues many occupations thus grows clear only when the entire process is reconstructed. At that point, one can appreciate the extent to which the fragmentation of tasks in production operates as the mechanism that precipitates and justifies the fragmentation of the worker. By dismembering workers' personal and social identity, the process permits their domination.

The political impact that can result from the psychologist's work in the company, whether direct or indirect, deserves special emphasis. To take one example, the psychologist cannot define jobs according to the internal logic of the institution and the particular characteristics of individuals, while ignoring contributing criteria in a country's social, political, and cultural spheres; for if these are neglected, what functions as adaptation to the business risks becoming a variety of political submission, and what appears on the surface as nothing more than technical training bears within it the seeds of political and social alienation. Thus, when labor psychology fails to make empowerment one of its goals, or the active and organized participation of workers one of its principles, it runs the danger of falling into psychologizing and promoting alienation even in the act of disguising it.

The image of the "lazy Latino" alluded to at the start of this essay—so wholeheartedly embraced by the journalist Montaner—offers a striking example of a psychologizing analysis that serves clear political ends while posing as strictly technical interpretation. In a recent study of the problem, Sherry Cable (1988) examined subordination in labor relations and identified three types of response available to the worker: accept the situation without questioning it; accommodate to it and try to extract some benefit; or alternatively, rebel. In each case, the response varies according to what the worker identifies as the root cause of the state of subordination. Attributing the cause to one's own incapacity or lack of effort is an entirely different matter from attributing it to the justice or injustice of the labor system. Only in the case of rebellion, that is, when workers attribute their oppressive situation to an unjust social system, do they say they feel alienated from their labor. In the other two cases, whether for reasons of resignation in the face of destiny or because some small gain is won through accommodation, the workers exhibit no consciousness of feeling alienated (see Table 5.1).

Cable points out that primary socialization processes, which are general, as well as more specific secondary processes, such as training imparted in the workplace, both tend to incline the worker to accept subordination. In the best of cases, where they promote accommodation, they systematically undermine the rebellion inherent in questioning the fairness of the system. The image of the "lazy Latino" crystallizes the most negative causal expla-

Table 5.1. The worker's response to unequal power relations

Response	Attribution of the state of subordination	Effect on power relation	Expression of alienation
Acceptance			
Self-devaluation	Internal, to incompetence	Maintained	Low
The world is just	Internal, to own effort	Maintained	Low
Submission	External, to a just system	Maintained	Low
Accommodation			
Status recognition	External, to a just system	Modified	Low
Self-ingratiation	External, to a just system	Modified	Low
Collective negotiation	External, to a just system (unionized)	Modified	Low
Rebellion			
Individual rebellion	External, to an unjust system	Maintained	High
Coalition formation	External, to an unjust system (non-unionized)	Modified	High

Source: Cable, 1988.

nation a worker can adopt with respect to his or her position of subordination, namely the conviction that he or she is personally incompetent, which results in a devaluation of the self. The crushing conclusion is that workers are where they ought to be, because they're no good for anything else.

One tends to arrive at a similar conclusion in the analysis of the marginalized and unemployed. Apart from whether or not they hold themselves responsible for their marginalization or unemployment, the fact remains that people who endure prolonged joblessness succumb, more often than not, to progressive passivity and the tendency to self-denigration. And that self-denigration, together with the deterioration of their material conditions, inexorably produces a deterioration in their mental health.

As Ramsay Liem has shown in much of his work, this kind of analysis tends to view the consequences of unemployment in very partial fashion, turning the unemployed person into a mere victim and thus dodging a broader sociopolitical analysis of the labor conditions in each situation (see Liem, 1988). All this is not to deny the damaging consequences of occasional unemployment, much less the scourge of permanent unemployment suffered by the greater part of the Latin American population. Rather, we urge that the picture be fully drawn in order to make clear what it means to face life outside the formal economic system. What it means is developing tremendous ingenuity to survive and come out ahead socially, tapping into virtues that are completely excluded from the dominant system. Contemporary capitalism, as Sloan and Salas have shown (1986, p. 245), promotes development at the cost of "(a) near-total collapse of any sense of community, (b) meaningless participation in the provision of material goods and services, (c) passive consumption of canned entertainment that numbs the senses and eliminates the possibility of reflection," and only illusory participation in the organization and destiny of one's own society. For these reasons, as Liem notes, in many ways the unemployed are social critics as well as victims. They are living testimony of an erroneous and unjust socioeconomic system. But this interpretation is unacceptable to the established order, which at best opts for pity rather than trying to understand the unemployed: it commiserates or doles out charity rather than listening to the poor.

Conclusion

A political psychology of labor in Latin America must pay very close attention to the critical aspects of the prevailing labor system. With new eyes it must examine what is emerging from the sectors that suffer discrimination, from the marginalized and the unemployed, the exploited and the oppressed. To see them not as objects but as social subjects requires, as Liem would say, seeing them not so much as victims of a system—which they are—but as that system's critics. Such a view serves two ends. On the one hand, for those who are dedicated to the psychology of labor it reveals the full compass of labor processes in the formal sectors of the economy. And on the other, it permits the discovery of all the various ways of behaving and working that make it possible to survive in the so-called informal sector, under the burden of subhuman conditions—through the creation of values of community and cooperation, sobriety and persistence, simplicity and the capacity for sacrifice.

Paying attention to what comes out of communities that are marginalized and discriminated against allows us to recognize the value of alternative forms of fulfillment in work. It also compels us to consider the possibility of diverse technologies, better suited to the circumstances of our countries and our peoples. Thus, it comes as a surprise that industrial/ organizational psychology in Latin America has had so little interest in promoting more appropriate technologies, which would make better use of the labor force, and which, above all, are integrated more closely into our own cultural patterns and forms.

Finally, this kind of attention to sectors that suffer discrimination in the workplace should bring about a reconsideration of what constitutes mental health in the world of work. One of the chief concerns of industrial psychology is to watch over the mental health of all workers—whether they be executives, employees, or laborers—and this is exactly the point at which the concept of mental health must be redefined in light of the political whole, moving beyond purely individualistic or technocratic considerations. One can hardly equate mental health with the well-being, often more than a little artificial, enjoyed by those who reap all the benefits of a discriminatory system. Don't we have to recognize that this individual well-being is built upon the denial of others and willful ignorance of unjust privilege? I believe that if there is any way to interpret the plague of managerial stress that today spreads across the upper levels of business, it is by reference to the materialization of violent and asymmetrical structures, which dehumanize the people who are concentrating power as much as the people who find themselves out in the cold.

For years, Alfredo Moffat (1974) has said that a more just distribution of material goods must be paralleled by a more equitable distribution of mental health, and that all of us should share equally the material limitations as well as the distress and imbalance generated by the collective life of our society. This is to say, we must leave behind the notion of mental health as an individual state, and move toward a more social conception that locates health within the deeper meaning of being fully human, with all the ties and social relations this implies (see Chapter 6 and Martín-Baró, 1988b).

Political psychology does not mean to hurl invective at the accumulated knowledge of industrial/organizational psychology, but it does seek to have labor psychology add a new dimension to its work by placing business within the broadest context of the surrounding society. If that were accomplished it would be able to look beyond the boundaries of the workplace, to take class interests into account and address the destinies of an entire people rather than just certain individuals or social sectors. Only through this expanded view can personnel selection avoid discriminating against the permanently rejected, can training escape submission to a manipulative hierarchy, and can decisionmaking take the most basic needs of the popular majority, rather than the needs of a privileged minority, as its central criteria. While the task poses a great challenge to the creativity of psychologists, it is a historical challenge well worth the effort.

II

War and Trauma

"War and Mental Health" (Chapter 6), prepared in 1984 for a mental health conference held in El Salvador, is the seminal piece for several presentations made by Martín-Baró over the next few years and formalized as "La Violencia Política y la Guerra como Causas del Trauma Psicosocial en El Salvador" (1988b), variations of which have been reprinted in English (1989d, 1989e, 1990j, 1990k). In some respects Chapter 7, on the psychological trauma of the Salvadoran child, might also be considered an elaboration of that earlier piece, for like the essay on trauma it borrows from it rather extensively. Overlap between Chapters 6 and 7, and occasional other repetitions, have been preserved out of respect for the integrity of the writings, and as examples of Martín-Baró's talent for reworking older ideas to address new themes, events, concerns, or data.

At the time "War and Mental Health" was written, the Salvadoran civil war had claimed 50,000 lives. By the time peace accords were signed early in 1991, more than 75,000 were dead, among them Martín-Baró. A major offensive by the FMLN insurgency in November 1989 brought direct hostilities to the capital and into the wealthy neighborhoods of the oligarchy. With the November offensive it appeared that despite the $1.4 million a day the United States was pouring into the country to buy a military victory for the Salvadoran government, the FMLN would achieve its goal of a negotiated settlement. Among its demands the FMLN was seeking an end to the killing and human rights abuses, and a remedy for the structural conditions of poverty and political inequality that gave rise to the war— and November 11 looked like the turning point in its favor. The Jesuits at the University of Central America, as outspoken advocates for a political solution to the conflict and as people prepared to facilitate dialogue between the government and the FMLN, were branded by the military as subversives, or in the Cold War rhetoric of the day, "communists."

Had they lived, the academics of the UCA could perhaps have played a role similar to the one later played by the Norwegian research analyst whose instigation of secret talks between the Israeli government and the Palestine Liberation Organization led to a breakthrough in the Middle East conflict. It was of course in part to prevent such a development that the military ordered their assassination. The war, as Martín-Baró explains so well, was for some sectors of the society a profitable and desirable condition: it kept the military employed, the oligarchy secure, the old structures in place, and the U.S. sponsors content. When the news of the death of the Jesuits was brought to the joint headquarters of the CIA and the DNI (the Salvadoran security forces), the intelligence officers cheered.

For Martín-Baró, steeped in the collective wisdom of his academic field and convinced that psychology had much to teach, support for negotiations was inseparable from a commitment to conflict resolution as practiced in psychology. An application of the principle of conflict resolution was entirely consistent with his idea of a psychology in the service of life, undertaken through a praxis of liberation. For this he was murdered by a U.S.-trained death squad of the Salvadoran army, who came to the Jesuit residence in the middle of the night on November 16, 1989, and with high-powered weapons shot out the brains of six priests and killed the witnesses—their housekeeper and her daughter.

While some may acknowledge that psychology is a tool, how many would concede that it is a dangerous tool?

Searching for ways to link his professional commitment and competence to the struggle of the poor and oppressed for a more humane and just society, Martín-Baró directed his attention to the mental health effects of the trauma of institutionalized violence. He was particularly concerned with the pervasive and destructive impact of the war on children, who, he feared, were being socialized to think of violence as the way to settle disputes, and whose options in life were being shrunk as the perils to their lives expanded (Chapter 7).

The analyses of adaptive responses to "normal abnormality" (Chapters 6–7) are part of Martín-Baró's sustained effort to find a place for subjective experience as mediating between large-scale structural forces and collective consciousness and action. In arguing for the necessity of attending to the concrete circumstances of people's lives within their historical context, he moves forward in his attempt to transform psychology, expanding his critique of the ahistorical and individualistic biases of his discipline. The horizontal and vertical axes of religious thought described in Chapter 8, together with the insertion of an ideological dimension into the study of religious experience, carry even something so personal as religious conversion into a sociohistorical context. The dialectic was for Martín-Baró a useful platform for correcting the individualist bias of psychology while exposing the historical forces that influence human behavior.

Martín-Baró had no quarrel with bias per se. He took the position that bias, or partiality, is unavoidable, part and parcel of the human experience, because all of us peer through lenses supplied by our societies. But bias, he argues, need not foreclose objectivity in psychosocial analysis—a thesis he proves admirably in Chapter 8 as he, a Catholic priest, engages in no theological dispute with Protestant fundamentalism, and simply points out without polemics the role of the United States in driving both the war and the evangelical movement. His purpose is to expose the tactical use of evangelical proselytizing in Central America's low-intensity conflicts, as well as its imperfect results. For this there is no advantage in delving into (and indeed, much reason to steer clear of) questions of faith and dogma—matters about which he plainly was not impartial.

In the essays on war and trauma that make up this section, Martín-Baró takes a strong stand on the side of peace and social solidarity, yet never loses objectivity in his analysis. Chapter 9, however, seems to carry this virtue to the point of absurdity, as he asks, in a query worthy of Machiavelli, whether psychology can "help explain more scientifically the advantage or disadvantage of using repressive violence as a means of achieving political objectives." What are we to make of an exercise that puts out as its central topic the question of whether it is effective for a government to torture and kill its citizens—that claims a regime can defend and legitimate its practice of institutionalized repression if it can show on a cost-benefit calculus that the behavior is rational?

Using Martín-Baró's own framework for understanding human behavior and thought, we can see this atavism from the Enlightenment as a reflection of a particular man's experience within a particular historical context. Written in 1975 by a middle-class Spanish priest whose academic background was in philosophy, this was the work of a scholar who had not yet lived through the massive persecution of his fellow citizens in El Salvador, was not yet privy to the disasters of war, and was still a year away from finishing his Master's degree in psychology at the University of Chicago. Socialized to an old order, he was "the living result of a complex process" in which genetic endowment and social context interact and mutually shape each other, and, in terms explained in Chapter 4, had internalized a particular reality with regard to "a distribution of power, a hierarchy of values, an organization of social needs—that serve . . . the interests of the dominant classes."

To be fair, it must be acknowledged that in trying to reason with the generals Martín-Baró was in no way trying to apologize for the growing repression in El Salvador. On the contrary, he was hoping to change official policy by convincing the military that its real goal, of changing people's behavior, was not being served by the government's repressive policies. This was The Prince, advising the rulers of Florence in the spirit of civic virtue, not the author of the Kissinger Report proffering advice in the spirit of counterinsurgency. And it is very much to his credit that, unlike virtually all North American psychologists of the day, who ignored the catastrophic political repression sweeping the southern cone of South America, Martín-Baró was paying attention to it and reading in it, correctly, a warning sign. Still, his very approach, of invoking the scientific knowledge of psychology to appeal to the intellects of the ruling powers, bespeaks a certain ingenuousness, not only as regards those powers but also as regards psychology. By 1986 (Chapter 1) the illusions were quite shattered: he would be lamenting the discipline's acclaim for "contributions as trivial as some of the so-called learning theories," and exercising far more discrimination in his respect for the power barons, making sport now of the pistol-packing "macho" president of Ecuador, who fell apart as soon as he was kidnapped. "In similar circumstances a Fidel Castro or a Salvador Allende would have acted very differently," Martín-Baró observes, making an objective but not necessarily unbiased comparison.

Martín-Baró's early naiveté and conformity to many of the canons of psychology he was later to criticize had the effect, perhaps unanticipated but no less salutary for that, of establishing both himself and his discipline as having something to offer the government, by way of science. For the government this might represent no more than window dressing, but for Martín-Baró it led to a license to operate a science for the people. It was no coincidence that he received the government's blessing to open the university's Institute for Public Opinion Research at a time when the United States was threatening to discontinue aid to El Salvador if the government did not show signs of progress toward democracy. But it was an opportunity, and Martín-Baró used it to build mirrors to reflect a people's reality. His surveys (as we will see later in Part III) were a further example of psychology as a dangerous tool.

As we contemplate the subject matter of the essays in this section, it behooves us to ask how the tool of psychology is being applied by social scientists in our own consulting rooms and universities, which presumably stand at a safe distance from war and trauma. What happens to that margin of safety once we begin to look at structural forces that have hitherto been ignored? One wonders if attention to the political structures would help us understand how a militaristic foreign policy, with quick but extremely destructive wars or the slow fueling of military repression, combines with other conditions—such as unemployment, racism, the erosion of public education, censorship in the media, and the rise of religious fundamentalism—to contribute to a militarization of the mind. One wonders how this militarization of the mind, if it exists, manifests itself in the various sectors of the society. Urban violence, domestic violence, child abuse, violence against women, juvenile gangs: is it possible that these have been looked at too often as *problems,* requiring individual rehabilitation of perpetrators and victims, and not often enough as *symptoms* calling for a collective intervention? One wonders about the origins and ramifications of anti-immigrant sentiment, and its effects on the collective consciousness of a people, and especially its relationship to the educational system—from legislation that would exclude refugee children from the public schools, to policies that would dismantle ethnic studies programs in the universities.

Martín-Baró's critical examination of life in El Salvador points not only to the lessons to be learned from war and extreme repression but also to a methodology and perspective that can fruitfully be adopted in other countries and other situations. His most important message is perhaps not about El Salvador, or even about the Third World, but about what needs to be done everywhere if psychology is to make a place for itself in the continuing struggle for human liberation.

6

War and Mental Health

TRANSLATED BY ANNE WALLACE

Mental Health

Amid the hardships of a deadly civil war, with its accumulating problems of massive unemployment, prolonged periods of hunger, the displacement of hundreds of thousands of people, and even the annihilation of entire communities, it might seem frivolous to dedicate time and effort to reflecting upon mental health. Faced with a "limit situation" like the one in El Salvador, when the very historical viability and survival of a people are in question, it would seem a mockery, an act of a decadent aristocracy, to devote ourselves to discussing psychological well-being.

At the heart of this well-intentioned critique lies a very constricted understanding of mental health, defining it first as the absence of psychological disorders and then as the healthy functioning of a human being. From this perspective, mental health is seen as an individual characteristic, attributed in principle to those who show no significant disturbances in their ways of thinking, feeling, or acting while adapting to their environment (see Braunstein, 1979). Anyone who doesn't suffer paralyzing anxiety attacks, who can go about his or her daily work without hallucinating dangers or imagining conspiracies, who attends to the demands of family life without mistreating his or her children or submitting to the mind-numbing tyranny of alcohol, would be considered healthy and normal.

Given this understanding, mental health would clearly be a relatively secondary problem, for two reasons. In the first place, before concerning itself with anxiety, delirium, or compulsive escapism, any human community must concern itself with the survival of its members: when life itself is at stake, it would obviously be folly to speak of the quality of that life. *Primum vivere, deinde philosophare—before philosophizing about life, we must ensure life itself.* Second, this understanding of mental illness would make it a minority problem, a problem that would affect only a small segment of the population. Even if we agree that psychological problems trouble more people than those who are hospitalized in psychiatric clinics or seek the advice of specialists, we would still have to reiterate that, from this perspective, the majority of the population can be classified as mentally healthy; therefore, mental health problems concern only a few people. This is the reason it has been said, not unjustifiably, that mental illness is a disease of developed societies but not a problem of those who struggle with the more prosaic and fundamental demands of economically and socially underdeveloped societies.

In contrast to this partial and superstructural conception, I believe that mental health must be understood in broader, more positive terms. The problem is not due entirely to the use of the "medical model" (see Szasz, 1961; Cooper, 1967), for it seems that even the leading schools of psychiatry no longer subscribe to this model in practice (see Smith and Kraft, 1983). The problem is rooted in a limited conception of human beings that reduces them to individual organisms whose functioning can be understood in terms of their individual characteristics and features. Such a conception denies their existence as historical beings whose life is developed and fulfilled in a complex web of social relations. If the uniqueness of human beings consists less in their being endowed with life (that is, in their organic existence), and more in the kind of life they construct historically, then mental health ceases to be a secondary problem and becomes a fundamental one. It is not a matter of the individual's satisfactory functioning; rather, it is a matter of the basic character of human relations, for this is what defines the possibilities for humanization that open up for the members of each society and group. To put it more plainly, mental health is a dimension of the relations between persons and groups more than an individual state, even though this dimension may take root differently in the body of each of the individuals involved in these relations, thereby producing a diversity of manifestations ("symptoms") and states ("syndromes").

The *Diagnostic and Statistical Manual of Mental Disorders, DSM-III,* of the American Psychiatric Association (1980), which some consider the *vademecum* of those who work in mental health, has introduced significant changes into its taxonomic system since its two previous editions. Probably the most important change is that disorders are no longer considered pathological entities but rather configurations in which different aspects of human life converge; specifically, the *DSM-III* describes five axes on which to base a diagnosis (see Millon, 1983; Eysenck, Wakefield, and Friedman, 1983). Although they are assigned only an auxiliary role in the understanding of disorders, of particular interest is the incorporation of Axis IV, on psychosocial pressures and tensions, and Axis V, on the degree of the person's adaptation in his or her most recent past. Although the *DSM-III* tries to avoid favoring certain theories (and its editors went so absurdly far as to make decisions by majority vote or according to what would suit the insurance companies), there is at least the dawning recognition that neither mental disorders, nor mental health for that matter, are simply products of an individual's varying organic states; they are also particular ways of being in the world (Binswanger, 1956) and even of shaping the world.

The advance made in the *DSM-III,* though worthwhile, still leaves much to be desired, especially from the perspective of those who enter the field of mental health through psychology, not psychiatry (see Eysenck, Wakefield, and Friedman, 1983; McLemore and Benjamin, 1979; Schacht and Nathan, 1977; Smith and Kraft, 1983). As Theodore Millon (1983), one of the few psychologists who participated in preparing this edition, indicated, a fuller acknowledgment of the interdependence of behavior and environment is still lacking, and what is missing, above all, is the incorporation of the interpersonal dimension as the unifying axis of human existence.

There has been a tendency to consider mental health and illness as healthy or unhealthy outward manifestations of an individual's functioning, governed essentially, but not exclusively, by internal laws. On the other hand, as Giovanni Jervis (1979) points out, instead of speaking of mental disorder, it would be more useful and accurate to say that people may find themselves in a social situation that causes them problems they are not capable of resolving, and that leads them to act in a way that others recognize as inappropriate. Clearly, mental disorders or problems pertain not only to the individual but also to the individual's relationships with others. But if this is the case, then mental health should also be understood as a problem of social relationships—between people and between groups—which will provoke crises, depending on the case, within an individual or a family, inside an institution, or in a whole society.

It is important to emphasize that we are not trying to simplify a problem as complex as mental health by denying its personal roots or, in trying to avoid individual reductionism, replacing it with social reductionism. In the end, we always have to answer the question, Why this person and not that one? But we want to emphasize how enlightening it is to change the lens and see mental health or illness not from the inside out but from the outside in; not as the result of an individual's internal functioning but as the manifestation, in a person or group, of the humanizing or alienating character of a framework of historical relationships (see also Guinsberg, 1983). From this perspective, for example, it may be that a psychological disorder is an abnormal reaction to a normal situation; but it may also happen to be a normal reaction to an abnormal situation.

The first time I came into contact with groups of campesinos displaced by the war, I felt that much of their behavior showed aspects of paranoid delirium. They were constantly alert and hyper-vigilant, and they mistrusted anyone they didn't know. They were suspicious of everyone who approached them, scrutinizing gestures and words, looking for possible danger. And yet, when I learned about what had happened to them and the real dangers still preying on them, as well as their defenselessness and impotence against any type of attack, I quickly began to understand that their hyper-mistrust and vigilance were not signs of a persecution delirium born of their anxiety, but rather the most realistic response to their life situation (see Morán, 1983). This was, without any doubt, the most normal reaction one could hope for, given the abnormal circumstances they had to face (for a recent, paradigmatic case, see "El Exterminio de 'las Masas,' " 1984). [For an English-language discussion of the massacre at El Mozote, see Danner, 1994.—Eds.]

If mental health and illness are both a part of, and a result of, social relationships, the question of the mental health of a people leads us to analyze the specific character of their most common and significant interpersonal and inter-group relationships. This perspective allows us to appreciate to its fullest the impact that events which substantially affect human relations have on the mental health of a people—events like natural catastrophes, socioeconomic crises, and war. Of these three kinds of events, there is no doubt that war has the most profound effects, because as well as involving socioeconomic crisis and human, if not natural, catastrophe, it also engenders irrationality and dehumanization (See Spielberger, Sarason, and Milgram, 1982).

The Civil War in El Salvador

El Salvador has been engaged in a civil war for the past three and a half years [since 1980]—a war that is no less real for being officially denied, nor less destructive on account of its irregular character. Every day, the media report the number of dead or wounded in battle or in ambushes, or the destruction of bridges or communication lines, or the intensive bombing of mountains, fields, and towns. We know that the victims of repression, who make up the hidden face of the war, number upward of, perhaps more than, 50,000 people. The majority of these victims are civilians not directly involved in the conflict. Many of them were barbarically tortured before their execution, and reviled as terrorists after their murder or "disappearance." In addition there are the one million Salvadorans—in other words one out of every five of the country's inhabitants—who, to save their lives, have had to flee their homes, to become internally displaced or refugees in other countries (Lawyers' Committee, 1984; Achaerandio, 1983; Morales, 1983).

In order to examine the possible impact of the war on the mental health of the Salvadoran people, we must try to understand the war itself, the ways in which it alters and shapes social relations. The war can be described in three words: violence, polarization, and lies.

Above all, the violence. This is the most immediate fact, the most wounding, and for this very reason, the most susceptible to a rationalizing ideologization. War implies a conflict of interests between social groups that take up arms as a way of resolving their differences. As has often been said, in war it no longer matters how right each contender may be. What counts is that might makes right: military power, the ability to hurt and destroy the opponent. Thus, in the relations between groups, reason is displaced by aggression, and military operations take the place of the thoughtful analysis of problems. The best resources, both human and material, are oriented toward the destruction of the enemy. And the most damaging effect of all is that, as the war drags on, the recourse to violence, which at one time was considered only as a last resort and temporary solution, becomes a habit and the preferred response. Studies have proven that the use of violence can be attributed less to destructive impulses or psychopathic personalities than to its instrumental value in a given situation as a means of getting what one wants (Sabini, 1978; Martín-Baró, 1983a). Therefore, a society that becomes accustomed to using violence to solve its problems, both large and small, is a society in which the roots of human relations are diseased.

Secondly, war implies social polarization, the displacement of groups toward opposite extremes. A critical split is produced in the framework of coexistence, leading to a radical differentiation between "them" and "us," where "they" are from the outset the "bad guys," and "we" are the "good guys." The rivals contemplate each other in an ethical mirror that inverts characteristics and values, to the point that what is reproached in "them" as a defect is praised in "us" as a virtue (see Bronfenbrenner, 1961; White, 1966; Martín-Baró, 1980c). This polarization exacerbates differing social interests and, in the end, implicates the whole scope of existence. People, actions, and things are no longer valued in and of themselves, but rather on the basis of whether they are "ours" or "theirs," and in terms of what they have to offer either for or against our side in the conflict. Thus the basis for daily interaction disappears. No frame of reference can be taken for granted as valid for everyone; values no longer have any collective validity, and even the possibility of appealing to "common sense" is lost, because the assumptions of coexistence themselves are being put on trial.

By its very dynamic, the phenomenon of social polarization tends to spread to all sectors of a population. The already polarized nuclei seek and even demand that everyone define themselves in partisan terms. Thus, not making a commitment to certain groups is seen as a sign of commitment to certain other ones, and identifying with neither side entails the risk of being considered an enemy by both sides. It is very likely that the process of social polarization has already reached its climax in El Salvador, that is, unless there is an invasion by the United States. The prolongation of the war and the resulting weariness appear to lead more and more people to a conscious rejection of identification with both sides in the war. However, this does not prevent their feeling more sympathy for some people than for others (Martín-Baró, 1983c). But both polarization and dissociation crack the foundation of coexistence and induce an exhausting climate of socio-emotional tension.

The third characteristic of the war is the lie. The lie ranges from corruption of institutions to intentional deception in public discourse, and includes an environment of distrustful falsehood in which most people tend to hide their opinions and even their choices. Almost without realizing it, we have become accustomed to institutions being exactly the opposite of what they are meant to be: those responsible for guaranteeing our safety are the main source of insecurity; those in charge of justice defend abuse and injustice; those called on to enlighten and guide are the first to deceive and manipulate. The lie has come to permeate our existence to such an extent that we end up creating an imaginary world, whose only truth is precisely that it is a false world, and whose only pillar of support is the fear of reality, which is too "subversive" to be tolerated (see Poirer, 1970). In this environment of lies, thrown off balance by social polarization, with no place for sanity and reason, violence dominates life to such an extent that, as Friedrich Hacker says (1973), people begin to believe that violence is the only solution to the problem of violence itself.

The Impact of the War on Mental Health

This brief characterization of the Salvadoran war allows us to reflect on its impact on the mental health of the population. Our first conclusion must be that, if the mental health of a group of human beings depends primarily on the character of their social relations, then the mental health of the Salvadoran people must be in a state of serious deterioration, whether or not that deterioration clearly presents in individual disorders. As indicated above, if we look at mental health or disturbance from a perspective that moves from the whole to its parts, from collective behavior to the individual mind, the disturbance may be found at different levels and may affect different entities. In some cases the individual will be the one who is disturbed, but in others it will be an entire family, a specific group, or even an organization. No one doubts today that Hitler's national socialism presupposed a deep disturbance in German society, a serious deterioration of its mental health, which manifested in institutional behavior as aberrant as the massacre of millions of Jews. In the truest sense, Nazi society was a disturbed society, a society based on dehumanizing social relations, even in cases where this disturbance may not have manifested itself in personal disorders that could be diagnosed with the *DSM-III*.

I am not saying that Salvadoran society is sick; I believe that the medical metaphor would be even more deceptive here than it has been regarding traditional conceptions of mental health. What I am saying is that the roots of social coexistence in El Salvador are seriously damaged. How could it be otherwise in an environment where resorting to violence is the principal means for resolving differences between persons and groups, where common sense has been replaced by partisan sense, where unreason stifles the possibility of humanizing contact between different social sectors and prevents the development of a daily normality?

Freud's famous response when asked to describe a psychologically healthy person was: someone who is able to work and to love. In our country, the problem is not Salvadorans' undeniable capacity to work; the problem is that there is no work. The acknowledged rate of real unemployment is 20 percent; when added to underemployment, which in effect is also unemployment, the figure reaches 60 percent of the economically active population (UNICEF, 1983; El Salvador, 1984). It isn't a play on words to say that the main occupation of most Salvadorans is to find an occupation, to find work and employment. Work is the basic source for the development of the human personality, the process that shapes the identity most, the fundamental context for our human fulfillment or failure (Martín-Baró, 1983a). So what will become of all those Salvadorans, half of our population, who are unable to find jobs no matter how hard they look? And something similar must be said about the ability to love. If Salvadorans have proven anything, it is their immense capacity for self-sacrifice, empathy, and solidarity. In the final analysis, love is a mutual union and giving of oneself. But this love finds itself blocked by the personal and social lie, by the simplistic schemes that divide the world into black and white, by the violence that corrodes the foundation of respect and trust between people and groups.

Without doubt, of all the deleterious effects of the war on the mental health of the Salvadoran people, the undermining of social relations is the worst, for our social relations are the scaffolding we rely on to construct ourselves historically, both as individuals and as a human community. Whether or not it manifests in individual disorders, the deterioration of social interaction is in and of itself a serious social disturbance, an erosion of our collective capacity to work and love, to assert our unique identity, to tell our personal and communal story in the history of peoples. The war is corroding our human roots to such an extent that it is not inappropriate to ask ourselves, as some already have, whether the historical viability of our country is in danger (Agonía de un Pueblo, 1984). And we can't very well speak of the mental health of a people unable to guarantee their own survival.

Through this undeniable collective erosion of social relations, the war is causing many personal crises and disorders for those who, for one reason or another, cannot adequately cope with the demands of their life situation. Because it cannot be assumed that the war has a uniform effect on the whole population, coordinates for analysis must be established, and I would propose three as paramount: social class, involvement in the conflict, and a time factor.

Social Class

Neither the direct nor the indirect effects of the war are the same for the different sectors that make up our society. Military conscription is discriminatory and recruits most heavily from the humblest sectors, and therefore the great majority of those who die on the battlefields, day after day, are the poor. The poorest sectors, especially the campesinos, are also the ones who suffer the war's direct impact, through the destruction of their homes and crops, just as it is they who are most affected by the machinery of repression, by the work of the "death squads" and military operations of all types. And, once again, the poorest sectors are the ones who are most brutalized by the increase in the cost of living, by rising unemployment and declining health care—damage added to a socioeconomic situation that is already very serious.

This does not mean that the middle or upper classes of society do not feel the impact of the war. Although to a much lesser degree, they have also been battered by repression, assassination, kidnapping, the decline in living conditions, the sabotage of the economy, and the harassment of police checkpoints and searches. However, I would say that the most painful consequence of the war for the dominant sectors of society has been the radical questioning they have felt directed at their social position and way of life. First the peaceful uprising and then the armed uprising of the masses have undermined the very foundations of the social system. This has caused its main beneficiaries to fear the loss of their lifestyle, which was built behind the backs, and indeed on the backs, of the misery of the majority. At first this radical questioning unleashed great anxiety, and later, when the initial moments of discomfort were overcome, an aggressive denial of reality. In some cases, this denial has become the driving force behind violent activism; in many others, the reaction has been characterized by an insatiable orgy of pleasure that has led people to build artificial castles to amuse themselves. Years ago, Karl Jaspers (1962) recognized this symptomatic behavior as an enormous mania for pleasure and an unbridled passion for living life for the moment.

Involvement in the Conflict

The second important variable in analyzing the differing consequences of the war on the mental health of the population is the involvement of groups and individuals in the war itself. Thus far, the consequences of the war have undoubtedly been different for the inhabitants of departments [in FMLN zones of control] like Chalatenango and Morazán than for people living in Ahuachapán or Sonsonate. In some cases it is difficult to meet anyone who has not been directly affected by the war, while in other cases communities have been relatively free from combat. But it is also important to differentiate between the possible effects on those who have participated in combat and those who have suffered from the war as civilians. There is ample knowledge of the effects that the tension and danger experienced on the battlefront can have on soldiers; it was first called "war neurosis," then "combat fatigue," and finally a "stress reaction" (Spielberger, Sarason, and Milgram, 1982; Watson, 1978). The problems the soldiers face in re-adapting to normal life are also well known, especially when the war has left them crippled or disabled for life. All of this affects the mental health not only of soldiers themselves but also of their families and neighbors, because it will be everyone's task to rebuild the framework of life with these weakened links [for an elaboration of this problem, see Chapter 2].

Though different, the effects on the civilian population are no less important. The experience of vulnerability and danger, of defenselessness and terror, can leave a deep mark on people's psyches, particularly on children. The spectacle of rapes or tortures, of assassinations or mass executions, of bombings and the leveling of entire villages is traumatizing almost by definition. As we said earlier, reacting to such events with uncontrollable anxiety or with some form of autism must be considered a normal reaction to abnormal circumstances, perhaps the only way a person can cling to life and withstand such a suffocating knot of social relations. Jervis (1977, p. 152) wisely asserts that "on not a few occasions, a certain degree of psychological discomfort and a certain permanent 'dose' of psychiatric symptoms are the expression of the greatest mental health and well-being attainable in a given situation of sclerosis of human relations, extreme material difficulties, misfortunes, solitude and social marginalization."

The prototype of the civilian population affected by the war is the groups of displaced persons and refugees, most of whom are the elderly, women, and children (see Lawyers' Committee, 1984). They have had to leave their homes, which in many cases have been razed; and making this decision is always difficult because it distances them from their roots, from their dead, and perhaps from their relatives in the countryside. Often the flight, or *guinda,* is made under deplorable conditions, walking at night and hiding like wild animals during the day to avoid being massacred, sometimes for one, two, three, up to four weeks, without water or food, hushing the cries of children and leaving along the way the mortal trail of those who get lost or weaken and die. Following the flight, the displaced must deal with life outside their environment, without resources of any kind. Sometimes they are crowded into settlements where the food received ends up engendering a dependency and the lack of self-sufficient work can lead to listlessness and passivity. Certainly, not all of the displaced and the refugees go through such tragic circumstances, but it is hard to imagine that the experience of displacement will leave no mark on people's psyches, particularly on those of the weakest and youngest (Cohon, 1981). And we cannot ignore the fact that there are already one million Salvadorans affected by this condition.

The Time Factor

The third variable in analyzing the effects of the war on the mental health of Salvadorans is time. To put it simply, some effects are immediate and others can be expected in the medium and long term. Of course, the longer the war lasts, and at present there is no end in sight, the more profound the immediate effects will be. The deterioration in the material conditions of life; the persisting climate of insecurity and, in many cases, of terror; having to construct a life on a foundation of violence; polarized or ambiguous references; the awareness of falsehood or fear of the truth—these effects of the war ultimately break down resistances or encourage adaptations that, in the best of cases, reveal an abnormal normality, formed from alienating and depersonalizing social ties.

Even if the war were to come to a rapid end, we must think of the mental health consequences that reveal themselves only in the long term. For example, we know that the so-called refugee syndrome has an initial period of incubation in which people manifest no major disorders; instead, it is precisely when they begin to rebuild their lives and return to normal that the critical costs of the war experience must be paid (Stein, 1981; also see COLAT, 1982). The group that should command our attention most is the children, those who are constructing their identities and their life's horizons in the fabric of our present social relations. They are truly the "children of war," and we have the difficult task of ensuring that they do not structure their personalities by learning violence, irrationality, and the lie.

Although it may seem paradoxical, not all of the effects of the war are negative. It has been proven repeatedly that periods of social crisis spark positive reactions among certain sectors of the population. Faced with "limit situations," there are those who bring to light inner resources they weren't even aware they had, or who reorient their lives toward a new, more realistic and humanizing horizon. During the social crisis of 1968 in France, or the 1972 earthquake in Nicaragua, psychiatrists and psychologists observed a significant decrease both in the demand for their services and in the crises of some of their regular patients. Viktor Frankl, founder of what is known as the Third School of Viennese Psychotherapy, survived the experience of the Nazi concentration camps in which he lost his entire family, and with his logotherapy developed Nietzsche's profound intuition that "[one] who has a *why* to live can bear with almost any *how*" (Frankl, 1946; see also Frankl, 1950; 1955).

We know of many Salvadorans who have been led by the cataclysm of war to face the meaning of their own existence and to change their life's horizons. Certainly, this crisis has also offered many campesinos and those marginalized by the social system the opportunity to break the chains of their submissive alienation, of their existential fatalism and dependence, even though the liberation from a servitude imposed and maintained with violence may have forced them to resort to violence (Fanon, 1963). Therefore, in analyzing the effects of the war, it is essential that we pay attention not only to its harmful consequences for mental health but also to the new resources and options that have emerged in response to the "limit situation."

A People's Mental Health

This final observation leads us to the crucial question: What should we do, as mental health professionals, given the situation now confronting our people? How do we begin to respond to the serious questions posed by the war, when perhaps we haven't even been able to offer an adequate response in times of peace? Without a doubt, we are facing a historical challenge, and we would be wrong to deny this by diluting it into prefabricated formulas or by trivializing it into the schemata of our routine work. We don't have ready-made solutions. But this reflection allows us to offer some ways to channel our professional activity.

In the first place, I think we must seek or develop models capable of comprehending and addressing the uniqueness of our problems. This requires us to take a closer look at our reality, the painful reality of our people, which takes more diverse forms than is assumed in our usual working schemata. This is not a matter of proposing some ingenuous psychological nationalism, as if the Salvadorans weren't human, or as if we had to add a new personality theory to the many that already exist. It is a question of turning our scientific gaze, enlightened by theoretical knowledge and directed in a systematic way, toward the concrete reality that is the Salvadoran man and woman within the historical framework of their social relations. On the one hand, this obliges us to examine our theoretical assumptions, not so much from the standpoint of their intrinsic logic as from their historical logic; that is, in terms of whether they work and are truly effective in the here and now. But on the other hand, it forces us to cast off the veil of lies we move about in, and to look at the truth of our social existence without the ideological crutches of our routine work or of professional inertia.

In a conversation with Salvatore Maddi, a professor at the University of Chicago, I recall hearing him say that, ultimately, the healing power of any psychotherapeutic method depends on the dosage of its break with the dominant culture. The value of Freudian psychoanalysis, when it scandalized the European puritanism of the early twentieth century, would have been rooted in such a break. Another example is the best of Rogerian "nondirectional" therapy, in response to the one-dimensionality of the postwar North American therapeutic style. Perhaps this is what is lacking in present-day psychotherapeutic methods, including psychoanalysis and "client-centered" psychotherapy: a dosage of rupture with the dominant system. Once again, this intuition brings us back to the fact that mental health is found not so much in the abstract functioning of the individual organism as in the character of social relations where the life of each person is founded, constructed, and developed. For this reason, we must work hard to find theoretical models and methods of intervention that allow us, as a community and as individuals, to break with the culture of our vitiated social relations and put other, more humanizing, relationships in their place.

If the foundation for a people's mental health lies in the existence of humanizing relationships, of collective ties within which and through which the personal humanity of each individual is acknowledged and in which no one's reality is denied, then the building of a new society, or at least a better and more just society, is not only an economic and political problem; it is also essentially a mental health problem. By the very nature of the object of our professional work, we cannot separate mental health from the social order. For this reason, I believe there is an extremely urgent task of education for mental health. And this task consists not so much in teaching relaxation techniques or new ways of communicating, however important these objectives may be, as in training and socializing so that people's desires truly conform to their needs. This means that our subjective aspirations, both as groups and as individuals, must be oriented toward the satisfaction of our true needs; in other words, toward the requirements that lead us down the path of our humanization, and not those which tie us to compulsive consumption, to the detriment of many and the dehumanization of all. This would perhaps be the best psychotherapy for the effects of war and, surely, the best mental hygiene for building our future.

In the final analysis, this is indeed the issue: to contribute with our professional knowledge toward the building of a new future. The war situation we have lived in for almost four years has brought out the worst and the best in Salvadorans. The war continues to gnaw at our material and social roots and threatens our very survival as a people. If, like Freud (1930, p. 92), we were to say in the end that we hope the eternal Eros "will make an effort to assert himself in the struggle with his equally immortal adversary," Thanatos, we would openly be sharing his pessimism and resigning ourselves to death. In the midst of the destruction, the Salvadoran people have sown enough seeds of life to be able to trust in the possibility of a tomorrow. Let us gather those seeds to cultivate the plant of mental health. Let it not be said that while humankind moves its life forward, we mental health professionals resign ourselves to living in the past. There will be healthy, free, and creative minds in our country to the extent that we enjoy a free, dynamic, and just social body. For this reason, the challenge is not limited to addressing the destruction and disorders caused by the war. The challenge is to construct a new person in a new society.

7

War and the Psychosocial Trauma of Salvadoran Children

TRANSLATED BY ANNE WALLACE

Psychosocial Trauma

There are those who consider psychology to be no more than a technology—not a science—designed by modern industrial societies to remedy some of the damage inflicted on people by the conditions and lifestyle of the prevailing social system. Some of the harshest critics claim that psychology is no more than a "recombinant ideology," a type of oil, a slow lubricant that allows the capitalist system to continue reproducing in spite of its negative consequences (see Deleule, 1972).

Our objective here is not to examine the validity of this critique. What interests us is to take it as a warning about what psychologists accomplish while they are at work, particularly in situations like civil war. The curative work of the psychologist is necessary, but if psychology's work is limited to curing, it can become simply a palliative that contributes to prolonging a situation which generates and multiplies the very ills it strives to remedy. Hence, we cannot limit our thinking to the question of what treatment is most effective for children who have suffered the traumas inherent in war; we cannot limit ourselves to addressing post-traumatic stress. Our analysis has to extend itself to the roots of those traumas, and therefore to the war itself as a social psychopathogenic situation.

To this end, our first task must be to reexamine our concept of psychic trauma and look at what we mean when we say that the damage to the human psyche produced by war should be called "psychosocial trauma" (see Martín-Baró, 1988b).

The Meaning of Psychosocial Trauma

Etymologically, trauma means wound: a traumatized person is a wounded person, whatever the causes and the type of lesion incurred. Nevertheless, when in psychology we speak of trauma we are not referring to just any type of suffering or behavioral disorder, but rather to the psychic problems brought on by the impact of a particular experience or life situation. We assume that this means a difficult experience, generally occurring unexpectedly, and always pathogenic in character; that is, it causes a psychic injury. But this injury or wound is not organic, or at least not merely organic. It can be simply functional: no body organ is affected but one begins to suffer disorders in one's normal functioning, in one's thinking and feeling, in one's behavior or abilities.

These are some of the assumptions that are more or less implicit in our understanding of psychic trauma. I will discuss three of them here: the harshness, the unexpectedness, and the individual character of the traumatic experience.

That there are unforeseen traumas goes without saying: traffic accidents, or someone's home burning down, are harsh and sudden experiences which may be traumatizing. But are they unforeseeable? Let us say that they are, at least in principle, for the people who are affected. Obviously, if an automobile accident could be foreseen, one would try to avoid the circumstances leading up to it, and if it was anticipated that the house would burn down, one would try anything to keep it from happening. But this does not mean that the accident and fire were not foreseeable, for taking the precaution of correcting one's driving or the conditions of the house shows that the possibility, at least, was foreseen. Let's assume, nevertheless, that those traumas really are sudden, unexpected, and unforeseen experiences.

Can the same be said of all traumas? Not at all. For example, I contend that today many Salvadoran civilians, among them many children, are suffering traumatizing experiences that are perfectly foreseeable and, unfortunately, perhaps even foreseen and planned by the exigencies of a counterinsurgency war such as the one we are living through. This is why it is not enough to direct our attention to the post-traumatic situation, and why we can and must orient our analysis toward the pre-traumatic situation, including an analysis of trauma as the normal consequence of a social system's way of functioning.

The most misleading of the presumptions about trauma is the implication that the traumatic experience is individual. Traumas are assumed to be individual, not only in the sense that it is individuals who suffer them but in the sense that they are by their very nature individual—as if psychic trauma were like organic trauma, best understood by examining the affected individual and his or her individual wound or injury. I fear this "medical model" still holds sway in the American Psychiatric Association's (1980) definition of "Post-traumatic Stress Disorder" in the *DSM-III.*

Those who speak of *social traumas* were the first to call attention to the inadequacy of the medical model's perspective on trauma, by looking at experiences that affect a whole population, not only as individuals but as social beings in a social context. Social trauma affects individuals precisely in their social character; that is, as a totality, as a system. What is left traumatized is German society or Palestinian society, not simply Germans or Palestinians.

The individualistic view of psychic trauma shares the problem inherent in the medical model, of abstracting sociohistorical realities and insisting on locating disorders in the individual (naming them as organic or functional, according to the particular case), and giving too little consideration to humankind's social nature. For this reason, I have proposed that, at least concerning psychological problems tied to the situation of war, we speak of *psychosocial trauma* (see Chapter 6 and Martín-Baró, 1988b). With this conceptual blend, I mean to encompass three aspects that seem to me essential for an adequate understanding of the reality of psychic trauma: its dialectical character, its social origins, and the cause of its chronicity.

Trauma has a dialectical character. This means not only that it is produced by society, although it is the individual who is the principal victim, but also that the nature of the trauma resides in the particular social relations of which the individual is only a part. Precisely because trauma must be understood in terms of the relationship between the individual and society, one cannot simply predict that a given type of social situation will automatically produce a trauma in anyone, or that a particular type of person will never suffer a trauma. We also have to underscore the possibility that exceptional circumstances, just as they may lead to deterioration or injury, may also lead to people's growth and development. In other words, in asserting the dialectical character of trauma, we necessarily affirm its historical character.

Trauma is socially produced. To speak of psychosocial trauma is to emphasize that trauma is produced socially and, therefore, that understanding and resolving it require not only treating the problems of individuals but also treating its social roots, in other words, the traumatogenic structures or social conditions.

Trauma is chronic when the factors that bring it about remain intact. The social relations of individuals are not only the *cause* of trauma; maintaining these social relations is what feeds and multiplies the number of traumatized individuals.

Psychosocial trauma thus constitutes the concrete crystallization in individuals of aberrant and dehumanizing social relations, like those prevalent in the situation of civil war (Martín-Baró, 1988b). This means that the chain tends to break at its weakest link (the most unprotected social sectors), or the link subjected to the greatest stress (the sectors most directly affected by the conflict and warfare). It follows that the particular character of the trauma will vary according to the concrete nature of the relations within which it materializes.

These reflections lead us to propose two theses that should be applied to a reality like the one endured in El Salvador at the present time. First, psychosocial trauma can be a normal consequence of a social system based on social relations of exploitation and dehumanizing oppression. In other words, psychosocial trauma can be part of a social "normal abnormality." And second, this social "normal abnormality" especially affects children, who must construct their identities and develop their lives within the network of these dehumanizing relations. In order to understand the implications of these theses, let us look at what it means for a child to confront the tasks of childhood in a country at war, and then apply this analysis to the particular situation of the Salvadoran war.

Childhood and War

Before examining the specific problem of the children of El Salvador, let us briefly review some of the most significant results of psychosocial research on the problems of children in war situations (see Hoppe, 1985).

Proximity to Zones of Conflict

It is possible to distinguish the impact of warfare on children living in the zones of greatest conflict from the impact on those living in less conflictive zones, or areas where strictly combat operations are less prevalent. In some cases the most characteristic reaction is fear; in others the most common reaction is anxiety (Fraser, 1983). Fear is a negative emotion felt in the face of a known threatening object. Anxiety, by contrast, is an emotion felt in the face of an undefined threat, an object whose characteristics are not well known. Thus, children who live in the areas most directly affected by military action will most typically react with problems related to fear, while those who live in zones that are only occasionally or partially affected by the warfare will tend to display problems more associated with the experience of anxiety.

Traumatizing Experiences

There are two major types of traumatizing experiences for children: the experience of destruction and violence, frequently steeped in cruelty and horror; and the experience of physical and personal separations. The damage caused by seeing one's own house burned down, or a family member being killed or directly suffering violent aggression, is one thing. The damage produced by separation, temporary or definitive, from one's own land or home and, even worse, from one's closest family members, is something else (see Engestrom, 1983). Although they have elements in common, there are also important differences between childhood trauma that comes from violence and that which comes from separation.

Emotional Responsiveness

Although children's immediate reaction to traumatic events tends to be strongly emotional (screaming, crying, terror), they also characteristically develop a relatively stable pattern of emotional insensitivity. That is, the excessive emotional cost of their experiences causes a defensive desensitization which makes them appear cold, insensitive, and even lacking in emotion in their daily lives (Punamäki, 1982; Lindqvist, 1984).

Symptomatology

Children's disorders caused by war tend to take classic forms: night terrors, deterioration of the ability to concentrate, regressive behavior, the emotional paradox of the manifest daily insensitivity and the eventual emotional overflow mentioned above, irritability in general, sensitivity to sudden noise, and, above all, multiple types of somatization. The prolongation of traumatogenic experiences frequently causes children to seek a psychic flight into fantasy (Lindqvist, 1984). In some cases, these flights lead to the development of schizoid syndromes of varying severity, which permit the children to escape from a reality they are unable to handle.

Family Relations

Children's closest family members filter the impact of the war experience (Fraser, 1983; Ressler, 1984). Hence the harmful or traumatic character of the warfare depends in large part on the way the older relatives closest to the child react to events. If family members react calmly and serenely, the negative impact is much less than if they react with anxiety and panic. This is why it is important that the child confront the war from the bosom of the family, although family may be understood in a broad sense. It is a commonly held opinion that, although war marks a child, there is no reason for it to stigmatize or traumatize, as long as the necessary support of relatives is available. As Margareta Holmberg states about Lebanese families, the problem is that among family members there occur "too many separations," and there exists "too much closeness" (1984, p. 27). War tends to deprive children of the presence of their parents and siblings, through death or through their absence because they are fighting at the battlefront. But even when their presence can be counted on, it is generally difficult for adults to maintain the kind of balanced behavior that children need, since the dangerous circumstances or the situation of being refugees forces them into a permanent closeness and overcrowding.

Attitude Formation

Growing up in the context of war teaches children that violence is the most important response for solving the problems of existence; their attitudes tend to fluctuate between the use of violence and impotence, depending on the capabilities they ascribe to those around them. Mentally, to develop in the context of war leads one to accept as a given the legitimacy of violence (Hietanen, 1983), if not the militarization of one's own mind (see Freud and Burlingham, 1942, 1943; Martín-Baró, 1988b).

Psychic Resistance

War leads children to develop various types of resistance in the face of traumatizing experiences. The character of this resistance depends on other factors, such as the age at which a child begins to experience the war, or the presence and reactions of his or her closest relatives. One resistance already mentioned is the flight into fantasy, which can culminate in paranoid syndromes of greater or lesser severity, although there are those who maintain that a certain amount of isolation is therapeutic (see Fraser, 1983). Other, more positive forms of psychic resistance are a strengthening of internal control and the development of political commitment to a cause (see Punamäki, 1987). Although researchers have not paid much attention to the possibility that war might have a positive impact on people's development, undoubtedly, like any "extreme situation," war offers the possibility that some people, and even whole groups, may develop virtues that would not have arisen under other circumstances. The much discussed heroism of soldiers, or of the civilian population victimized by warfare, is frequently no more than a patriotic idealization of war. But it is true that situations generated by war offer opportunities for people to bring out the best in themselves through altruistic behavior, and to develop the virtues of solidarity that get so little stimulation from the dominant system's values in times of peace.

Deprivation

Ultimately, for many individuals, the most tragic consequence of war is that they have to go through childhood unable to live it as children: a childhood without love, without toys, without affection or dreams for the future.

The Children of the Salvadoran War

El Salvador at War

It would seem unnecessary to emphasize something as obvious as the fact that El Salvador finds itself submerged in a terrible and protracted war. Nevertheless, it is necessary to remember some basic facts, not only because the state's propaganda apparatus systematically attempts to deny them, but also because the immediacy and everydayness of the war paradoxically render these facts less conscious. We incorporate the war, like everything else, into our daily routines and accept its existence as a commonsense fact, if not the doings of a presumed human nature or some preordained social order.

The reality of the war. El Salvador has been in a *state of real war* since 1980. This is conveniently denied by some heads of the military in order to deprive the revolutionary movements of insurgency status. It is also denied by those U.S. government agencies which attempt to present El Salvador as one of the model democracies achieved by the Reagan administration in Latin America. But it is strongly reaffirmed every time the request for continuing military aid comes up for renewal before the U.S. Congress or the continuous human rights violations produced in the country must be explained. In fact, the war is the thing that best defines the present reality of the country. Moreover, the seeming calm or normality so noticeable in the nation's capital is part of that state of war. The truth of San Salvador's involvement must be denied before the collective consciousness, precisely in order to be able to carry on without raising serious political, much less ethical, questions [about why the capital, where the oligarchy is concentrated, was not under military attack].

The character of the war. The war lived in El Salvador is a *civil war,* not a war of external or international aggression. But the geopolitical situation of El Salvador, located in the security area the United States considers its backyard, puts this civil war in the broader context of the conflict between the rich North and the poor South, or between the socialist East and the capitalist West. Nevertheless, it must be reiterated that the essential character of the Salvadoran war is civil, that is, that what is happening is a violent rupture of society and the struggle arises, or at least is carried out, brother against brother.

The victims and beneficiaries of the war. The Salvadoran war, precisely because it is a civil war, affects the various social sectors very differently. The majority of Salvadorans feel the effects of the war primarily in its economic consequences, that is, its damaging effect on the cost of living or on job opportunities (see Martín Baró, 1987a; IUDOP, 1988). However, there are sectors that not only do not suffer the economic consequences of the war but actually profit and make money from it. Overall, it is the poor, particularly the campesinos, who are most affected by the war: they are the ones who replenish the opposing armies; they are the principal victims of the armed confrontations; they are the most battered by the massive unemployment and the dizzying rise in the cost of living.

The war's consequences for the social order. The prolongation of the war carries with it serious consequences for the very social order of the country.

I shall mention some of the most destructive consequences with the greatest psychosocial impact:

• The corruption of institutions, particularly those agencies involved in the war, which find themselves obligated to perform functions often contrary to their very nature and which handle large amounts of easy money.
• The growing destruction of the country's means of production and even of its scarce natural resources (for example, the deforestation of certain zones as a result of military operations).
• The loss of national sovereignty, which the militarist interests pledge to the United States as payment for their survival, thereby mortgaging the Salvadoran people's ability to resolve the conflict according to their own interests, rather than the interests of the North American government.
• The growing militarization of the diverse institutions and organizations of the state's formal apparatus, and even of the social order.
• Acceptance of the war as part of the normal functioning of the life of the nation (see McWhirter, 1983) and as a result, people's internalization of its inevitability and legitimacy.

An appraisal of the gravity of these consequences and the possibly irreversible nature of some of these evils must bring us to the conclusion that it is urgent that the war be ended and that this national goal should take priority over the partisan interests of the opposing groups. This is in no way a declaration in favor of peacemaking at all costs; it is the recognition that prolonging the Salvadoran civil war makes it ever more difficult both to end the war and to resolve the causes which give rise to it and sustain it.

Existential Dilemmas of Salvadoran Children Facing the War

In this context of war, Salvadoran children today face three important existential dilemmas as an essential part of the tasks of their development. We can sum up these three dilemmas in terms of action-flight, identity-alienation, and polarization-tearing apart. Let us briefly examine these three dilemmas.

Action-flight. There are two principal ways in which children become involved in war: as active participants, and as victims. These two ways are not mutually exclusive, since many children fall as victims on taking an active part in warfare, or they join the armed struggle upon feeling themselves to be victims of the war.

Just a few days ago, a terrifying report on the use of children for wars came to light. The child soldier is a universal phenomenon and, clearly, a phenomenon that occurs in El Salvador, not only in the ranks of the FMLN but also in the armed forces. The child soldier is instructed and formed in the use of violence; his mind is filled with polarized and Manichean images of absolute goodness or evil; he is taught to understand existence in terms of hostility toward an enemy; and, as an ideal, he is asked to risk his life under the guise of patriotic heroism.

How many child soldiers are there in El Salvador? It is hard to say, since the FMLN does not give out the numbers of its combatants and the methods used by the armed forces to hunt down recruits do not discriminate by age, so long as those they trap look like young men. Certainly the images occasionally offered on television and the faces we see when we come across a military unit of either side both confirm the presence of adolescents and even pre-adolescents in their ranks.

The other side of the coin is that of the child victims of the war, who, as we have said, can come from or end up in the military ranks. The child victim is the one who suffers the disaster of the war in his or her own flesh: experiences of violence and scarcity, bombings and combat, the death or injury of close relatives, destruction and persecution, the lack of food and affection. In general, the child victim has no choice but to flee, to get as far away from the places of armed conflict as possible. These forced flights, or *guindas* as they are called in El Salvador, sometimes take place under terrifying conditions (see Martín-Baró, 1985i).

Child victims are tortured by living with fear and horror. For them, heroism is not possible, only impotence and deprivation. For them, violence appears not as a manifestation of power, but as destruction. For them, all that is military represents the permanent threat, the symbol and bearer of death, society's rejection of their place in the world. The child victim is the incarnation of the human and social disaster that is war. Let us ask ourselves, how many child victims are there today in El Salvador? We do not have, or at least I do not have, reliable figures, though the number of children among the displaced and refugee populations is a valuable indicator of their magnitude (see Instituto de Investigaciones de la UCA, 1985; Montes, 1986).

It is possible that the majority of Salvadoran children are confronted with the dilemma of actively participating in the war as soldiers or of fleeing as victims of it. But there is also a minority of Salvadoran children whose privileged social situation saves them from that dilemma. Some of them benefit from this privilege. But others incur a form of flight whose benefit is highly questionable; these are the children who are confined in artificial worlds, gardens with high walls that isolate them from the surrounding reality, from the hunger and suffering of others. In and of itself, there is nothing wrong with protecting the child from the sad dilemma of action-flight; there are even therapists who recommend this behavior as a "treatment of the context" (see Fraser, 1983). As in the case of the child victims, the problem lies in the fact that, for them, too, the impact of life experiences is mediated by the closest adult relatives; and that filter is frequently one of repressed anxiety and manifest hatred, of discriminatory goodness and mental militarism (see Martín-Baró, 1988b). Obviously, that filter cannot be psychologically constructive, nor can it favor the humanizing development of children. These children, too, can be victims of the war, through a social escape that is certainly physical and mental, although of a very different nature from the violent flight of the poor.

Identity-alienation. A second dilemma Salvadoran children face because of the war, and above all because of its prolongation, is having to confront the processes of socialization primarily in a context we have described as "normal abnormality." The fact that El Salvador assumes war to be a part of the normal process of daily living has a strong impact on the child, who has to construct his or her identity in a context of generalized violence. Children must make an untenable choice: either aggressively adopt a socially stigmatized identity, or accept the closing of options and submit to an imposed identity that is full of dehumanizing elements.

This problem has been examined in depth by the team of Chilean psychotherapists currently working in ILAS, the Latin American Institute for Mental Health and Human Rights of Santiago (see Lira, 1988; Lira et al., 1984; Lira, Weinstein, and Salamovich, 1985–86; Weinstein, 1987; Weinstein et al., 1987). The basic premise centers on the climate of fear, if not of outright terror, in which people considered by the established power to be enemies and even potential "enemy" sympathizers must develop and act. Fear limits the possibility of developing a personality according to the social and personal options freely exercised by each individual. Thus, among other consequences, a collective political apathy is produced, no less real for being unavoidable. Subjectively, the renunciation of a political identity one considers desirable, but must give up because it is socially stigmatized, creates a feeling of inauthenticity toward oneself and of guilt toward one's abandoned comrades. But in taking on that desired identity, one must carry the burden of the objective risk of repression and subjective fear, as well as a feeling of guilt toward one's own family, who are endangered by that personal political choice.

To be socialized in the context of war, whether the war is strictly military or psychological, puts the child in a dilemma, both parts of which are untenable. One choice is to construct an identity that internalizes violence, the institutionalized lie, and dehumanizing social relations. The other is to construct a socially stigmatized identity, frequently no less violent, with a need to resort to the social lie, the game of public falsehood and clandestine authenticity, in order to survive. The dilemma is even more harmful when, as frequently happens, neither the children's parents nor their teachers are aware of it and therefore give the children no help in facing it constructively and creatively. Punamäki (1987) has found that, among Palestinian children, ideological clarity and political commitment are a great help for positively facing the traumatogenic circumstances in which they must live and develop.

The children's dilemma is not simply a Manichean choice between desirable authenticity and undesirable alienation, since identifying against the social system implies obvious objective and subjective costs and therefore cannot be considered an ideal option. Rather, the dilemma demonstrates how children in a war situation must make existential choices whose normal dynamic tends to produce harm in the form of psychic disorders, in other words, what we have called psychosocial traumas.

Polarization—tearing apart. The preceding dilemma is closely tied to the character of sociopolitical polarization that reigns in El Salvador (see Chapter 6 and Martín-Baró, 1988b). Both armed groups make a conscious and systematic effort to gain the sympathy and support of the civilian population, thus positing social existence in terms of the unconditional acceptance of some and the absolute rejection of others, who are considered "enemies." The pressure on the civilian population is particularly intense in the most conflictive zones, where people have to endure the presence of one side one day, only to receive a visit from the other side the next, suffering in both cases the demand for allegiance and the suspicion of betrayal. This situation can tear one apart, especially when, as the years pass, the polarized choice becomes an excessive and unending requirement for the majority of the people, blocking the development of the individual's own life, subjugating it to the extremist fluctuations in the conflict.

Salvadoran children live and must develop in this climate of polarization, with the danger of structuring their minds in dichotomous terms, so little conducive to the creative solution of problems and so easily predisposing them toward violent behavior. Today there is debate about whether a simplistic cognitive style, such as the intolerance of ambiguity, is or is not related to authoritarianism and, therefore, to the most extreme political options (Sidanius, 1985, 1988a, 1988b; Ray, 1988). In either case, it doesn't seem to be the style most psychologically favorable for the healthy development of the personality or for daily psychosocial functioning.

Recently I advanced the hypothesis that situations like war zones, where the climate of polarized tension is experienced with greatest intensity, are a particularly favorable culture medium for psychosomatic disorders (Martín-Baró, 1988b). Somatization would indicate that the social polarization had taken root in the body and would be a sign that the person is incapable of handling the stressful situation. This kind of internalized polarization can occasionally lead to autism in children and to problems of a clearly psychotic or schizophrenic character in young people.

Conclusion

Salvadoran children today find themselves overwhelmed by a war situation whose "normal abnormality," faced every day, tends to produce some kind of psychosocial trauma. This trauma arises because, as part of their development, the children are obliged to face some dilemmas whose terms are always unsatisfactory. Whether children end up as soldiers or victims (or as soldiers and victims), whether they construct aggressive/stigmatized or aggressive/alienated identities, whether they opt for one or the other of the two sides in the conflict or are trapped between them—in every case they face the possibility of some trauma or psychic damage. And the creative solution, though possible, generally requires some conditions and social resources which are available to very few Salvadoran children, in large measure for the same reasons that the war exists.

Therefore, as psychologists, we cannot be satisfied with treating post-traumatic stress. This is necessary and especially urgent with children. However, the underlying problem is not a matter of individuals but of the traumatogenic social relations that are part of an oppressive system that has led to war. So it is of primary importance that treatment address itself to relationships between social groups, which constitute the "normal abnormality" that dehumanizes the weak and the powerful, the oppressor and the oppressed, soldier and victim, dominator and dominated alike. If in the El Salvador of tomorrow we want our people to be able to raise their voices with dignity and assert their historical presence, we must today contribute toward creating conditions for our children to develop and construct their identities without being subjected to traumatizing and, in short, dehumanizing dilemmas.

8

Religion as an Instrument
of Psychological Warfare

TRANSLATED BY TOD SLOAN

"The Salvadoran Church has experienced great growth since 1978, when socioeconomic problems became more acute as the country stood on the brink of civil war. Since then the nation has opened itself to the gospel and people have opened themselves more to God and try to quench their spiritual thirst by joining the evangelical churches."

Thus begins the introduction to a recent study of the growth of the "evangelical" (pentecostal and fundamentalist) churches in El Salvador (Salcedo, 1987, p. 1). According to that study, 22 percent of Salvadorans belonged to such churches in 1987, an increase of approximately one-fourth since 1985.

These data are very questionable—in part, because they do not take account of desertion. In fact, successive surveys indicate that the number of Salvadorans who describe themselves as evangelicals oscillates between 10 percent and 15 percent of the adult population (Martín-Baró 1987a, 1989a). Nevertheless, these data do indicate a striking growth of evangelical churches in a traditionally Catholic country during a period of civil war. According to Salcedo's interpretation, Salvadorans convert to the evangelical churches in order to "quench their spiritual thirst," which historically neither Catholic nor Protestant churches seem to have satisfied.

Religious conversion and/or affiliation on such a large scale is of major significance. Its psychological meaning cannot be reduced to the individual or group experiences of the people involved. Nor can it be seen as mere cultural change. To be understood, its political character has to be examined as well, and this is where the dominant social psychology of religion tends to grow slack.

The principal theories of religious conversion examine the phenomenon on three dimensions: (1) The *process* dimension includes characteristics of the conversion process, such as whether it is sudden or gradual, whether the person seeks out the change or experiences it passively, and whether it is primarily a rational or an emotional (irrational) experience. (2) The *motivational* dimension focuses on what leads the person to religious change, in particular, whether such change is the consequence of an existential crisis, a traumatic incident, or an interpersonal or even communal process. (3) The dimension of *generality* considers whether the change is partial or total; whether it is limited to the religious sphere or affects the totality of referential schemata (see Lofland and Skonovd, 1981; Richardson, 1985; Snow and Machalek, 1984).

The typologies of conversion offered by various authors differ in their emphasis on these dimensions. Using only these three dimensions, though, it is difficult to achieve a specifically psychological perspective on religious conversion, for the typology reduces conversion to a process of individual change, abstracted from its social context and its network of interpersonal relations. A truly psychosocial perspective must consider the *ideological* dimension of human behavior—the determination of action by social forces and interests (see Martín-Baró, 1983a). Ideology cannot be reduced to a group of ideas and values that more or less guide a person's existence; it must include the system of social forces that impinges on each person. These effects can be seen in, but cannot be reduced to, cognitive schemata, value frameworks, behavioral habits, and lifestyles. Obviously, social forces are historical realities, and it is precisely this historicity that tends to be ignored in the dominant psychosocial analyses, or worse, incorporated as a "situational variable" and not as an intrinsic determinant of the nature of the behavior being analyzed.

That is why, in analyzing religious conversion, it is necessary to add a fourth dimension—*ideology*. This dimension requires an examination of the particular social forces that converge in the phenomenon of conversion: What social group or class benefits, at a given time, from the conversions? What interests are served, and, most important, what are the social effects? Is conversion an alienating, or a de-alienating, experience? That is, does it function like Marx's "opium," or rather as a consciousness-raising force?

Analyses of the other three dimensions (process, motivation, and generality) immediately change once the ideological dimension is included. The conversion process can no longer be seen as something that is simply interpersonal or individual; instead, it is seen as social, and even political— the decision of a person who is the subject and object of the play of power in society. Individual motivations take on a wider historical sense when they are situated in the network of social forces that either humanize or dehumanize the person. Conversion, in this broader perspective, has ramifications that cannot be reduced to simple relations between abstract variables. The process can be understood only in the light of a personal and social history.

From this psychosocial perspective, my working hypothesis is that the massive religious conversion to pentecostal groups (evangelical or Catholic charismatic) during El Salvador's civil war represents not only a way for certain individuals and groups to try to satisfy their psychological ("spiritual") needs, but also a political instrument for those who hold power, and more specifically, an element of psychological warfare.

Psychological Warfare

By psychological warfare, I mean operations carried out during war that aim to achieve victory through mental changes in the enemy (Watson, 1978). These changes include demoralizing the rival (military or civilian, individual or group), convincing the enemy that it would be useless to continue fighting, or bringing about a new understanding of the conflict that leads to other forms of resolution. These are therefore aggressive acts, but not in the strictly military sense.

El Salvador has been in a state of civil war since January 1981. Given the small size of the country (about the size of Massachusetts) and the involvement of the government of the United States in the conflict, the insurgency has opted for an informal sort of war, often called a "prolonged people's war." As a result of the government's failure to smash the rebel movement by exclusively military means, the Salvadoran armed forces, financed, trained, and directed by the United States, have applied a model known as "low-intensity conflict" or LIC (see Barry, Castro, and Vergara, 1987; Benítez, 1988; Bermúdez, 1987; CRIES, 1986). The LIC strategy assumes that the ultimate roots of a conflict lie in the dissatisfaction of the populace, and therefore a military victory is not enough; it is essential to win the "hearts and minds" of the people who generate, feed, and support the insurgency. LICs are thus basically sociopolitical rather than military wars (Bacevich et al., 1988).

Psychological warfare is a part of this sociopolitical confrontation. Its most typical operations include propaganda campaigns, the open or clandestine transmission of news, rumors, and interpretive schemata; and civic-military actions that meet the material needs of the populace or change images either of the enemy or of one's own forces. These strategies are accompanied by threats and systematic acts of harassment and torture that demonstrate the futility and dangerousness of supporting the resistance.

Thus, a basic mechanism used to gain objectives in psychological warfare is the unleashing of personal insecurity: insecurity about one's own beliefs, judgment, and feelings, about right and wrong, and about what should or should not be done. This insecurity finds an immediate and tranquilizing response in the solution offered by those in power: to accept the "official truth" and to submit to the "established order." In this manner, psychological warfare becomes a substitute for, or a complement to, the so-called dirty war of paraofficial repression. The psychological means to the desired objective is not fear or terror in the face of a cruel authority, but instead insecurity in relation to an authority who is simultaneously powerful and magnanimous (Lira, Weinstein, and Salamovich, 1985–1986; Martín-Baró, 1988a).

In order to make people feel insecure, psychological warfare tries to penetrate their primary frame of reference—their basic beliefs, their most precious values, and their common sense. It is here that religion begins to play an important role, since it forms part of the world view of any population and it is certainly central for most Salvadorans. Popular culture in El Salvador encompasses an abundance of religious values, practices, and symbols. Salvadorans use religious schemata and categories both to organize their lives and to interpret events (with variations, of course, according to group membership and personal circumstances).

Religion in the Salvadoran Conflict

The Salvadoran conflict cannot be understood without taking the religious element into account. The assumption that "liberation theology" is one of the principal causes of the Salvadoran revolution is simplistic, and in general, biased (see Bacevich et al., 1988; Bouchey et al., 1981). But there can be no doubt that the changes in the Catholic church begun in the Vatican Council II and concretized at the Medellin episcopal meeting (*Los Textos,*

1977) have had profound repercussions in Latin America. In El Salvador, the main consequence has perhaps been that the rural and urban working-class sectors most closely tied to the church have abandoned the traditional belief that their miserable oppressed situation is the will of God, or is at least tolerated by God, and have begun to think that faith in God should guide them toward the construction of a more just and humane society (see *La Fe de un Pueblo*, 1983; Martín-Baró, 1987b). This new religious consciousness alone did not incite Salvadorans to revolution, but it did leave them without a justification for passive acceptance of oppression, and it offered them a religious basis for their search for profound social change. Additionally, the experience of the "Christian base communities" (CBCs), the thousands of small lay-led groups working to improve their local communities and to establish a more just society (see Berryman, 1987), offered the poorest Latin American sectors an organizational model that could be easily translated into the social or even the political sphere (see Hurtado, 1986; Lona, 1986; Madruga, 1987; Richard, 1983). It is inter-esting to note that this religious posture was shared by majority sectors within the main Protestant churches.

That this change represented a potential danger to the social order was soon perceived by local governments as well as by the U.S. government, which saw in it the specter of communism—see the famous "Rockefeller Report" (Vidales, n.d.) or the report of the Santa Fe Committee (Bouchey et al., 1981). The systematic persecution that the more progressive sectors of the Catholic Church have suffered since then in various Latin American countries (Bolivia, Ecuador, Colombia, Panama, Guatemala, El Salvador) confirms the assertion that they are perceived as constituting a threat to the "national security" of the established regimes (Comblin, 1978).

Persecution campaigns against the Church were not sufficient to erad-icate the seed of religious "subversion" and even ran the risk of producing the opposite effect by creating martyrs. Thus early on a decision was made to substitute as much as possible a psychological war of conversion for the dirty war of religious repression. Latin Americans were channeled toward the "true salvation" and the "true faith" grounded in individual change, leaving to God the task of transforming the "world of sin." The recourse to pentecostal fundamentalism, frequently imbued with intense anticom-munism, was logical, since it entailed a religious world view that postulated direct intervention of the Holy Ghost in the solution of human problems. More or less explicit governmental invitations were accepted gladly by various North American evangelical churches, which greatly intensified their missionary efforts in the nations to the south (see Domínguez and Huntington, 1984). The case of Guatemala during the regime of Rios Montt is paradigmatic and well documented, but it is not unique nor perhaps the most significant example.

Faced by the growth of the evangelical churches, the Catholic Church introduced a movement that could be interpreted sociologically as a sort of "ideological counteroffensive": charismatic renewal. As various authors have pointed out (see McGuire, 1982; Diamond, 1989), there is little difference between the operative beliefs and practices of evangelical pentecostalism and Catholic charismatic renewal. Thus, the religious battle shapes up in one of the most ideologically heated arenas to be found in Latin America, and is part of a much larger set of sociopolitical conflicts. It is not at all strange, then, that in a psychological war aimed at conquering the "hearts and minds" of Latin Americans, religious campaigns should be part of the strategy.

In general, the notion of a relationship between religious attitudes and sociopolitical attitudes is consistent with either a Marxist or a Weberian perspective. Yet it is difficult to define the character of this relationship or its concrete determinants. Gibbs, Mueller, and Wood (1973), for example, maintain that religion influences political attitudes only when it is central to a person's ideology. What is more, they hold that such influence is not due to religiosity in general but to specific religious beliefs, and, as Marx seemed to believe, that the influence would always be in a conservative direction (see Hoge and De Zulueta, 1985).

It may be the case that this relationship between religious and sociopolitical attitudes is conditioned by the particular situation being studied. Certainly, religion is prominent in the Salvadoran frame of reference and would thus affect attitudes there, whether or not Gibbs and the others are right. Nevertheless, the effect has not always been conservative. For example, Cabarrús (1979, 1983) found that religious *concientización* among Salvadoran campesinos in the 1970s made possible, and in certain cases precipitated, progressive political activity.

The conclusion, then, is that religion does not necessarily have a uniform "alienating" sociopolitical impact, as would follow from mechanical Marxist theorizing, but rather, its impact depends on the type of religiosity involved and the meanings that religious values, symbols, and practices acquire for individuals in given sociopolitical situations (Martín-Baró,

1987b). Piazza and Glock (1979, p. 76), who maintain that "the kind of God in which one believes is more relevant to political and social positions than the mere fact of belief," hold that individuals who barely believe in a transcendent force tend to be more liberal, while those who believe that God instituted the social order are more conservative. Neal (1965) found that the responses of Boston-area Catholic priests on social justice issues depended on whether they experienced God as remote, far from the earth, and acting *on* people, or, instead, as immanent, in the world, and acting *through* people. Those who conceived of God in more horizontal and historical terms tended to be more concerned with problems of justice than those who saw God in more vertical and extrahistorical terms. Likewise, Tamney (1984) found, among 91 pastors and priests in "Middletown," that there was a significant relationship between religious ideas and attitudes on current sociopolitical problems.

An example closer to home, and closer to the subject of our study, comes from Brazil. There, according to Rolim (1980, p. 193), "the pentecostal posture is one of submission, marginalizing its converts and driving them away from any form of protest . . . [In contrast] the CBCs gradually assume a critical tendency . . . thus criticizing the social order." A recent study by Valverde (1987) arrived at a similar conclusion regarding evangelical churches in the banana plantation zones of Guapiles, Costa Rica, where aggressive labor unions have traditionally held sway. There, the "Christians" (as they call themselves) not only do not join political or labor organizations but also oppose the struggles of working people and frequently work as scabs or strikebreakers. These Christians have become the banana bosses' trusted workers, and the bosses throw all their support behind the local evangelical churches and pressure their workers to join them.

Why would conversion to pentecostalism lead to political submission to the established order? Carrasco (1988) analyzed the accounts of 18 converts to evangelical Protestantism in Central America and concluded that rather than looking to submissiveness as the critical variable one should focus on the converts' rejection of politics. Central American fundamentalists pursue intense individual religious activity rather than politics in order to solve their life problems. Thus separated ascetically from the rest of society, the fundamentalists may achieve personal well-being, but they become dependent on the sociopolitical analyses of their religious leaders, the same leaders who furnish the symbols and practices that are necessary for their salvation. This translates, in general, into "the radical and permanent abandonment of civil life understood as a critical commitment to a society condemned to destruction" (Carrasco, 1988, p. 41); however, it can eventually evolve into more active forms of critique or political support. In any case, conversion has a clear political impact, serving one social force or another depending on the circumstances.

If the relationship between religion and politics depends on the type of religiosity being practiced, one may postulate at least two directions of impact. The first is *vertical* religiosity, which leads to alienation and social submission; the second, *horizontal* religiosity, leads to a critical consciousness and social liberation. Both types of impact can exist in combination with other religious practices, but the direction taken reflects an essential aspect of religious conversion: its ideological dimension.

Faced with the possible "subversive" effect of horizontal religiosity, the directors of the psychological war in El Salvador have tried to promote forms of religious conversion or membership that contribute to political passivity toward the established order. What the present study attempts to demonstrate is the differential impact of religious conversion, and the need to take into account the ideological dimension if we are to understand the phenomenon of massive conversion to pentecostalism (evangelical or charismatic) in the midst of the Salvadoran war.

Empirical Studies of Religion and Politics

In a series of empirical studies in El Salvador begun in 1984, we have examined the relationship between religious beliefs and other attitudes, the relationship between type of religiosity and sociopolitical choices; and processes of religious conversion and socialization. These studies include, among others, a study of members of various CBCs (N = 54) in 1985; a comparison of members of CBCs (N = 78) with a group of evangelical pentecostalists (EPC; N = 51) in 1986; and a comparison of CBC members (N = 12) with charismatic Catholics (N = 11) in 1987.

These studies were based on participant observation, depth interviews, and personal questionnaires. In all cases, before the research was carried out, the objectives of the studies were discussed with the groups and persons involved, and afterward the results were submitted to them for analysis and criticism.

Overall, the results tend to demonstrate a clear connection between religious and sociopolitical attitudes. The connection is even more apparent when the respondents claim to have undergone some form of religious change. Thus, for example, the longer a person had been a member of a CBC (for the group interviewed in 1985) the greater was his or her political consciousness (F = 3.8, p < .005). For those interviewed in 1986, between 76 percent and 100 percent asserted that they had undergone changes in their family, educational, work-related, and political attitudes in connection with joining a CBC or an EPC (see Table 8.1).

These attitude changes were not unidirectional. As Table 8.1 shows, the type of social attitude change that occurred was related to the type of religious affiliation. The data presented here were drawn from a questionnaire administered to each of the individuals contacted in 1986, in which each attitudinal item required two Likert-scale responses, one for "before belonging to the religious group" (whether CBC or EPC) and another for "after." The difference between the before and after scores on the attitudinal scale was taken as an indicator of change, whether real or retrospectively imagined. Almost all of the CBC members changed toward more progressive sociopolitical attitudes, while EPC members were divided between those whose attitudes moved in a progressive direction and those who moved toward the conservative pole. (Examples of specific items on these scales are shown in Table 8.2).

The data in Table 8.1 do not show clearly enough how the attitudes of either group changed, because all changes are taken into account, regardless of their magnitude. Table 8.2 shows more clearly the mean size of the

Table 8.1. Attitude changes by group, type of attitude, and direction of change (%)

Type of attitude	Religious group	Direction of change			χ^2
		Progressive	No change	Conservative	
Family	CBC	98.6	1.4	0.0	34.9
	EPC	58.8	19.6	21.6	
Education	CBC	89.8	3.8	6.4	42.2
	EPC	35.3	23.5	41.2	
Work	CBC	97.4	1.3	1.3	42.7
	EPC	49.0	13.7	37.3	
Politics	CBC	97.4	0.0	2.6	65.9
	EPC	31.4	13.7	54.9	

Note: CBC N = 78; EPC N = 51. All values of χ^2, with 21 degrees of freedom, were significant at $p < .0001$.

Table 8.2. Mean attitude change by group of key items from four attitude areas

Attitude item	Group				
	EPC	CBC	*t*	*df*	*p*
To achieve harmony at home, children should obey without question.	−0.50	1.27	−5.83	123	.000
Professors should dedicate themselves exclusively to teaching and not join strikes and demonstrations.	−0.55	1.23	−5.74	127	.000
A good worker must accept the opinions of his or her boss.	−0.64	1.60	−8.02	126	.000
The citizens of a country should not oppose the decisions of government leaders.	−0.26	1.49	−6.70	126	.000

Note: Negative values indicate a change of opinion in a conservative direction, while positive values indicate a change in a progressive direction. Maximum possible change was four points in either direction, with zero indicating no change at all.

changes reported by both groups on one important item from each of the four areas examined: family, education, work, and politics. In each of these cases, the mean changes reported by the members of CBCs were in a progressive direction, and were double or greater than those reported by EPC members, all of whom moved in a conservative direction. During a situation of civil war such as we have in El Salvador, if people tend to believe that one "should not oppose the decisions of government leaders," this is clearly an important ideological support for those who happen to be in power.

To what may we attribute these differences in attitude changes associated with religious change? Our hypothesis is that this sociopolitical differentiation is related to the type of religiosity (vertical or horizontal) that each group stimulates in its members. As Table 8.3 shows, there are clear differences between the meanings that the CBC members give to the principal religious symbols and schemata and those given by charismatic renewal Catholics (CRCs), who are similar in beliefs and practices to the evangelical pentecostal church members (EPCs). These findings are similar to those achieved through depth interviews (Flores and Hernández, 1988) and in comparative studies of religious discourse of the CBCs and EPCs (Delgado et al., 1987a, 1987b).

Table 8.3. Meanings in the religious consciousness of charismatic renewal Catholics and Christian base communities

Topic	Meaning for	
	CRC members ($N = 11$)	CBC members ($N = 12$)
God	Creator and provider of all things; bountiful and mysterious; pardons those who admit their sins and accept his will.	Creator and transcendent being; can be found in and among people.
Jesus	Same as God; is strength and love; died for the truth and to save us.	Son or part of God; died for denouncing injustice and subverting the social order.
Sin	To be out of communion with God; to disobey His word or reject His will.	Personal sin due to mistakes; social sin due to omission or structural evil.
Salvation	To achieve the eternal life promised by God.	To create the Kingdom of God through work.
Kingdom of God	All churches together or the Promised Land.	Building a more just society through structural changes.
Church	House of prayer where one goes to communicate with God.	The people of God, who have the mission of denouncing injustices.
Mission of the Church	Evangelize to bring people together with peace in their hearts; to teach people to trust God and accept his will.	To accompany the people; to denounce injustice and raise the people's consciousness.
The Church and social conflict	No. The Church should only speak of God.	Yes. The Church must "concienticize" the people.
Social system of El Salvador	An evil system due to man's sins.	Unjust system; corrupt, alienating, and unfair to the poor.
The civil war of El Salvador	The war is the product of divine will and the sinful nature of man. Only God can end it; man can only pray and ask for mercy.	The war is due to consciousness of structural injustice. It will end as people organize, enter a dialogue; *concientización* is thus critical.

CBC members articulate a religious discourse that is fundamentally horizontal: God is among us, the church is the people, salvation means the construction of a more just society. This stance induces a political commitment to change the unjust social system. In contrast, CRC members maintain a predominantly vertical discourse: God is the creator of the world, the church is a house of prayer, salvation means achieving eternal life. This induces political passivity and an interest only in individual changes, leaving the task of judging this "world of sin" to God.

The data presented demonstrate that the impact of religious conversion is not mechanical. In fact, many of the EPC members showed attitude change in a progressive direction (see Table 8.1), especially in the spheres of family (59 percent) and work (49 percent). And, although the data in Table 8.2 show EPC attitude changes in the direction of conservatism, we must take into account that these are group means that do not display individual changes. Unfortunately, we do not yet have enough data to connect the direction of individuals' attitude changes with their personal type of religiosity, that is, with the personal form in which they have assimilated their groups' religious symbols, practices, and beliefs.

Analysis and Reflections

The data presented here support the validity of the following assertions:

1. In the case of Salvadorans, a significant relationship exists between religious belief and sociopolitical attitudes, and therefore religious change (conversion or joining a new group or church) is related to other changes in sociopolitical attitudes. The data do not allow us to confirm whether this relationship is due primarily to the importance of religion in El Salvador.
2. The relationship between religious belief and sociopolitical attitudes is not uniform; it depends on the type of religiosity that predominates in each religious group. In El Salvador, vertical religiosity (for example, believing in God as being in heaven and a salvation beyond this world) is connected with conservative sociopolitical attitudes and political submission, while horizontal religiosity (for example, belief in God as a brother and salvation in this world) is linked to more progressive sociopolitical attitudes.

3. While Salvadoran CBC members use a predominantly horizontal religious discourse and tend to move toward more progressive sociopolitical attitudes as a result of joining the CBCs, the pentecostal groups use vertical religious discourse and their members tend to move toward conservative sociopolitical attitudes.

These data say nothing about why Salvadorans join these groups, nor about the process of conversion itself or the scope of the changes the converts experience. We could, however, anticipate that there would be differences between the groups in these areas. The data also fail to show us what personal meaning conversion or membership has had for Salvadorans in recent years. What the data do bring to light is the distinct psychosocial meaning of the conversion/membership phenomenon—its ideological dimension. The fact that for individuals conversion may represent an existential consolation, a refuge, a new meaning in life, or an experience of community says nothing about the psychosocial meaning of the process—that is, its impact on historical realities, how it is mediated by social forces, and what social groups benefit from it.

Ideological analysis shows that even though conversion may represent an experience of new meaning that makes individual life more fulfilling, this new meaning can alienate individuals from their reality and from the history of their people; or conversely, it can make them conscious of that reality and inspire them to become subjects of their own history. The ideological dimension does not deny the individual meaning of conversion, but does furnish a concrete historical context for interpreting it, and thus defines a truer reality. The conversion that the individual lives as a purely individual process has important social meaning, and as such becomes an object of interest to political forces, which try to manipulate it to their benefit.

There is abundant evidence regarding the intimate ties between some pentecostal evangelical churches and the most conservative of North American political groups. It is not strange, then, that regardless of individual will or motive, the "missionary" efforts of these churches would be used as part of the ideological offensive against Central American revolutionary movements and, concretely, as part of the psychological war of the "low-intensity conflict."

If our data demonstrate the potential political efficacy of religious mediation of attitudes, they also show that religious conversion does not affect sociopolitical attitudes in a direct, mechanical fashion. A small percentage of the CBC members become more conservative and, more significantly, a relatively large percentage of the EPC members report progressive attitude changes. It cannot be assumed, then, that conversion to or membership in a pentecostal group will in itself make a person more politically conservative, though it does greatly increase the probability of such a change. We can only speculate on what brings this about. It is quite possible, for example, that the direction of attitude change is connected to a person's initial motives for conversion or membership, as could be the case with the personal elaboration of certain religious symbols relating to the social order at a given moment in history. These issues should be studied in future research. The work of Carrasco (1988) stresses that the sociopolitical posture of the EPC members is closely linked to their religious leaders' interpretation of the social order. Even when such leaders seem to assume a distanced, metahistorically critical stance, in practice they forfeit their critical religious posture and are submissive to the political authorities. But a study currently being carried out indicates that certain Salvadoran evangelical groups have been gradually evolving toward more progressive sociopolitical positions.

In view of the ideological dimension of religious conversion/membership in El Salvador, the attempt to be scientifically neutral quickly becomes a form of collaboration with the established powers, masking the conflicts of interest that come into play in the apparently "apolitical" religious sphere. This is true not only with respect to research on religious conversion but even more so with respect to other social research—and not only in El Salvador but in other countries as well. Eliminating the ideological dimension—the relationship any social process has to the whole historical milieu in which it evolved—turns psychology into a blind enterprise with a scientific expertise that is led into the service of the established order. Clearly, a psychologist who allows this to happen is making a value judgment about his or her people and country, just as the decision to follow paths more conducive to growth and humanization is a value judgment. But in any case, one cannot claim technical or methodological independence from such processes; there is a substantial change of perspective at stake in the application or non-application of the ideological dimension, and the perspective one chooses changes what one can see. Objectivity is not the same as impartiality with regard to the processes that necessarily affect all of us. Thus, for an objective psychosocial analysis it is more useful to become conscious of one's own involvements and interests than to deny them and try to place oneself on a fictitious higher plane "beyond good and evil."

Our studies were not done from an ivory tower. In each case, the individuals and groups studied were consulted about the objectives of the research, and their opinions about the findings were sought. Thus, the "objects" of the study were able to become, at least partially, the subjects of important knowledge about their personal lives and their futures as members of a people. Still, we have to recognize that Salvadoran psychologists have not yet confronted all the dimensions of the problem of religious conversion/membership. Some have taken it on from purely political platforms at a distance from work as psychologists; others have ignored it as unworthy of psychological attention; and still others have studied it as affecting only the inner life of the individual, not as a psychosocial phenomenon. But this failure merely mimics the dominant orientation in psychology, which is prone to disregard the historical reality in which we live, particularly if it means having to take a political stand.

9

The Psychological Value of
Violent Political Repression

TRANSLATED BY ANNE WALLACE

The Institutional Use of Repressive Violence

Day after day, in the media, we hear about governments using violent repressive methods against both real and presumed members of the political opposition. These measures include imprisonment, beatings, mistreatment, torture, and even the outright and systematic elimination of dissidents, mainly the leaders of organized movements. Some countries have become world-famous for the massive scale of their repressive violence: Chile under the dictatorship of Pinochet; South Vietnam when it was ruled by Thieu and his U.S. advisors. But these are not the only countries that have used or are now using repressive violence. In Latin America the roster closely resembles the list of the existing "democracies," from Guatemala to Paraguay and including Nicaragua [under Somoza], Uruguay, and Brazil.

Although much of this repressive violence is carried out indirectly, by forces and organizations that the government does not acknowledge as institutional, they are backed, promoted, and protected more or less openly by the government, and their actions are therefore identified as "official" government policy. In other words, for better or worse, governments are responsible for their actions.

Repressive violence is widespread; this has been proven many times and no one questions it. The question is whether the use of repressive violence does or does not aid the governments in achieving their objectives. Our purpose here is to learn whether the results of violent repression are beneficial or not, politically speaking.

Political order implies coercion and, at least in today's world, it is idealistic or naive to think that an absolutely noncoercive political regime can exist. The political constitutes the "ordering of the orders," and all ordering implies some constraint. From a psychological point of view, Freud (1921, 1927, 1928, 1930) intuited this when he held that social life required placing a series of barriers and limitations on individual tendencies.

Our effort here is not to make an idealistic judgment on political coercion in the abstract, but rather, from the perspective of psychology, to establish some criteria for determining the rationality or irrationality of particular forms of political coercion in use today. With this we should be able to assess the conditions and circumstances that render repressive violence psychologically rational, with its benefits outweighing its costs. For institutionalized violence to be politically legitimated it would have to have this kind of social rationality.

To determine whether repressive violence is rational, we must first know its results. If we neglect to examine the results, we run the risk of favoring the violence irrationally or a priori, either because it is easier to continue already established practices than to look for possible alternatives, or because short-term interests are better served by justifying what is currently being done than by reflecting on what ought to be done.

In principle, the effects of repressive violence are not at all obvious, at least not in the medium and long term. Seemingly contradictory cases can be cited, cases that even lend themselves to opposite interpretations, depending on one's point of view. Thus, while in Brazil repressive violence seems to have produced positive results (at least from the point of view of development), in Uruguay it seems to have helped bring about almost total socioeconomic chaos. While in Czechoslovakia the dominating violence of the Russians and their allies seems to have generated a new, stable situation, in South Vietnam the paranoid violence of Thieu and Nixon resulted in one of the most incredible political collapses in history. And whereas in Spain the violence of Franco's regime seems to have made notable economic progress possible, the same violence in Portugal enabled an entire empire to crumble in a couple of days.

Obviously, the effects of a whole political system cannot be attributed simply to the variable of repressive violence. Many other more important factors come into play and determine those consequences in a more immediate way. Nevertheless, we need to calculate as best we can the extent of the influence of repressive violence and the kind of sociopolitical conditioning it may cause, precisely in order to clarify its advantages or disadvantages.

To talk about the advantages or disadvantages of repressive violence is to make a value judgment. This implies the need for criteria, which in this case would be political in nature. *Political* must be understood in a broad sense here, to encompass the whole historical existence of humankind. Clearly, politics is not free from value judgments; a given option and its results can be valued as more ethical than another option that was rejected or one that was blocked. For example, the fact that an act of violent repression allows a government to stay in power does not therefore mean it is politically rational or ethically acceptable. Partial efficiency cannot automatically be identified with ethical goodness or political rationality.

The political advantage or disadvantage of a given measure will depend on its rationality in relation to a particular society's historical objectives. That rationality is in turn indicated by the various social sciences (economics, sociology, psychology, and so on), which must enlighten the path of political options with their knowledge. Thus, for example, a government's political plans have to include a position on the value of education, but the conditions and means by which to achieve educational objectives should be determined by educators.

The case of violent political repression is exceedingly complex and is often judged too superficially. Generally, the very violence condemned in the enemy is praised in the friend. And in the final analysis, repressive violence is not judged on the basis of its political rationality (that is, whether its benefits for society are greater than the harm it causes), but rather on the basis of whether it serves certain interests.

This is generally the case in our countries, where violence is practiced officially or quasi-officially while the same type of violence, when it comes from dissident sectors, is condemned. There is a tendency to assume that this practice is logical, since—or so it is thought—it allows the government to maintain power. But is it really logical? Does it really help a government maintain power? This is where the social sciences should come into the debate, because the logic or rationality of this political practice must be measured by its real effects, by its cost-benefit ratio, as a function of the objectives of a concrete historical society and not merely as a function of the short-term ambition of a dominant elite.

There is a well-known expression from the early period of the Christian expansion: "Blood of martyrs, seed of Christians." On observing some contemporary cases (Vietnam or Portugal, for instance), one is tempted to transform the phrase: "Blood of the repressed, seed of dissidents." This phrase seems to be confirmed as soon as governments offer their people the possibility of relatively free elections: the cases of El Salvador in 1972 and 1974 and Guatemala in 1974 are too recent to be ignored. And, as we know very well, frequently these elections do not so much represent a positive opinion of the candidates elected as the rejection of the official candidates who represent the government.

What is psychology's opinion of repressive violence? Does this science have any data that can help us better understand the effects of repression, its effectiveness for people and groups? Can psychology help to explain more scientifically the advantage or disadvantage of using repressive violence as a means of achieving political objectives?

In attempting to answer these questions, we will try to limit the discussion to data that have experimental proof and that therefore yield findings with greater scientific reliability (see Guiton et al., 1973). We do not mean to claim the absolute validity of these data, particularly not when applying them to a phenomenon as complex as repressive violence in the context of different political situations. Nevertheless, we have no doubt that such data can help us think more objectively about repressive violence and aid us in making decisions that are more ideologically coherent and more rational in terms of political practice.

We should reiterate that we are limiting ourselves to a psychological focus here, realizing that this is only one of several ways to look at the problem. This means that a global judgment about repressive violence in politics would require a broader frame of reference and that this small study therefore offers answers only of a limited scope. We certainly do not mean to claim that psychology must have the final word on the advantage or disadvantage of violent repression. What we are saying is that psychology is necessary for understanding the rationality or irrationality of the application of repressive violence in each specific case. And in a situation where violent repression increases every day, as in our Latin American countries, this is a crucial task.

The Effects of Repressive Violence

As different individuals, in one way or another, enter into the process of repressive violence, it is useful to identify the persons involved and see how each grouping, respectively, is affected by the violence. First, the executors or authors of the violent acts; second, the persons who are the objects of the violence, who become targets of the repression; and third, the persons who, in some way, become spectators, whether immediate or indirect, of the repressive violence. We are using the term *spectator* here in a broad sense, to refer to anyone who is aware of the repression, whether by direct or indirect knowledge.

The Effects of Violence on the Repressor

In principle, the first effect of violent acts on those who carry them out is *cognitive dissonance.* Cognitive dissonance is the psychic discomfort of an individual facing two or more contradictory thoughts that in some way imply an incongruence or inconsistency within the self (see Festinger, 1957; Aronson, 1969). Thus, for example, a dissonance would be produced between two concepts such as "I am a pacifist and I have voluntarily enlisted in the army," or "I believe in democracy and I am working to prevent union organizing among campesinos."

Cognitive dissonance is an imbalance that the individual feels impelled to overcome. In fact, dissonance can be resolved in widely differing ways. It can be resolved by changing one or the other of the dissonant thoughts through a change in beliefs or behavior. For instance, "I am in favor of war and I don't believe in democracy," or "I refuse to be a soldier and I support union organizing among campesinos." Or new concepts can be added to compensate for the dissonance in some way. For example, "Although I am a pacifist, I believe the enemies of peace must be eliminated," or "Although I believe in democracy, I think one must be educated for it and the campesinos aren't," and so on.

In the case of repressive violence, it is evident that the repressors have to find a way to resolve the inescapable internal dissonance between the use of violence against other individuals and one or more of the following precepts: democratic principles, the supposedly accepted principles of social coexistence, or the belief in their own goodness (for, psychologically, we all need to consider ourselves good). Moral inconsistency is, precisely, one of those things that have been systematically shown to unleash dissonance. In the case at hand, dissonance would be produced between the social precept of respecting the health and life of others—a precept that is strongly underscored by the ethic of our societies—and the act of destroying the health or life of some particular individuals.

This dissonance is generally taken into account in the training of those who, like soldiers, will be obligated by trade to kill other human beings (see Berkowitz, 1975). The most common way the dissonance is prevented is through denial of one of the concepts: the humanity of the victim. So, although the soldier subscribes to the idea that "thou shalt not kill," he is taught to believe that "this person I'm killing isn't really a human being." It has been substantiated many times that this kind of dehumanization of the victim not only works as a compensatory preventive mechanism but above all is the effect of dissonance (see Lerner and Simmons, 1966). In other words, one of the consequences for the repressors is the tendency to devalue their victims: either their victims are not really human beings or they are such bad people that they don't deserve to go on living.

This may be the psychological reason that, in certain environments where violence is taken for granted, the devaluation of certain human groups is implicitly and at times even explicitly incorporated into the dominant culture. Thus, when Freire analyzes the myths of the oppressors and the oppressed in Latin American countries, he finds that the oppressors perceive themselves to be the only persons—only people like them are persons—whereas they perceive the oppressed to be instruments, objects, or individuals that acquire meaning only to the extent that they serve the purposes of the oppressor (see Freire, 1971). Obviously, in this environment, an act of violent repression against the oppressed has a prior justification that prevents any type of dissonance from presenting.

Whether cognitive dissonance manifests or the mechanisms of compensation are already institutionalized in society, the fact is that repressive violence causes a cognitive distancing between repressors and their victims. "If they're punished, it means they deserve to be punished"; "If they are repressed, it's because they are evil and a danger to society." The tendency to devalue, which produces a *progressive distancing between the groups,* justifies the repression and thus resolves the possible cognitive dissonance in the oppressor. Observe for a moment the twist in logic that this implies: the use of violence generates its own justification and not the other way around, as would be rational. And it is this lack of logic that is consecrated in the mythology of the oppressor, subtly hidden behind the great liberal values—the naturalizers of unacceptable historical situations.

But repressors cannot always devalue their victims, and the closer or more immediate they are, the harder it becomes. Conversely, the less contact there is with the victims, the easier it is to behave destructively toward them (see Kilham and Mann, 1974). Therefore, repressive acts often leave the repressors with a psychic dis-ease, a need for congruence, that can result in the need to compensate the victim in some way. Not infrequently this leads the repressors to turn against those who are forcing them to use repressive violence. The harder it is for repressors to achieve cognitive congruence by devaluing their victims—either because they know the individual or can personally verify the falseness of the devaluation—the more likely is this reversal to occur. In part, this is what happened on a daily basis in South Vietnam during the Thieu regime, and what happened to the Portuguese soldiers in Angola and even to certain Peruvian soldiers in their repressive action against the guerrillas in their country.

A second consequence that repressive violence may have for the repressor is the *learning of violent habits* as a preferred response for resolving interpersonal conflicts and confrontations. This learning of violent models would explain why certain veterans of wars like the one in Vietnam feel inclined to solve social problems in an abrupt way or demand a little more from the authorities, or even how they can evolve into violent criminals or near criminals, as has happened in Guatemala.

Certain ethologists and psychoanalysts consider that exercising violent behaviors (which they call "constructive" because of their socialization), can provide an outlet for aggressive instincts and, therefore, serve as a cathartic escape valve. However, numerous studies disagree, demonstrating that practicing or watching violence leads instead to its being learned and becoming a fixation. Thus, for example, Walters and Brown (1963) proved that aggressive games can increase the probability that aggression will occur in real situations. Bandura (1972) insists on the importance that social reinforcement can have in the fixation of aggressive behaviors. When parents reinforce their children's violence frequently, they are probably training future juvenile delinquents (see Bandura and Walters, 1959). Similarly, university students who are praised for their toughness can become very aggressive toward their victims (see Geen and Stonner, 1971).

There are many studies that prove the value of social reinforcement in the learning and generalization of responses; in this case, of aggressive responses. If individuals are specially compensated for committing violent acts, if they are encouraged and rewarded by their social group or their superiors for it, there is clearly a very high probability that in similar situations they will resort to the same type of behavior. In other words, in cases of confrontation, discrepancy, or conflict, their most likely response will be aggressive violence, thus corroborating what we observe in our daily experience in El Salvador, of aggressive responses becoming generalized. This can lead to the deceptive conclusion that there are "human instincts" of aggression, even "naturally" aggressive personalities.   .

The Salvadoran press recently published a communiqué from the office of Press and Public Relations of the National Guard which stated that, for various reasons, over a two-year period "more than four hundred members of the Institution [have been] dishonorably expelled" (see *El Mundo* [San Salvador], June 26, 1975, p. 2). The context of this note (the expulsion of certain guards for committing violent acts), seems to imply that these expulsions are motivated, at least in some cases, by violent behavior which is not institutionally acceptable or endorsed. Now then, the fact that four hundred members (an estimated 5 to 10 percent of total active personnel) are dishonorably discharged from an institution in which there is strong military discipline is an index that corroborates the statement about learning violent habits and then wantonly generalizing them to situations that are not institutionally sanctioned. Someone who learns to behave violently in one situation, and is reinforced for doing so, will tend to repeat this type of behavior in other situations. In fact, environments in which violence is systematically practiced become closed groups where the highest value is placed on the brutality of aggression and where individuals internalize that evaluative criterion to such an extent that later they will need no greater reward than the knowledge that they have reached the "ideal" level of aggression.

Certain pragmatic politicians may consider the existence of such dehumanized groups at the service of the regime to be a minor and socially necessary evil. What should be challenged is both the conviction that they are a minor evil and the more or less implicit assumption that the benefits they produce for a given regime compensate for their social costs. This debate is intensifying now that the image produced by any given regime can influence not only its chances for success but also its national and international stability. At the same time, the progressive degeneration of social groups that is caused by the growing presence of violence in their lives casts serious doubt on the political legitimacy of a regime. The recent history of Guatemala is a case in point.

The Effects of Repressive Violence on the Repressed

By repressed, we mean the subject who personally suffers the impact of violent repression. We do not mean repressed in the psychoanalytic sense of an individual who displaces from the conscious mind to the unconscious any knowledge or feeling that causes discomfort. Obviously, when repression consists of the elimination of dissidents, the one consequence for them is death. We must not lose sight of these cases, but because our purpose here is to examine the effects of violent repression on the repressed subject, we will refer to cases in which the aggression does not result in death.

The physical impact can vary greatly. For instance, there is the recently reported incident of a Basque priest who, after being "interrogated" by the Spanish police, had to be admitted to a hospital emergency room and, in order to survive, must use an artificial lung and be under continuous medical observation (see *Excelsior* [Mexico, D.F.], May 14, 1975, p. 3A). In other cases the effects are limited to a few contusions, hematomas, or small lesions. Between the two extremes, there is the whole possible gamut of wounds, mutilations, and impairment. Clearly, the greater the physical damage caused or the more delicate the injured parts (the nervous system, genitals, and so on), the longer the imprint of the repression will last and the more disabled the subject will be. It is the *psychological impact,* however, that generally tends to be most profound, and this is the damage the repressors are most interested in inflicting. Thus, it has recently been reported that in Chile they are systematically torturing political prisoners with drugs, presumably because the drugs bring about the desired psychological impairment while leaving fewer signs than physical torture (see Diego Ferrat, 1975). In any case, the greater the damage caused, the more disabled the individual will be.

Does violent repression have any psychological effect other than simply rendering an individual useless to a greater or lesser degree? As a tentative first step toward answering this question we can interpret repressive violence as the application of physical punishment for the purpose of modifying an individual's behavior. From this psychological perspective one can see in repressive violence the same properties, and therefore the same advantages and disadvantages, as punishment has in a learning context.

First, we know that punishment is more effective for learning avoidance than for learning from the punishment per se. The difference between the two types of learning is that in the former the individual learns to do something to avoid being punished ("If you don't do this, you will be punished"), while in the latter the individual is punished following an action, with the aim of eliminating that action ("If you do this, you will be punished"). The difference may seem subtle, but it is important. In the first case the punishment functions as a threat before the behavior takes place, and can therefore serve as an orientation for seeking another type of behavior to satisfy one's motivation while avoiding the punishment. In the second case the behavior has already taken place in response to some motive and, as we will soon see, the punishment by itself is not effective for eliminating an already acquired mode of behavior. What in fact happens with repression is this: it applies punishment to certain already existing, already learned behaviors.

The punishment tends, however, to generate an emotional conflict; the greater the individual's motivation to carry out the punished behaviors, the greater this conflict will be. This emotional conflict tends to result in various kinds of serious disorders. In the case of violent repression, this is confirmed by the frequency with which people who have been tortured "go crazy." Obviously, in these cases there has been no positive modification of behavior; the individual has simply been "eliminated" as an active subject in society.

As we have just indicated, the most important thing is that *punishment in itself cannot eliminate learned behavior.* What punishment achieves is to inhibit or block the execution of the behavior. But when a learned and punished behavior responds to one of the individual's true needs, if another behavior that allows for the satisfaction of that same need does not present itself, the punished behavior will tend to reappear. In this sense, the punishment is effective only to the extent that it offers subjects the opportunity to satisfy their needs with socially acceptable alternative behaviors—not theoretical alternatives, but concrete and real ones. If, in spite of promises and good wishes, no alternatives are offered, the punishment will be ineffective and will act as an inhibitor only so long as it is felt to be stronger than the need whose satisfaction it is blocking. On the other hand, maintaining this violence over a long period of time produces a growing passivity among the population subjected to it (see Berkowitz, 1975).

In many cases, political repression is directed against behaviors that, ultimately, express and seek the satisfaction of people's most basic needs: food, shelter, work, and so on. This means that repressive violence will be effective only in the short term, and that over time an increasingly higher dose of violence will be necessary to hold back the pursuit of the fundamental need. Frequently, the repressed find themselves opting for the lesser evil of a double bind: it is not unusual nowadays, in certain campesino sectors, to hear people say, "It is better to die fast from a bullet than slowly from hunger."

The systematic application of violent repression does not discriminate sufficiently between subjects and the behaviors it attempts to punish. We know, for example, that the reputation for "ferocity" and "effectiveness" of a special corps of South Koreans that operated in Vietnam from 1965 to 1973, was based on a policy of deliberate assassination of the civilian population (for example, killing one out of ten civilians in every occupied village; see Chomsky and Herman, 1975). There are also the numerous programs of "counterrevolutionary" terror directed by the U.S. forces in Vietnam, such as the celebrated case of "Project Phoenix," which, sadly, can be credited with more than 20,000 murders (ibid.). This type of indiscriminate repression renders the punishment totally ineffective, because people are not able to distinguish which characteristics (what types of behavior) the repressors are trying to eliminate with the punishment.

In these cases, repressive violence is effective only insofar as it manages to inhibit behavior through fear. However, it is very possible that if people have no way of distinguishing which behavior is being punished, the stimulus they will come to fear is *the repressor*. That is, they will fear the police, the army, the government, or whatever the repressive force is, but they will not fear taking actions that they have never identified as provoking punishment. In other words, the result of indiscriminate violence is that it inhibits behavior as long as people think their actions can be observed, controlled, or known. As already indicated, this kind of inhibition can lead to progressive passivity. But as soon as the opportunity arises for the behavior to be enacted without the danger of punishment, the behavior will recur. The only discrimination achieved with punishment of this kind is that people will be able to recognize the agents of repression and will become increasingly adept at eluding them (Bandura, 1969).

There is another important aspect to consider when evaluating the psychological effects of repressive violence on the victim. Numerous experimental studies as well as clinical experience show that the more external the punishment imposed, the less an individual tends to internalize the ethics and ideology of the authorities. To the extent that the punishment imposed is internal or psychological, rather than external or physical, the tendency is for the individual to internalize the authority figure's evaluative criterion and, consequently, to experience guilt each time he or she violates it. Stated differently, when people are taught predominantly through physical sanctions, what develops, instead of an internalization of the model and a tendency to experience guilt when it is violated, is a tendency to keep their transgressions from being discovered (Wallace and Sadalla, 1966). Physical punishment tends to generate aggressive responses rather than anxiety responses: just the reverse of psychological punishment. This brings us to the final effect we want to analyze in people who are violently repressed.

According to the now classic thesis of the Yale team, "aggression is always a consequence of frustration" (Dollard et al., 1939, p. 1). This does not mean that whenever frustration occurs it will inevitably result in an act of aggression. It means more specifically that a particularly important consequence of frustration is an incitement to aggression, which will express itself under the right circumstances, depending on what other environmental factors exist and what else has been learned.

The authors themselves state that "the strength of inhibition of any act of aggression varies positively with the amount of punishment anticipated to be a consequence of that act ... In general, it may be said that, with the strength of frustration held constant, the greater the anticipation of punishment for a given act of aggression, the less apt that act is to occur; and, secondly, with anticipation of punishment held constant, the greater the strength of the frustration, the more apt aggression is to occur," because "anticipation of failure is equivalent to anticipation of punishment" (ibid., pp. 24–25). To put it more simply: frustration incites aggression. If aggression is punished, then whether or not an act of aggression occurs will depend on the strength of the frustrated need.

Applying the theory of frustration-aggression to the case of repressive violence, the latter clearly constitutes a punishment for the victim, but it is also a cause of frustration; therefore, it is a frustrating punishment. On the assumption that it is built on top of another frustration, repression produces a double incitement to aggression: there is an incitement in the frustration of the aspiration and then a new incitement in the frustration produced by the repressive violence. (Such is the case with political repression in Latin America, which tends to destroy people who work for change because their most basic desires are frustrated). What we can conclude from this is that one of the effects of repressive violence is an instigation to aggression; that is, an increase in the level of existing aggressiveness and, consequently, an increased probability of aggressive responses. Whether or not these responses occur will depend largely on the degree to which individuals anticipate that punishment will follow from their actions. But it is evident that if the threat of punishment decreases the aggressiveness will tend to express itself with greater vehemence than ever. This also confirms the common experience that violence is a continuously growing spiral and that the maintenance of political control through force will demand an increasing application of repressive mechanisms.

The Effects of Repressive Violence on the Spectator

Repressive violence will have very different effects on both direct and indirect spectators depending on their possibilities for identifying with, or distancing themselves from, the victims. When spectators can clearly distance themselves emotionally from victims, the devaluation mentioned above occurs, converting the victims into "scapegoats": "If they've been punished, it's because they deserved it," "It's the right thing to do," "Subversion must be punished," and so on. This also produces a feeling of well-being, of comparative self-esteem: "I am good," "I am not like them." This is precisely the type of reaction people have to movies about the "good guys" and the "bad guys," even though the "good guys" may in fact be no less violent or criminal than the "bad guys."

But, for this distancing to occur, there must be at least some minimal definition of the factors related to the punishment. It is necessary to be able to identify the victim as "subversive," "communist," "guerrilla," "criminal," "antisocial," or any other attribute that society considers punishable, based on a series of more or less clearly defined traits that spectators can find in the others but not in themselves.

The problem arises when the attributes used to categorize the victims are not clearly defined features, characteristics, or behaviors, but instead remain ambiguous and vague. When the attributes for justifying repressive violence are just generalizations, or are arbitrarily assigned, this impedes the process of recognizing punishable features and behaviors. As a result, spectators cannot adequately achieve emotional distance from the victim.

When the spectators identify in some way with the victims, when they perceive in themselves some or all of the features and behavior for which other individuals have been repressed, vicarious learning occurs. In other words, the punishment applied to the victim also serves as a modeled learning situation for the spectator. As Bandura and others have abundantly demonstrated, the experience that permits the formation and fixation of habits does not necessarily have to occur in the subjects of the learning themselves; it can occur in other subjects, who serve as models (see Kilham and Mann, 1974; Bandura and Walters, 1963; Bandura, 1971). Seeing behaviors, control stimuli, and positive and negative reinforcement in others, individuals learn "through someone else's body."

In the case of repressive violence, if the spectators identify in some way with the victims, they learn from what they see modeled. As with the victims, however, this learning can take different forms. For the spectator, the spectacle or knowledge of repressive violence can produce an *inhibiting fear* of the punished behavior. But it is also likely to lead to *situational rather than behavioral discrimination,* causing individuals to learn that certain acts must be carried out in secret (clandestinely) by eluding the repressive forces, rather than that they must not commit these acts. Similarly, in addition to fear there may be an increase in aggressiveness of the spectators, to the extent that they see in others the frustration of their own aspirations, even though they may not suffer the physical impact of the repression personally.

Assuming, however, that the spectators identify with the victims, they may experience a cognitive dissonance which is the inverse of the dissonance produced in the repressor—a dissonance that will lead them to disqualify the aggressor morally and politically as "fascist," "murderer," "oppressor," and so on. Thus, the same distancing that the repressors establish between themselves and their victims, the spectators who identify with the victims establish between themselves and the repressors. There is a growing abyss between repressors and potential victims, which—from the government's point of view—means a serious deterioration in its image and its political possibilities.

Finally, the spectator *learns*—also by seeing it modeled—*the value of violent power.* Experiments have proven that violence on the screen can serve as a model from which people learn to respond violently as a way of solving social problems. Because movies not only show violent behavior but also repeatedly reinforce it by presenting it as successful and praiseworthy (the strongest or most violent person tends to win), this success serves as a vicarious reinforcement that fixes the pattern of behavior in the spectator, who, in similar circumstances, will tend to respond in the same way. In addition, watching violence on the screen produces a lack of inhibition of aggressive tendencies. Thus it has also been proven that individuals tend to show more aggressive behavior after watching violent scenes than after watching peaceful ones (Berkowitz, 1965; Walters, 1966).

If watching cinema violence teaches people to behave aggressively and makes them less inhibited about acting violently, the effect is even greater when the violent behavior they see is direct and real. The daily spectacle of violence committed by repressive forces teaches and encourages spectators to use similar behavior to solve their own problems.

The power of example leads spectators to the conclusion that the best way to resolve social conflicts is through the immediate use of violence, violence that may even take the lives of opponents. Simply because this behavior is learned does not mean it will be put into practice immediately. But it does mean that when circumstances are favorable, and given certain instigating stimuli, the customary response for solving problems will tend to be violent aggression. Once again, then, society is being thrown into a spiral of growing violence, with the immense deterioration in the conditions of social existence that this implies.

Final Reflections

With the following propositions drawn from the study of psychology, we can synthesize the effects that repressive violence may have on a given society:

- As a punishment, repressive violence is capable of inhibiting certain behaviors, at least as long as the threat of the violence is stronger than the need or aspiration those behaviors are trying to satisfy.
- Repressive violence in itself does not produce any change in behavior. Unless there is a simultaneous possibility of satisfying the need or aspiration in question through some alternative behavior, the repressed behavior will reappear, with greater force, as soon as the violence ceases.
- The effectiveness of repressive violence in blocking certain actions is greater in repressed people than in spectators, primarily because of its incapacitating effects. Politically, however, the effect of repression on the spectators is of greater interest, if only because there are many more spectators than repressed people—unless the violent repression is carried out on a massive scale. To the extent that repressive violence does not achieve its goal of inhibiting the spectators, its effect can be even more counter-productive for the objectives of the repressors.
- Although it is effective, repressive violence maintained over a long period produces a reaction of generalized passivity among the population.
- Repressive violence raises the level of frustration of various social groups and, therefore, increases their aggressiveness; that is, their instigation of aggressive acts.

- Repressive violence produces a cognitive polarization between social groups that carries the opposition between one's own group ("us") and the opposing group ("them") to an extreme. People begin to perceive everything as good or bad in simplistic and total terms, depending on whether it is identified with or opposes their own group. This extreme simplification of perception impedes an adequate evaluation of the facts, thereby obstructing all possible communication and social collaboration. It therefore blocks the success of any type of political measure people may later want to put into practice, as happened in Chile during Salvador Allende's popular government (Zúñiga, 1975).

- Finally, repressive violence constitutes a model that teaches and reinforces habits of violent response as the most effective way to solve social and political problems. This, in turn, fosters a deterioration in the conditions of social existence.

A careful consideration of these consequences leads to a very negative judgment of repressive violence from the point of view of its psychological effectiveness. The case of Vietnam, in which neither France nor Japan nor the United States was able to establish a human base for political domination, even when repressive violence was applied at extreme levels, corroborates the preceding conclusions. It is clear that other variables played a role in this failure (Vietnamese nationalism, for example). But that in itself is a sign of the political ineffectiveness of violent repression.

In my opinion as a psychologist—and again, this is only one point of view—it is primarily the determination of the second point above that will define the rationality or irrationality of the use of repressive violence in any given situation. In other words, the need to block certain socially harmful behaviors while the learning of alternative, socially advantageous behaviors is made possible is the criterion that should necessitate the use of repressive violence. Only this violence can be justified. Of course, the psychological justification will depend on what is really offered the subjects in the way of opportunities for learning alternative behaviors. If these opportunities are not offered, then, psychologically, repressive violence has no rational justification, and will cause the government more harm than good.

This is how the irrationality of certain recent acts of repressive violence in El Salvador manifests itself. The use of a huge repressive apparatus to eliminate barely a dozen campesinos or to break up a student demonstration has not only led to a considerable erosion of the government's image in the eyes of the spectators (the rest of the population). It has also led to a reinforcement of the learning of violence among some groups, and to support for the majority's ethical and political condemnation of the violence. All this has further weakened the current Salvadoran government's precarious base of social legitimacy.

There may very well be non-psychological reasons for imposing repressive violence in a given situation. It is not our purpose here to analyze them. Ultimately, when a government wants nothing more than to maintain power, the application of violence can be an irrationally effective weapon. The problem is that no regime can last very long purely through the exercise of violence. Sooner or later, any regime needs some kind of legitimation and, in the final analysis, legitimacy can come only from the good produced in the community. This is an elemental truth for the guerrillas who, before beginning their military operations, must ingratiate themselves and psychologically win over the population in those areas where they will be operating. If they do not succeed at this, their enterprise is destined to end in failure. The pure exercise of power for power's sake, whose only objective is to maintain domination and political control over a certain population, is condemned to perish sooner or later.

Our constitution proclaims and demands democratic consensus, that is, the support of the people as the ultimate legitimation of any regime. And although reality is always far from the ideal, it is nevertheless true that the constitutional principle expresses a politically rational criterion. For this reason, if in addition to *de facto* control there is an attempt to achieve control by law, if in addition to conquering there is a desire to convince, if there is a desire to exercise power not only through force but also through reason—in short, if there is truly a desire to be a government of the people, then what psychology is saying must be heeded. Because, among other things, history confirms its points of view.

III

De-Ideologizing Reality

The three chapters of this section move from polemic to data-based argument to exquisite synthesis—a journey whose way-stations gave the author time to earn a reputation as an activist with a vision of the future, a demanding professor with high standards of excellence, and an intellectual *extraordinaire.*

The polemic "The People" (Chapter 10), the earliest of the pieces collected in this book, was written in 1974 for *Estudios Centroamericanos (ECA)*, the intellectual journal published by the UCA. Martín-Baró had begun publishing in *ECA* in 1966, writing on topics whose range can be discerned by the titles: "A Strange Remedy for Homosexuality: Its Legalization"; "Who's Afraid of James Bond?"; "The Macho Complex, or *Machismo*"; "The Psychology of Shortage"; "From Alcohol to Marijuana"; "Some Psychosocial Repercussions of Population Density in El Salvador"; "Antipsychiatry and Antipsychoanalysis." (For his complete bibliography, see pp. 223–228 of this book.)

Snatching pieces of class struggle from Marx and glimpses of the New Human Being from Che Guevara, Martín-Baró produces in Chapter 10 a near reverie on the concept of *the people,* explaining that the *real* people do not exist but are rather a historical-political-socioeconomic potential to be realized in the future. In looking for a single meaning for this three-dimensional reality, this trinity that must cohere as a unified being, Martín-Baró the Jesuit finds *the people* as representing an opening to the other, and thus, without naming it, finds in liberation theology the principle that allows us to identify *the people* with freedom and justice for all. As always, the author is cautioning us to listen critically to what we are hearing, and to ask whose interests are being served by what is being proposed. And he is clarifying for us, if we had any doubt, what it means to live and act on behalf of the people.

Chapter 11 joins theoretical discourse with practical application, to provide a superb concrete example of how one can use one's professional knowledge and skills (in this case the social scientist's ability to conduct empirical research) to assist the people in their historical mission of creating a community of solidarity. Here Martín-Baró can no longer work from a context of demagogues deceiving people through their sloganeering, as he did in 1974; by 1984 the exigencies of civil war require a more formidable base, and he must produce arguments first to justify doing research at all amid the legions of lame and wounded whose needs are crying for attention, and second to justify survey work to psychologists, who have never placed much stock in the public opinion poll.

The historical perspective Martín-Baró advocates in all his writings is here demonstrated not only in the base for his arguments, formed by the realities of the day and the conditions that produced them, but also in the argument's direction and the destination of its conclusions—toward a future whose realities social science research can help bring about. With data from the polls themselves Martín-Baró illustrates his point that such surveys are critical in breaking down the prevailing discourse (The Lie), and invaluable for helping people to develop a new collective identity. He argues convincingly that collective consciousness can play a role in prolonging or ending the civil war and, more important, in ending the unjust social conditions whose prolongation caused the war to erupt.

Embedded in the discussion of the utility of public opinion polls are certain data about the current situation as Martín-Baró and his student survey workers were living it: in El Salvador it was dangerous to ask questions, dangerous to attend to the victims of war, dangerous to admit support for a dialogue between the FMLN and the government. He mentions that his house (the Jesuit residence) had been bombed five times. Modestly, he does not mention that each of the firebombings occurred at a time when he was at home. Martín-Baró was letting psychologists see that outside those "safe and sterile little academic boxes," their work held the promise of making a real contribution to building a just society.

In lauding the courage of his co-workers, Martín-Baró was not saying we should all be risking life and limb for the sake of social science research. Rather, he was making a case for commitment, and vision, whatever our circumstances may be. What he meant was that researchers, professors, and students need to examine and evaluate the kinds of contributions they are actually making, and to weigh these against the potential they have for effecting real change. When we resolve to carry out a project, for instance, are we thinking beyond our reputations and careers, our publications and grades? Are we mindful of the implications of our research, of the socialization that led us to undertake this project rather than a different one? Are we attentive to whose interests are being served by what we are doing, and whose interests ignored? Are we so thoroughly caught up in an ideologized view of what counts, what needs to be studied, what it means to do good work, that we have forgotten a commitment to truth and justice? He does not mention, but we should not forget, that an intellectual in a little place like El Salvador writing in Spanish is in many ways a marginalized being whose greatest credibility would normally come from an identification with, and acceptance by, the people ensconced in safe and sterile academic boxes. He resisted the temptation, and a whole world opened up to him. Are we willing to endure a few raised eyebrows and a possible barrage of unkind words, for the chance of participating in that world? Or will the university remain a place like the Latin America described in Chapter 12, where people seem to have "fallen into a forced siesta, a state of semi-wakefulness that keeps them at the margins of their own history, where they are made to participate in processes that others control"?

War and violence were at the center of Martín-Baró's professional and personal life, because they were what for many years defined life in his adopted country. His arguments drew strength from his analysis of the particular features of the society in which he was living, even as ours can draw strength from our own particular circumstances. Undaunted by El Salvador's small size and relative insignificance, he often used his country as a case in point for illustrating larger issues, and through that technique sometimes made startling discoveries. In Chapter 12, "The Lazy Latino," Martín-Baró offers El Salvador not as a mere object lesson but as the crowning example, for Latin America and the rest of the world, of a country where a significant proportion of the population has broken away from the oppressive cognitive frameworks of fatalism and dared to form social organizations through which they can design, and possibly achieve, a collective future based on justice. From his own position in the "limit situation" of El Salvador, which gave him foresight as well as insight, he perceived the struggle for justice as achievable on earth.

"The Lazy Latino" brings together, in an elegant package wrapped up in a discussion of fatalism, themes we have seen separately and mixed, fully displayed or lightly folded through the many pages of this book. Commonsense knowledge and the social lie, stereotypes and concrete realities, socialization and *concientización,* labor and liberation, fundamentalism and individualism, propaganda and alienation, power in social relations and the recovery of collective history, the culture of poverty and alienating social structures—all this and more is delivered to the reader with a note from García Márquez and a final seal of revolutionary change.

The profound optimism that informed all of Martín-Baró's work is especially poignant in the essays of this section, where he shows that the recovery of historical consciousness is possible even under the most extreme, most repressive of conditions, when reality is so thoroughly ideologized that the official discourse is the only voice that speaks. In pointing out to us that those with access to resources can control and manipulate the psyche through their control of what is projected as "reality," he demonstrates the psychological consequence of our responding in an adaptive manner: we become the bearers of labels (learned helplessness) or the objects of negative stereotypes (fatalistic), and when we internalize those characterizations we fall victim again to the same social controls that manufactured them. We become alienated from our own personal and social reality. Because this destructive historical process is played out through a psychological transformation, it is psychologists who have the responsibility—and, more important, the *resources*—to combat it. Martín-Baró saw in the theory and practice of psychology the potential for de-ideologizing artificial realities and for re-empowering people to interpret and shape their own histories. In the end the question is, do psychologists dare to be empowered?

10

The People: *Toward a Definition of a Concept*

TRANSLATED BY ADRIANNE ARON

Introduction

Everyday political life seems to move on an ideological plane marked by a number of unquestioned and contradictory central concepts that nobody ever bothers to explain and that have hidden under them, as we know from experience, a number of different realities. This might not matter so much if in each case we knew which reality was under discussion, but the problem is that most of the time the terms that are used contain troublesome ambiguities, and under the guise of conveying an objective picture of reality they actually present something that is incomplete, biased, and even hostile to reality. Some have already caused crises among us. Take for instance the concepts of democracy, peace, violence, development, and apoliticism. But not the concept of The People! Still encircled by a "progressive-subversive" dynamic that fits around it like a halo, this mythical standard-bearer of revolutions and "popular" uprisings continues to evoke misty fantasies.

We hear "the people" when politicians want to justify and legitimate ("for the good of the people") things that then usually proceed to leave the people out. Under the banner of "the people" the most disparate decisions come to be made: those who plan a *coup d'état* invoke the people, just as do those who try to stop it; defenders of agrarian reform claim to represent the people, and so do those who attack it; the officials who administer justice use the people as their shield, but so do those who accuse these same officials of corruption—and so on. This continual use of the term "the people," under the most contradictory of headings, robs it of all meaning, leaving it as an empty vessel that may be filled by any political interest whatsoever. But its persistence, and its obligatory use by everyone—reputable and disreputable alike—who wants a turn in the political arena, indicates the presence of some kind of categorical imperative conditioning public life to some Entity X called "the people." But really, who is this "X"? Who do we mean when we say "the people"?

In many speeches and declarations the term "the people" is obviously nothing more than a euphemism for those in power or their direct beneficiaries. When we hear about "the good of the people," or "what the people have claims to," all that is really meant is the well-being and claims of certain special interests within a given country. In other cases, especially among certain political idea-makers of the "nationalist" persuasion, the term "the people" seems to be indiscriminately identified with everyone living inside a particular geographic space (bounded by national borders, sometimes uncertain), where inhabitants, grouped together more or less arbitrarily in a political entity called a nation, supposedly share a common destiny. "The people" then comes to refer to all those who belong to that particular nation, under the assumption that common biological roots (marked by some common borders) override all kinds of differences and offer the most authentic guarantee of a community with a shared destiny. Understood this way, the concept of "the people," in a malicious (though not necessarily conscious) blindness, can in one fell swoop cut away the irreconcilable conflicts that may exist among a nation's different sectors.

This is not the place to take on those cases in which, thanks to nationalism, the concept of The People is identified with a religious choice, a party affiliation, or worse yet, a race. Those cases tend to consecrate a static and adialectical blindness in a pattern that tries to escape history. They force a perpetuation of the existing order, an order obviously damaging to the basic rights of "minorities"—who statistically are frequently the oppressed majorities. This use of the concept of "the people" is more or less characteristic of totalitarian regimes, whether they are fascist or not.

The most generalized use of the term "the people" ties it to the less-well-off pole of the elite-mass dyad. As opposed to those who are outstanding in one life situation or another, the people are the ones who don't stand out, who represent the norm, the statistical mean; the people are the "common person," the man on the street, "John Doe," "Pablo Campo." Against the "exception," the people are the rule. In this line of reasoning "the people" are presumed to have, *par excellence,* the traits of a putative national identity.

In this same contrapuntal view, in certain more specific cases, the people come to be the most needy of all the groups that make up a particular society: the impotent ones, the needy ones, those who in one way or another are the "have-nots." Thus, Marxism identifies the people with the working class, as distinguished from the bourgeois-capitalist class, since workers are robbed of the fruit of their labor by the plundering capitalists. The people, then, are the proletariat, necessarily resentful (with resentment understood here as a positive revolutionary potential for social redistribution), though perhaps still unconscious of their rights, and even of their just claims in the redistribution.

Like trick mirrors, all these indiscriminate applications of the term "the people" seem to hide ambiguities that allow people to take the rights implicitly attributed to *the demos* (*the people,* who supposedly have the last word in political matters) and distort them for their own personal gain. If a government, a party, or certain individuals have the backing of The People, by virtue of that fact their actions become justified: they are democratic, in the most authentic sense of that term, no matter what they have done in the past to be unworthy of that label. Hence the need of politicians of every stripe to speak "in the name of the people," and to back up their acts with a good appearance, protecting their decisions behind the shield of popular demands and needs.

It is important to clarify as much as possible the determining characteristics of this entity called "the people," so as to be able to recognize when the term is being used objectively (and sincerely) and when it is not. Or, what is the same thing, to know who are the people and who are not, and to be able to judge when an endeavor that wants and claims popularity is really popular and when it is not. Hence, any reflection that might shed some light on this question does an urgent and necessary service. The following reflections, offered with full consciousness of their precariousness and sketchiness, are an attempt to collaborate in this effort at illumination.

Three Aspects of the Concept of *The People*

The various uses mentioned for the concept "the people" locate its meaning in one or more of three closely interrelated areas: the historical, the political, and the socioeconomic. Over and beyond the bias surrounding the arbitrary usage within each of these areas' boundaries—that is, the distortions of reality introduced by each interpretation—this triple reference identifies fields in which the concept is meaningful.

It is fitting, then, to assert that "the people" has a historical meaning, a political meaning, and a socioeconomic meaning, and that each of these meanings is simply an aspect of the concept, trying to define the reality of *the people* from its particular perspective. Each in its own way describes characteristics of the same entity, *the people*. The entity is therefore real only to the extent that it integrates (at least implicitly) all three aspects of its meaning. This has to be underlined because public oratory with its semantic half-truths would suggest otherwise. If, and only if, these three features are present as elements of a single structure of meaning, can the entity under discussion be objectively called the people. To absolutize a single feature is to falsify the theoretical concept, not only because the other features have been omitted but also because when such an excision is performed the absence of the complimentary aspects changes the feature that is retained. Thus, for example, to identify the concept of the people with the concept of nation absolutizes the historical factor. This not only ignores the dynamic tensions within the nation but also, by omitting them, falsifies the historical reality itself, turning it into something static and fatalistic; that is to say, mythifying it. Mythified as nationals or universals, "the people" then become in practice an instrument of the prevailing interests.

Defining the people as constitutive of these three features does not mean, and in fact is far from meaning, that all three aspects will always have the same importance, or that we will not choose to emphasize one over another at some particular time. Such emphasis is a dialectical necessity, acceptable when knowledge is experiential and not simply theoretical. At a given time, for example, the people themselves may find it politically necessary to underscore the historical aspect of the concept, in order to juxtapose their national identity to that of the distant and alienating dominant interests. At another time, emphasizing the socioeconomic aspect may be important to make clear the political priorities of a government given to obfuscation, whose development policy favors growth over justice and beclouds an agenda for internal and external institutionalized oppression. Finally, at yet another time, it may be necessary to put the political aspect of "the people" in relief, so as to consolidate the truly revolutionary forces of the country and guide them toward the attainment of collective objectives (which seems to be the intention of the "populists").

Emphasizing the various aspects of the concept, then, does not mean falsifying the concept of *the people*. Falsification comes about when an absolutism is produced; that is, when a single feature is advanced and the others are ignored. When that occurs, the entity hidden under the name "the people" is not actually *the people*, but only a partial and biased representation of it, a representation not of an objective reality but rather of a subjective one—the subjective reality of the groups in power.

The Historical Aspect

The concept of *the people* expresses above all a historical reality. In other words, to speak of the people in general is to be quite imprecise, for what actually exists is not *the* people, but rather particular *peoples:* the Salvadoran people, the Tanzanian people, the people of the United States, or of China. Plainly, the Salvadoran people is not the same as the North American people, nor is the latter the same as the Tanzanian or Chinese people. We have intentionally used examples of peoples who are very different in order to show that, although it is right in every case to speak of the people, the reality is very different from case to case. To separate "the people" from its concrete historical situation is to idealize it (in the pejorative sense of that term), as if peoples were independent of, or removed from, the everyday realities—past, present, and future—that shape them. Such a separation treats peoples' peculiar traits as though they were only passing accidents, in no way determined by the structures that in fact condition their very being and existence.

Peoples are historical. It is history that has determined their present peculiarities, and history alone that can explain their current situations. "The people," therefore, does not mean the same thing in one country as in another. Through history very important variables have arisen: race, geographical boundaries, political systems, culture, the way the many groups fit together, and so on.

The people have not been ignored by history, much less stood in opposition to or on the sidelines of historical causation. In Latin America, the who, the how, and the why of what constitutes "the people" has been determined by the Conquest, by relations to metropolitan centers, by independence struggles, liberalism, and neocolonialism. For each of the peoples of Latin America, *who, how,* and *why* are three separate, concrete determinations. In saying that each people has a history we are rejecting chance and fatalism as explanatory principles for what we see today in our nations.

It needs to be emphasized, though, that the history of the peoples of Latin America does not match what is dished out in the schools; indeed, the two histories are at odds. For instance, it is a commonplace that what are called independence struggles are not history for many of our Latin American peoples, and that many governments of today (conceived and plotted in flawless English-language dispatches) make "their" history at the expense of the people.

By putting the concept of "the people" in a historical context, we affirm the particulars, in terms of space, time, and characteristics, that in each case and each situation color the peoples' reality. Thus, it is not possible to generalize or pretend that all peoples at all times go through the same processes or make the same choices. Very simply, history affirms the present of a given people, insofar as that present is a product of a past and points toward a future. *The people* is, in this sense, a fact, but, above all, a challenge and a hope: the truth of the people is in the making. Hence the historical feature of a people indicates the objective of its yet-to-be-actualized freedom; it defines what a history of liberation demands. Because historically *the people* is called upon to be—to be itself—it must overcome its servitude, and must eliminate everything that stands in the way of its becoming itself. The historicism of a people is the fact and the promise of its struggles for freedom, and the self-determination of its axiological destiny. But what enslaves a specific people in a particular situation is not necessarily the same thing that causes another people to be enslaved, and therefore it is either naive or malicious to try transferring ideas from one situation to another. There are no ready-made models or miracle pills; each people must go about liberating itself, taking responsibility for its own history.

The historicism of a people, then, is necessarily tied to the vocation which that whole people has for freedom. Freedom—as liberties or the denial of specific freedoms—marks the road that the history of all peoples moves along, in a dialectic that determines what is the people and what is popular. All reference to "the people" that ignores its freedom and its servitude is losing sight of its place in history and, as such, is falsifying its reality.

The Political Aspect

The concept "the people" alludes in some way to a society, a particular society whose particularity is explained by history. But if the people connotes a society, it is to the extent that (1) there is a sector that is *not* the people, constitutive also of the same society, and (2) there exist some dynamic relations between the two sectors of the society.

In its political aspect, "the people" is a dynamic concept. The "polis" or society is made by a joining of forces or interests, some complementary, others opposing. It is precisely those forces and interests which fundamentally determine the configuration and characteristics of the diverse groups of a society. In this play of forces, *the people* is the human element *par excellence,* the social potential; that is to say, persons or groups essentially constitutive of the social community.

If by social community we mean that structure of human relations which makes possible an integral development for all its members through a harmonious and creative interaction, then obviously the objective of any healthy polity is the attainment of this communal structure. But everyday reality shows us that this kind of community is blocked and precluded by groups that manage to usurp power and, by marginalizing, oppressing, and crushing other groups, produce an anti-communal social structure, whose existence is the most patent demonstration of the irreconcilability of the interests of the various groups. "The people," in this context, is a politically conflictive concept, since it establishes the difference between who is and who is not *the people.* And who *is* the people? Simply stated, the people is all those whose presence is (or can be) a factor of communal integration. The people is all those objectively able and subjectively willing to shape an authentic social community, a new community, in which all individuals and all groups will be equally welcome.

It follows that the person who favors disassociation—the disassociator—is *not* of the people; and *not of the people* are all those whose dynamics or interests set them apart from the rest, opposing them to the others. But it is important to distinguish this concept of disassociation from antisocial or subversive behaviors as we are used to thinking of them. Behaviors that officially qualify as "antisocial" or "subversive," as we usually think of them, are in opposition to the present society because of its denial of community; what "subversion" tries to subvert is the present society's anti-communal values. In making this clarification we do not mean to approve indiscriminately of every "subversive" act that is committed (among other reasons, to avoid the ideological practice of the mass media, of lumping together political stories and detective stories, and turning political crimes into common crimes or attributing political inspiration and perspective to acts carried out by common criminals).

The Anti-People, or, what is the same, Anti-Community, is the individualist who rejects union; the competitor for whom getting ahead necessarily involves leaving others behind; the capitalist whose wealth is founded on the exploitation of the worker; in a word, the master who can be master only if there is a slave. Against the disassociator, the people is the integrator of the community, who is capable of integrating a social community, who can really be in solidarity with the other on an equal plane. The people is not, nor can it be, those whose interests in one or another way undo solidarity with others: those who, to be, must eradicate equality from the social structure.

If the people is that which presents the dynamic potential of a new and universal community (in the sense implied by an equality of all groups and persons), it is clear that the people represents more of a promise for the future than a present reality. The people is the depository of communitarian social values that cannot yet flower except as a plan or a repressed possibility. The people, therefore, is the bosom of a society's identity, but not as a present reality so much as an opening toward the collective future. The people is a denunciation of today's lack of solidarity, and the annunciation of tomorrow's community.

To speak politically of the people, then, is to make reference to its potential for collective solidarity, to its opening toward a new and different society, in which the energies of diverse groups join together in a common objective, in which special interests will not prevail and no sector will exist that is founded on the oppression of another. But, for all that, the political concept of "the people" represents a painful task.

The Socioeconomic Aspect

Finally, "the people" is a concept that points to the question of *being* in terms of *having*. The people are those whose reality is founded not on what they have but rather on who they are. In a situation of injustice, of radical divisions among the groups that make up a society, of opposing interests, of violence and plunder of some by others, the people can only be those who have not, though they are not *the people* simply for the fact of being Have-Nots. It can more readily be said that those who are the Haves in our society cannot be *the people,* for their *having* is exclusive and excludes those who have not; that is to say, they are able to have only at the expense of the Have-Nots. In this sense, to build a being on having is to build a being who denies others the chance to have, and as such, to build an egoistic being who is out of solidarity with the others.

It follows that the people is the dispossessed as opposed to the possessing, the oppressed as opposed to the oppressor, the exploited as opposed to the exploiter, the Have-Nots as opposed to the Haves, the miserable as opposed to the rich, the marginalized as opposed to those who belong, the slave as opposed to the master. The people is that which is lacking in power, in autonomy, in knowledge. The people is the negation of all those owners who make up the present violent society, those Haves who turn people into instruments for the advantage of others. The people is the absence of the word, the culture of silence.

Plainly, the mere fact of suffering exploitation does not automatically make an individual or a group a part of the people; but the act of exploiting others does remove an individual or group from the people. In our society one cannot both *be* and *have,* for both conditions are built on the concrete historical circumstance that today pits them against each other as incompatible entities. Understand, we are not judging *having* in the abstract; this is no mere ideological fiction. We are making a judgment about what *having* implies in our present-day society, and what it implies is the *non-having* of the other. Thus, so long as social having is achieved at the expense of the other, through the exploitation and plundering of others, *having* will necessarily be in opposition to solidarity, and alienating. Day by day, possession antagonistically separates people, creating the situation that underlies institutionalized violence.

It is for this reason that the concept of "the people" carries within it as an essential aspect the reclamation of an integral justice—the justice of a new social structure—in which *having* flows across egalitarian relations of being; in other words, a structure founded on a collective tenet, which enables all, as a community, to *be.* One cannot speak of "the people" while ignoring the fact that acquisitive and individualist economic power (capitalism) necessarily entails its denial.

The people, as an exigency of socioeconomic justice, represents a revolutionary potential, demanding a radical transformation of the structural relations of a society. The people is those who cannot remain anchored in the present, whose present is one of exploitation and violence. The people is necessarily the dissatisfied, the oppressed seeking an end to oppression. The people is the slave that seeks its own liberation, thus eliminating both master and slave. The people is those who are unwilling to accept the present, who are forced into feeling resentful. That they are accused in a self-justifying way of resentment is symptomatic. Are people supposed to suffer oppression, exploitation, and violence, and feel gratitude for it? For those who know how to read history, the people's resentment signifies the anguished and prophetic consciousness of a situation of injustice. It is the needed libidinal force that turns popular groups into generators of profound change, and enables them to put up with the many sacrifices that a revolutionary process demands.

To speak of "the people" in socioeconomic terms involves making manifest the immorality and injustice of prevailing social relations, placing the rich against the poor, and calling for a historical negation of all oppression and oppressors in order to be able to affirm every person and all of humanity.

Toward a Definition of the Concept of *The People*

In keeping with our analysis, the concept of the people involves three complimentary aspects: historical particularity, political solidarity, and socioeconomic exploitation. Each one of these three aspects moves in line with a social value: history seeks freedom, solidarity is marshaled to shape a community, and exploitation makes claims for justice. We are not dealing here with mechanical forces, or with automatic processes. And precisely because that is so, the concept of "the people" has meaning today, as it had yesterday and will have tomorrow. *The people* is a search and an effort directed at creating a concrete community of free people. *The people* is, in this sense, a denial of all slavery, not as an achieved present reality, but as a dynamic demand, as a vocation—a calling. It is important to understand that this calling can remain trapped in the unconscious, repressed by the jealous violence of the oppressor. Contemporary Latin American history gives palpable proof of how, when this communitarian vocation is awakened in the popular consciousness, the established powers become ever more violent in their efforts to repress and silence it: Brazil, Uruguay, Bolivia, Chile—the list goes on.

What remains is for us to try to find a single meaning for this three-dimensional reality of the people, a meaning that defines the people's relationship to the world, and that locates *the people* in its historical mission. In other words, we must ask what root attitude defines a social group (or a specific person) as the people.

Let us briefly review what we have observed as the attributes of the people. To begin with, historically, we have underlined the specific present of each people with respect to its particular future. In other words, we have identified the way the concept "the people" points to its existing state as one that must be negated, or dialectically overcome. Politically, through its calling to create a true social community, *the people* has been shown as the negation of non-solidarity. *The people* is the recognition of the existing dis-associating and egoistic individualism, but as a structure that must be eliminated. Finally, the socioeconomic aspect emphasizes the difference between present and future being, based on exploitation of others for gain. What is affirmed is a new being, a tomorrow, that does not demand the oppressive non-being of others, and that comes about through a *having* that is communitarian and united.

The three features have something in common: the negation of the present and the affirmation of a future; the rejection of the given, the established. But it should not be inferred from this that what the three definitive features of the concept have in common is a simple negativity, for a dialectical process of overcoming sees the negative as a necessity. If the present is denied, it is because the future is affirmed; today is rejected because tomorrow is embraced. Thus, the defining attitude of *the people* is the attitude of opening.

The people, in consequence, is an opening—an opening against all closure, flexibility against everything fixed, elasticity against all rigidity, a readiness to act against all stagnation. The people is hunger for change, affirmation of what is new; life in hope.

Socioeconomically, the people is those who accept the other and seek to become other. Politically, the people is those who are open to the other. Historically, the people is those who look for and struggle for the other. On the socioeconomic plane, the people implies an opening for personal growth. The self is open to becoming different, on a plane of equality, with neither privileges nor oppressive mechanisms.

On the political plane the people implies an opening toward the other, a readiness to let oneself be questioned by the other, as a separate being, to listen to his or her words, in dialogue; to confront reality in a relationship to and with (but not over) him or her, to unite in solidarity in a struggle in which both will be transformed.

Finally, on the historical plane, the people implies an opening toward that which is other: there is a disposition toward the new, an option for collective progress, for the creative realization of a common, fulfilling destiny. Socioeconomically, the people denies the viability of competitive individualism; politically, egotistical self-sufficiency; historically, the absolute end of the existing state. In short, the people is those who, in a specific historical situation, are open to others and *the other*, toward the end of becoming other.

A Kind of Conclusion

The above reflections are too sketchy to allow for definitive conclusions. Nevertheless, they give us a glimpse of certain places where the concept of the people can later be deepened and, case by case, made more concrete; and they offer us some criteria for judging the truth or falsehood of how the concept is employed.

1. First, "the people" cannot be discussed as a static, fixed, finite entity. If anything has become clear, it is that what is deepest in the structural meaning of *the people* is its dynamic opening. Thus, in spite of all the ideologizing of the concept of "the people," and in spite of all reductionist and absolutist efforts, the reality of *the people* is always out there. Its essence consists precisely in not allowing itself to be fixed in static categories, which in reality means that *the people* always escapes any attempt to hold back history for the benefit of any particular interest whatsoever.

2. It is not possible to reduce the reality of the people to a specific social class, though in a given historical moment or situation a particular social class may constitute *the people par excellence,* and even identify with it. "The people" is a concept that, without avoiding the reality of historical conflict (which saves it from the accusation of idealism), embraces or can embrace more than the concept of social class (working class; proletariat). The simple fact of being proletarian does not make the people the proletariat, though it is true that it would be hard under the present circumstances to become the people without having suffered the impact of proletarianization.

3. The concept of nation, and above all, nationalism, needs to be looked at together with the category of the people as it has been understood here. That is the only way to get rid of the privatistic coloration so common in present-day nationalist movements, and to be able to affirm identity without denying community. In addition to guarding against the denial of community, it allows for community to be claimed,

together with the personal, as one's own. Che Guevara once said that one does not belong to the people of one's birth, but rather to the people for whom one struggles and dies. It is this radical posture—to serve a people—which defines the nationalism of a particular individual or social group, and not their birth certificate, accent, or gesticulations, however flamboyant those may be.

4. It seems that the concept of "the people" as described here is adequate for application to practice. On the one hand it explains the historical variety and diversity of concrete entities we call peoples; on the other, it offers a conceptual base that can serve as a satisfactory platform for revolutionary work, giving the people a consciousness of their own identity, not as a simple fact but as a historical vocation.

11

Public Opinion Research as a De-ideologizing Instrument

TRANSLATED BY JEAN CARROLL AND ADRIANNE ARON

Social Psychology in Times of Crisis

Symptomatic Expressions of the Social Crisis

For social scientists today [1985], the grave conflicts being endured in Central America, particularly in El Salvador and Nicaragua, create some very special demands, for which an incorrect response can be as counter-productive as no response at all. Social scientists are having to analyze things in a context of political struggle and to go so far as to take a personal stand, and are thus being pushed out of their safe and sterile little academic boxes (see Zúñiga, 1975). They are coming face to face with dire emergencies, and this pushes them into positions of great responsibility, for if they do not act quickly their hesitation may cause someone to suffer irreparable damage.

Perhaps the most obvious example is the combatants on both sides of the conflict who are in need of psychological attention (see Spielberger, Sarason, and Milgram, 1982). Five years of civil war in El Salvador have generated a veritable army of young people traumatized by war and forced to rethink their existence while coming to grips with wounds, amputations, or permanent paralysis. The task of reintegrating the war wounded into civilian life is not strictly an individual problem; it is a community problem too, requiring adjustments, sometimes radical adjustments, by the entire family and the whole collective environment. To receive the disabled individual, to help compensate for the handicap and deal with psychological problems that may exist, calls for the involvement of the whole community, and all this requires help—a specialized kind of help for which the Salvadoran psychological community has not been trained.

Less obvious, yet no less serious, are the problems attendant to displacement and forced relocation (Stein, 1981). Various estimates calculate that more than half a million Salvadorans have had to leave the country in order to survive, and no fewer than another half million—the number grows every day—find themselves far from home, after having had to abandon their houses and lands to the violence of war. In resettlements and refugee camps or scattered in among the rest of the population, the displaced need immediate material aid and urgent psychosocial intervention. Their flight (often an inhuman Calvary), leaves their social roots violently destroyed, and they find themselves lacking in all types of resources, including not only employment but the skills that would allow them to get work. Moreover, given their campesino origins, most of the time they are poorly equipped to take advantage of what few opportunities open up in this new environment so saturated with misery and unemployment.

A situation like the one faced by the displaced people of El Salvador calls for immediate attention from community organizations, and for collective resettlement efforts. But for these, too, Salvadoran psychologists are not adequately prepared. The problem is aggravated by the fact that in practice, to work with this population or the population of combatants marks one politically and puts one's life in danger.

Compared to the gravity and urgency of these problems, other tasks the social psychologist undertakes may seem rather insignificant. But crisis situations bring out basic, underlying problems, of which the wounded and the displaced, as victims of war, are merely symptoms and consequences. Hence, while emergency intervention is vital, it does not eliminate the necessity of attending to more basic problems—problems that, from the very roots of the social order, vitiate the possibilities for a humanized common life. These problems, by justifying domination and producing collective alienation, form the basis for the continuing civil war.

The Need to De-ideologize Consciousness

One of the most serious problems faced by people of a country like El Salvador is the lack of a "social mirror" for looking at themselves: something to help them recognize themselves in the reality they know, and to become aware of their own identity as they work at constructing their own world. But just as the process of developing a critical consciousness *(concientización)* cannot be reduced to the simple notion of "being informed," so can a "social mirror" not be equated to what is reflected by the mass media. Collective alienation exists at the macro level, in the power mechanisms of the social structure, but it exists also within the cognitive schemata that are part of individual psychological structures (see Montero, 1984). Thus, in addition to seeing themselves as deprived of the product of their work and forced to accept someone else's definition of their personal being and social existence, people also lack adequate schemata to look at themselves and interpret the meaning of their existence as individuals and as a community.

In El Salvador the established power structure has concealed reality and systematically distorted events, producing a Collective Lie. Further aggravated by the civil war, the schizophrenia of everyday life becomes more acute, with the population living a daily experience that differs greatly from the "official" definition of what their lives are about (see Martín-Baró, 1982c).

The Social Lie as a determining factor is nothing new; it is part of the structural order of the country. It consists in constructing a reality that is ideologically compatible with the interests of the dominant class. It sets limits on how far the collective consciousness can move in any given situation, thus putting a ceiling on the growth of social consciousness. In El Salvador this has had at least three consequences: the country's most serious problems have been systematically hidden from view; the social interests and forces at play have been distorted; and people have internalized the alienating discourse as part of their personal and social identity.

The problem does not lie in the credibility or lack of credibility of the Official Discourse, for Salvadorans are obviously quite capable of understanding that what they are told does not correspond to how they live. They know there is an imbalance between the realities of their experience and the "realities" of the discourse, even when it applies to situations where they have no personal experience and they have to work from a position of ignorance or suspicion. The problem is that the Salvadorans are unable to see themselves and their circumstances reflected back to them, and, kept from these reflections, are handicapped in building a realistic personal and collective identity that would foster growth and progress. Problems can hardly be overcome when their causes are relegated to the Will of God and the demands of human nature (fatalism), or when the behaviors of the leadership are attributed to their personal peculiarities, or when the reality of what is happening is denied, plain and simple.

The purely formal manner in which the democratic processes function contributes to a ritualization, if not sacralization, of the Social Lie: elections are held, but the real control of power is not in contest; political parties proliferate, but merely represent segments of the same monolithic social interests; parliamentary debate takes place, but its very existence signifies that the disputes in question have already been settled.

For the most part, as UNESCO has partly intuited, the mass media are a docile instrument of the dominant interests. In El Salvador, for example, there are four commercial television channels, but for all practical purposes, all of them belong to the same owner. The existence of the four stations creates an illusion of diversity and pluralism, even when all are filled with the same canned series of "Starsky and Hutch" or "Dallas"; the same soap operas of "Ligia Elena" or "La Fiera"; and the same special programs of "Miss Mundo" or Julio Iglesias. In the best of cases, all the radio stations broadcast the same news and offer only partial and superficial reflections of what is happening. Very rarely does the radio supply data that would allow one to arrive at an interpretation that differs from the Official Discourse, and for these select cases the powers that be have at their disposal an effective mechanism of control: the person responsible for discrepancies is classified as a "disinformer," and can wind up in very serious trouble.

Given this environment of the Social Lie, there arises a need to increase critical consciousness through a process of de-ideologization [*desideologización concientizadora*]—to which social psychologists can and should be contributing. What this involves is introducing into the ambience of the collective consciousness elements and schemata that can help dismantle the dominant ideological discourse and set in motion the dynamics of a process of de-alienation. The need for this is particularly urgent in times of crisis such as we have in El Salvador, where expanding the horizons of consciousness can affect the choices made by social groups and the direction taken by the de-alienation process. In this light, I believe public opinion surveys can play a small yet significant role, as one instrument among others, in contributing to the process of shaping a new collective identity.

Public Opinion Polls

While public opinion polls are widely utilized in sociology (see Sudman, 1976), their use in social psychology is more often secondary and limited. Judging by the absence of public opinion research articles in the field's most prestigious journals, it could be said that the prevailing social psychology does not consider the public opinion survey as "scientific" or "serious," or in any case, useful. Possibly, to those who are used to laboratory experiments, knowledge obtained through surveys may seem lacking in rigor. It may also be that some people think information acquired from public opinion questionnaires is too superficial and transitory to serve as a basis for any important understanding of psychosocial processes. There are some, too, it would seem, whose "scientific modesty" might be offended if their work were reduced to the level of *New York Times* or CBS reports. But it is possible that the real reason for the scanty utilization of the survey method in social psychology research is to be found in something other than its presumed lack of scientific rigor, for the fact is, there is little difference between a poll sampling and the attitude surveys or other types of surveys that are used extensively in social psychology.

I suspect that the underutilization of the opinion poll in psychological research has to do with two characteristics that dominate the principal psychosocial models of the field: individualism, and a lack of a sense of history (see Tajfel, 1981; Martín-Baró, 1983a). Collective consciousness, as a transindividual phenomenon, is not much valued by the dominant theories in social psychology. Likewise, neither are the concrete forms that psychosocial processes necessarily acquire in every situation and all historical circumstances.

I believe public opinion polls can serve as an important de-ideologizing instrument, and that just as they are used by big commercial enterprises and political parties to market their products or stimulate support for all kinds of candidates and policies, so they ought to be used to start tapping popular consciousness. In El Salvador's situation, and perhaps in somewhat similar situations in other Latin American countries, systematic opinion polling can become an outstanding instrument for dismantling the alienating discourse of the dominant social sectors, and letting grassroots organizations strike up a constructive dialogue with the community consciousness, to search for a new collective identity.

One might object that, in light of the serious problems the civil war has caused for the Salvadoran population, spending time on public opinion is truly frivolous. But, if we consider the role collective consciousness can play in prolonging or ending the war, and, above all, in prolonging or ending all the social conditions that make up the unjust social order and lie at the root of the war, that objection is overruled. One need only look at how much emphasis the dominant sectors place on controlling the mass media, and the money they invest in propaganda, to be convinced that these subjective factors play an important part in determining a country's social processes.

In El Salvador an Official Discourse works to justify the oppressive social order and the repressive war. If public opinion research is to help break down that discourse and assist people in confronting their reality, it needs to meet certain criteria. My own experience points to four conditions as essential: systematization, representativeness, wholeness, and dialectic.

Systematization. First, public opinion polling should be carried out systematically, because for the ends being pursued here, very little is gained from quick and random surveys. The "social mirror" is useful, valid even—by which we mean historically correct—when it captures the evolution of collective consciousness over a period of time; absent a time framework it is difficult to distinguish a transitory or purely circumstantial idea from a state of opinion or a collective attitude (see Glenn and Frisbie, 1977). In any case, the road to a new identity requires periodic reflection on what has been achieved, and on the impact collective praxis has had on consciousness.

Representativeness. A public opinion poll should strive to represent the whole population or, if it falls short of that, to specify which sectors it does reflect. This may sound superfluous and even offensive to the average educated person. Nevertheless, it is important to emphasize this point, given the particular social make-up of populations like those of El Salvador and other Latin American countries. Too often a public opinion poll is limited to the urban sectors, ignoring the fact that the majority of the population are campesinos and that even in the cities, most of the population is poor working class and otherwise marginalized. Polling these sectors is clearly much more difficult, since they do not have telephones, do not go to school, have low or nonexistent literacy levels, and are frequently confused and inhibited by the questionnaires themselves. Because this is the case, representativeness cannot be taken for granted when a poll is taken, and there has to be a full awareness of the heavily urban, petty bourgeois skew of most of our psychosocial data.

Wholeness. Public opinion polls should strive for a sense of wholeness. Anything less runs the risk of becoming a merely superficial reflection of circumstantial opinions that are fairly homogeneous, more or less in line with the needs of those who hold power, but purely factual in content. Wholeness means that the poll not only exposes attitudinal configurations, showing how opinions relate to one another rather than presenting them as isolated entities, but also exposes the social soil in which these attitudes and opinions may possibly be rooted. With this, each separate attitude and opinion acquires its true sense as a historical certainty or as a joint mediator in a process that is structurally determined. I might add parenthetically that in my opinion this is the only way of doing real social psychology.

Dialectic. Last, but certainly not least, the results of the public opinion poll should be made available to the population. This is a complex problem since those in power control the mass media. Moreover, they could use the survey data to manipulate things in their own favor, against the popular interests, as happens with market research and polls taken by political parties. But the people need to be able to confront their own image, to see their own opinions and attitudes objectified. That is the only way they will be able to examine with a more critical eye the contrast between what they are living and thinking and what the prevailing discourse is pronouncing. Once they have that, with their own ideas and the events that are occurring, they can assume a new attitude, either continuing as they were or breaking off. Let us take some specific examples from our current work in El Salvador to illustrate the possibilities and problems of public opinion research as a de-ideologizing instrument in times of social crisis.

Public Opinion in El Salvador

I have chosen three problems that during these years of civil war have ignited campaigns to mold national and international public opinion so as to show that the Salvadoran population supports a particular position. The selected topics are United States intervention, the role of elections, and dialogue/negotiations between the government and the insurgent forces of the FDR/FMLN (the Democratic Revolutionary Front and the Farabundo Martí Front for National Liberation). It has been consistently claimed with respect to these topics that public opinion in El Salvador is homogeneous (with a few dissenters—"bad Salvadorans") and in line with official policy, and that the force of this public opinion is what has sustained the political and military decisions that have been made.

With regard to the intervention of the United States in Salvadoran politics, growing ever stronger and more lordly since 1980, the official version can be synthesized in two points: (1) there is no intervention by the United States; rather there is foreign aggression against El Salvador and Central America, and Cuba and Nicaragua are simply instruments of it; (2) U.S. economic and military aid cannot be considered intervention; it is a legal response to communist aggression, necessary to defend the "national security" of El Salvador and the United States. In one way or another this version has been reiterated in all the mass media and, more important, has been the premise on which all political thought about the conflict has been based, meaning that there has been no "civil war" at all; instead, there has been a struggle against the "communist subversion" launched from Russia, Cuba, and Nicaragua. (One is reminded of the shameful U.S. White Paper of 1981, which published lies that were quickly exposed in the press).

All that notwithstanding, data from various polls agree that in real life people followed an altogether different course of thought. In April of 1981, barely three months after the formal outbreak of the war (the "general offensive" of the FMLN was launched in January 1981), among a population of 750 university students, 31.9 percent considered the country's dependency on the United States as the principal obstacle to a peaceful solution to the conflict. Moreover, 51.7 percent of those same students felt the position of the United States on the war was "very unjust," while only 25.1 percent saw the FMLN position that way. In May of 1983, shortly after Mr. Reagan's famous pragmatic speech on Central America in which he proposed a type of "holy war" against the Communist Aggressor, a survey of 750 professionals and university students showed that 65.4 percent did not agree that Russia, Cuba, and Nicaragua were responsible for the war, while 81.4 percent thought the country was being run by the United States Embassy. For 69.1 percent of those surveyed, the only reason the United States was involved was "to smash the revolutionary movement"; and 55.4 percent blamed the North Americans for the failure of peace talks to come about. The opinions of these sectors, while certainly not representative of the whole population, do represent certain "middle sectors," and could not depart more from the official opinion.

In 1982, under pressure from the United States, the Revolutionary Government Junta called for elections to select members for a Constituent Assembly, and again in 1984 the government convened two rounds of presidential elections. The U.S. propaganda machine took it upon itself to broadcast to the world that this electoral process was democratic, despite the fact that opposition parties, including even the most moderate social democrats, were barred from participating. According to the official version, the elections were a way to bring about peace, and the propaganda efforts stressed this point: "Your vote is the solution"; "Vote for peace, vote for ARENA" (ARENA is a party of the extreme right, with half-macho, half-fascist airs, whose clearest objectives were the defense of private property and support for a military victory by the armed forces).

Against this official line, a poll of 1,754 high school students taken on February 9, 1983, found that only 5.8 percent believed the elections could put an end to the war, though 55.9 percent thought that what motivated people to vote was a desire for peace. In the poll mentioned above, only 7.3 percent of professionals and university students believed that elections could stop the war, and barely 17.5 percent believed the elections had been free. In fact, only 15.4 percent believed that the government which resulted from the previous elections represented the will of the people. In February of 1984, in a survey of 1,588 high school students, 82.2 percent considered the 1982 elections fraudulent and 70.8 percent thought that the presidential elections would not be fair either. And although 71.1 percent indicated their willingness to cast their vote, 66.1 percent did not believe that the elections would help bring about peace. Finally, in a survey taken of a representative sample of 2,178 Salvadorans in March of 1984, just a few days before the presidential elections, only 32 percent expected any improvement in the situation, and even fewer, 28.5 percent, thought the elections would be useful in bringing about peace. Taking into account the intensity of the official propaganda and the pre-election climate of optimism promoted by all the media, these opinions clearly reflected the skepticism felt by the majority of the population about the election results.

The third topic, the dialogue and negotiation between the government and the FDR/FMLN, is perhaps the most chilling. From 1981 to 1984 any mention of dialogue as a means of ending the war meant identifying oneself, practically speaking, with the insurgents' position. On a personal note, it may be mentioned that the last bomb to explode in the home of this author (the fifth in three years) came from his having publicly defended the need for dialogue. Only after the first round of talks in October of 1984 between government and rebel representatives did the word "dialogue" cease to be taboo and become an acceptable part of the Official Discourse.

But while dialogue and negotiation were rejected not only because they were alleged to be tactics of the insurgents but because they were also seen as a betrayal of the popular vote, the public consistently showed its preference for dialogue over a military option. As Table 11.1 shows, this preference has been steady.

It could be said that the most representative poll of the population, that of March 1984, presents the lowest percentage favoring dialogue, relatively speaking. However, it was also the least anonymous survey (the interviews were held on a one-to-one basis in private homes), and the time when it took place was the most dangerous period for defending dialogue as an option, because at that time a defense of dialogue could be interpreted as a rejection of the elections (see Martín-Baró and Orellana, 1984a). Finally, it should be noted that this poll yielded the highest ratio of supporters of dialogue to supporters of a military solution: for each person who considered military victory the best way to end the war, there were more than 5 (5.3 to be exact) who supported a negotiated solution.

Polls of public opinion on the three topics of U.S. intervention, the elections, and dialogue show clearly that the Official Discourse lies when it claims to represent the political views of the population. The contrast between the opinions attributed to the people and those voiced by the diverse sectors surveyed reveals the ideological and manipulative nature of the Official Discourse. Reflecting this contrast back to the people involved has played an important role in helping them feel they are members of a unique, identifiable collectivity, thus confirming that their experiences and their attitudes are not unusual, or silly. Of course, giving people back their own opinions is no easy matter under a reign of terror. Those few media sources which are available have been used, and despite their limited circulation they have reached some nerve centers of opinion. An effort has

Table 11.1. Opinions about the best solution to the war

Date of survey	Population polled	N	(A) Favor dialogue	(B) Favor military solution	A/B relationship
April 1981	University	719	57.9	14.4	4.0
March 1983	Pre-university	1,754	70.3	18.5	3.8
May 1983	Professional and university	780	70.1	14.9	4.7
Feb. 1984	Pre-university	1,588	62.3	15.3	4.1
March 1984	General population	2,178	22.7	4.3	5.3

also been made [via press conferences at the conclusion of each major survey] to maintain a constant flow of information to other more or less independent news networks with higher circulation. And finally, [by making our results available through published reports], an attempt has been made to allow all kinds of groups—academic, professional, religious, whatever—to use the information as material for collective reflection.

It is difficult to gauge the degree to which this effort toward de-ideologization has succeeded. Plainly, not all the polls examined meet the conditions outlined above, particularly the demands for representativeness and dialectic. It is hard to take surveys when asking certain questions, and even the simple fact of asking questions at all, can cost you your life. Nevertheless, there are indications that the information collected has caused some uneasiness among those who are responsible for the Official Discourse, especially the U.S. propaganda machine, which is so intent on maintaining a facade of objectivity and impartiality. There are also indications that the surveys have served as a looking glass for some insurgent sectors, who at times have been too quick to see objective social conditions as immediately transforming subjective conditions or class consciousness. Finally, it is known that the published and broadcast results of our surveys have helped more than one group to locate itself with respect to its experience and specific long-term objectives during the war, and to take positions more in accord with its members' personal and collective choices.

Final Reflections

Despite its limitations, our research clearly shows that what the Official Discourse tries, through its use of the mass media, to impose on the Salvadoran people as if it were their own opinion and their own assessment of reality, is a lie. This proves that public opinion polls are a potential de-ideologizing instrument, and as such, can help in some measure to reduce social alienation, by forging a connection between what is lived and what is seen, what is felt as personal experience and what is received as collective experience. Public opinion polls make it possible for people's and groups' life consciousness of reality to become articulated without losing all meaning in the process.

Taking and using public opinion polls clearly involves questions of power: working out a formal version of what is real—of what does or does not constitute reality in a given circumstance and society—is fundamentally in the hands of those who hold social power. Yet power is not something that one just has or does not have; it is the force that emerges in human relations as a differential in resources (see Martín-Baró, 1984f). In this sense, it is something dynamic and multifaceted. Any social order has its strong points and its weaknesses, and in the case of countries like El Salvador one of the most fragile areas of all is the one that has to do with the mechanisms of ideological control.

The importance that public opinion polls can have in times of social crisis may be appreciated from the impact of the homilies of Monsignor Romero, the murdered Archbishop of San Salvador. His homilies simply told the plain truth about what was happening every week, stating in public what people were experiencing day after day. In Monsignor Romero's voice, Salvadorans heard a formal account of their experience, an objectification of their consciousness, and this permitted them to affirm their condemnation of and opposition to the repressive regime.

Public opinion polling can be a way of giving back a voice to oppressed peoples (Mattelart, 1973). It is an instrument that, by reflecting popular experience with truth and feeling, opens consciousness to a sense that there is a new historical truth to be constructed. It would be no small public service if social psychologists founded institutes of public opinion—however modest they might have to be at the outset—to help people articulate their experience and gain an objective awareness of their oppression, by dismantling the Official Discourse and thus opening pathways to building more just and human historical alternatives.

12

The Lazy Latino: The Ideological Nature of Latin American Fatalism

TRANSLATED BY PHILLIP BERRYMAN

> *Dear philosophers,*
> *Dear progressive sociologists,*
> *Dear social psychologists:*
> *don't screw around so much with alienation*
> *here where what's most screwed up*
> *is the alien nation.*
>
> Roque Dalton, *Poemas Clandestinos*

The Fatalistic Syndrome

Latin American Torpor

In the Latin American world as recreated by García Márquez, the most flamboyant things come to look normal and the most colorful anachronisms seem matter-of-fact and timeless. As for the colonel who has no one to write to him, time seems to stand still in these towns plopped down between tropical jungles and Andean peaks. Isolated and lonely are these towns where the morning was yesterday, tomorrow will be too late, and nothing can be done to change inexorable destiny.

Is this a novelist's imagination? Of course it is—but it is one that very accurately captures a world forced to live seemingly on the margins of history. We need only take a look at everyday life in Latin America—from the Rio Grande to Tierra del Fuego—to realize that the literary imagination has simply distilled something essential in the way things are around us. In El Salvador, for example, nothing surprises us. If the civil war that has been laying waste to our country since 1981 has done anything, it is to turn what is strange into everyday occurrence. In 1981 the children of one of the junta members were guerrilla combatants; the head of the national police, who was accused of "sheltering death squads" and systematically practicing torture and murder, became a member of the Human Rights Commission; a government minister said on television that the Salvadoran revolution had no peer in history except perhaps the French Revolution; as prisoners were being exchanged, an undersecretary of the foreign ministry saluted a guerrilla commander with, "Yes sir, *comandante*"; there was a large tree growing out of the wall of the church in Tenancingo, which the war had turned into a ghost town; the national head of the tourism agency said that war would be very helpful for tourism in the country, since foreigners could be taken to see the *tatus*, the trenches the people dig in the ground for taking cover during the military's bombing raids.

This list of historical absurdities could be extended indefinitely. As is the case with the Freudian unconscious, all contradictions are possible in the Latin American world, since logic does not seem to count, at least the kind of logic based on reason and not on special interests. It could be said that the people of Latin America have fallen into a forced siesta, a state of semi-wakefulness that keeps them at the margins of their own history, where they are made to participate in processes that others control. As they are only semi-conscious of their own situation, their movement is confined to occasional jerks of the head, like someone trying to keep from falling completely asleep. The periodic coups that take place in some of these countries are an integral part of "Latino folklore," and simply amount to flipping the tortilla to cook it on the other side, that is, so that another faction can take its turn. Meanwhile, for ordinary people, everything stays the same.

Because historical time apparently stands still for Latin American peoples, social realities come to resemble the world of nature. Each object has its own predetermined cycle, and the only changes are those imposed by the minimal demands of evolution. Things are as they are, as they were yesterday, and as they will be tomorrow. Only the present counts, and not because of the fullness of experience the Latin poet sought *(carpe diem)*, but owing to the forced narrowing of life opportunities. Cast there as they are, with no historical memory and no overall project promising greater life, Latin Americans seem to have no prospect but to accept their destinies as inevitable.

Fatalism. The term "fatalism" comes from the Latin *fatum*, which means "fate," that is, prediction, oracle, and therefore, unavoidable destiny. Fate denotes inevitability, but it also suggests misfortune or disaster. In Spanish, accordingly, *fatalidad* has this double connotation of a future that is both hapless and unavoidable. Fatalism is a way of understanding human existence as a condition in which everyone's fate is already predetermined and everything happens inescapably. Human beings have no choice but to defer to their destiny and submit to the lot that their fate prescribes for them.

The fatalistic understanding of life attributed to broad sectors of the Latin American peoples can be understood as a basic stance, a way of facing one's own life. As such, fatalism makes manifest a particular relationship of meaning that people establish with themselves and the events of their lives (see Martín-Baró 1983a), and that will be translated into conformist and resigned behavior, no matter what the circumstances, however negative they may be. We can look at fatalism in terms of ideas, feelings, and behavior.

The most common *ideas* associated with the fatalistic attitude are as follows:

- The main aspects of people's lives are defined by their destiny the moment they are born: what people will and will not be able to be is already "inscribed" within them; hence individual existence is nothing but the unfolding of this life direction that is already predetermined by each individual's fate.
- Persons can do nothing to elude or change their fated destiny; the life of human beings is ruled by higher forces that are outside their power and control.
- In the predominantly religious framework of Latin American peoples, it is God who is regarded as defining people's destiny, a distant all-powerful God against whom it is futile to resist, and whose infinite wisdom in the creation of the world and society a mere creature may not presume to question.

The three *feelings* that appear most often in the syndrome of Latin American fatalism are as follows:

- The destiny that befalls each individual must be accepted with resignation; that is, one must take one's existence as it has been laid down, with neither resentment nor rebellion, which are utterly futile.
- The fact that the events of one's life are unavoidable nullifies the importance of any particular event. Hence there is no point in feeling

any great emotion, in being swept away by joy or sadness; what counts in life is to accept one's fate bravely and to bear it with dignity.

- Thus, life is a demanding and painful test, one that is tragic in nature, with the experience of suffering becoming the normal situation of human beings, to the point where destiny is identified with suffering: "you are born to suffer."

Finally, the three most characteristic traits or *behavioral tendencies* of Latin American fatalism are as follows:

- *Resignation with regard to the demands of one's own fate.* Since the circumstances in which one finds oneself and what happens to one are unavoidable, there is no alternative but to be resigned. Being resigned to what destiny imposes, that is, carrying out as faithfully as possible what is required of one, and in the way required, is the only proper way to accept one's fate and avoid further problems.
- *Passivity toward circumstances in life.* Since nothing can be done to change one's fate or to prevent the most significant events of life from happening, there is no point in trying to improve one's lot, take the initiative, or strive to change the course of things. From the standpoint of reason, passivity is the most convenient way to adapt to inevitable fate.
- *The narrowing of the life horizon to the present.* The only thing that counts is the here and now, for both good and evil. Knowing the past or predicting the future serves only to confirm the inevitability of fate. Since nothing essential can be changed, it is useless to plan or to strive for that to which we are already predestined. We have to respond to life's most immediate needs, trying to lessen the negative impact and getting the most out of the positive opportunities.

Table 12.1 sums up the features of Latin American fatalism conceptualized as a stance. Although the point is obvious, we should note that the ideas, feelings, and behavioral tendencies listed here represent an analytical breakdown of a way of being, a way certain persons relate to themselves and take their stand in their world. This existential reality could be analyzed in other ways and hence the features pointed out should not be reified as entities in themselves; each must be understood in reference to the whole person (those persons who are "fatalistic"). Each feature will appear more or less clearly in each individual, and its meaning should be analyzed in the context of each historical circumstance.

Table 12.1. Characteristic features of Latin American fatalism

Ideas	Feelings	Behaviors
Life is predefined	Resignation to one's own fate	Conformity and submission
One's own activity cannot change this fated destiny	Not letting oneself be affected or worked up over what happens in life	Tendency to be passive, to avoid effort
A distant and all-powerful God decides each person's fate	Acceptance of the suffering caused by the harshness of one's own fate	Focus on the present, with no memory of the past and no planning for the future

This description of the fatalistic syndrome can serve as a sketch of the stereotypical image of Latin Americans above and beyond particular nations or groups. Not only is this image widespread in countries in North America and Europe, it has become internalized as a frame of reference and cultural standard even in Latin American countries: the Latin American who is lazy, unreliable, irresponsible, ready for a party, and very religious. Over this "stereotypical matrix" various other types are sketched: the oligarch, cosmopolitan and freespending, the pampered child of a well-off father or a relative of some dictator; the military coup plotter, half populist and half gorilla, who can be bribed in everything except his machismo, which is visceral and a matter of principle; the shiftless and simpleminded Indian, who seems obsequiously submissive but is treacherous, spiteful, and vindictive.

It is important to distinguish fatalism as a stance people might take toward life from fatalism as a social stereotype applied to Latin Americans—even when Latin Americans are applying the stereotype to themselves. In other words, we must examine whether fatalism actually corresponds to a real attitude on the part of Latin Americans, or whether it is instead a quality attributed to them, which, by that very fact, has an impact on their lives, even though the way they really behave is not in accord with that characterization.

Studies of Latin American Fatalism

Although the stereotype of Latin American fatalism is quite widespread we do not have many empirical studies focusing directly on this issue. Most of the analyses one finds are theoretical reflections on the nature of fatalism, often regarded as one more feature of the "Latin American character" or of the particular character of the inhabitants of one or another Latin American country. In other cases, fatalism is simply taken as a given, so obvious that there is no need to examine it or to verify it empirically. Hence not only are there surprisingly few studies of fatalism, but most of them look only indirectly at the topic, when dealing with issues related to popular and marginal sectors. Let us have a look at some of the most important of these studies.

In his anthropological studies, which are composed of the very words of the people he interviewed, Oscar Lewis has managed to transmit the characteristic ways of thinking, feeling, and action of the popular sectors in Mexico (1961), Puerto Rico (1965) and Cuba (Lewis, Lewis, and Rigdon, 1977a, 1977b, 1978). Many hypotheses on the mental texture of machismo have arisen out of, or found their confirmation in, Lewis's stories. In these autobiographical narratives we find some of the characteristic features of fatalism: a more or less explicit belief that the fate of an individual is a foregone conclusion; resignation in the face of the inevitable; and passivity and a focus on the present as ways of adapting to pressures on one's own life. It is especially interesting to observe the difference in these mental patterns in Cubans before and after the revolution.

From a sociological standpoint, fatalism tends to show up in the results of almost all surveys of the attitudes and opinions of popular sectors in Latin America. We may take as an example a study carried out by Reinaldo Antonio Téfel in 1972 with 450 heads of families in poor barrios of Managua (Téfel, 1976). Of those interviewed, 79.9 percent agreed with the statement "Making plans only leads to unhappiness because it is hard to carry them out" *(uselessness of planning)*; 66.8 percent agreed that "One should be concerned about the things of today and leave tomorrow's for tomorrow" *(focus on the present)*; and 93 percent thought that "The secret of happiness lies in not expecting much of life and in being content with the luck you draw" *(acceptance, resignation)*.

One of the first psychosocial studies of Latin American fatalism was done by Erich Fromm and Michael Maccoby between 1957 and 1963, in a small Mexican settlement of 162 families, utilizing Fromm's typology of social character (see Fromm, 1941, 1947). According to Fromm and Maccoby (1970, p. 37) the village people they studied "are selfish, suspicious of each others' motives, pessimistic about the future, and fatalistic. Many appear submissive and self-deprecatory, although they have the potential for rebelliousness and revolution. They feel inferior to city people, more stupid, and less cultured. There is an overwhelming feeling of powerlessness to influence either nature or the industrial machine that bears down on them." We thus find in these campesinos the typical features of fatalism: pessimism about the future, submission, and helplessness toward the world and society. Of course these traits are not absolute, for we find seeds of rebellion as well. Yet it is important to note that the tendency toward rebellion in itself does not negate fatalism, but can even serve to confirm it: the fatalism affirmed in everyday life is challenged only through occasional violent rebellion, which generally ends in a retrenchment to "fated normality."

By means of a "philosophy of life" questionnaire and other measuring instruments, Rogelio Díaz-Guerrero (1973, 1975) has come to the conclusion that, in contrast to Anglo-Saxon society, Mexican society tends to reinforce passive and conforming patterns of adaptation. Among the eight characteristic types of Mexicans, Díaz-Guerrero (1975) believes that the "passive obedient affiliative" is the most common. This type should not be equated with the fatalistic type that we have described, but it shows some of its traits, especially in its resignation and submission to the established social order. Fatalistic traits are accordingly related to the economic, political, and cultural conditions of each social system. More recent studies comparing equivalent populations of Mexicans in the United States and in Mexico confirm this relationship between social milieu and fatalism. Ross, Mirowsky, and Cockerham (1983), for example, compared a group of 330 residents in El Paso (United States) with 138 residents of Juárez (Mexico) ranging in age from 18 to 65, and found that the Mexicans from lower socioeconomic levels were more fatalistic than those from higher levels, and that subjects in Mexico as a group were more fatalistic than subjects in the United States.

Studies on the self-image of various groups in society are without doubt the most helpful for discerning the presence of the fatalistic schema. It is particularly in Venezuela, following the pioneering work of José Miguel Salazar, that such studies have been carried out. Traits such as "laziness," passivity, irresponsibility, pessimism, and the lack of a sense of history repeatedly show up in the Venezuelan self-image (Salazar, 1970; Santoro, 1975; Salazar and Marín, 1975; Salazar and Rodriguez, 1982; Montero, 1984). These studies show that the Venezuelan's self-image is not rigid and uniform throughout the population, and that it is very much related to socioeconomic status; but they do indicate that one of the most constant features of Venezuelans' self-image is that they see themselves as passive with respect to reality.

We may ask to what extent existing empirical studies confirm the validity of the Latin American syndrome of fatalism. On the basis of an admittedly incomplete examination of existing studies, three tentative conclusions can be drawn:

- Although no studies confirm the existence of each and every one of the traits making up the fatalistic syndrome as we have presented it, available studies demonstrate that various sectors of Latin America's population have a fatalistic posture toward life. How decisive it is varies according to historical and social circumstances.
- Several of the main traits of the stereotype of the fatalistic Latin American are found in the image that different social groups attribute to their own fellow citizens and to Latin American countries as a whole.
- The fatalistic stance tends to be observed especially at the lower socio-economic levels, among campesinos and other marginalized members of the population; that is, among the majority population in Latin American countries. The stereotyped perception of Latin Americans as fatalistic is found not only among these sectors but in other groups as well.

Psychologizing Fatalism

Considered dispassionately, fatalism is a very counterproductive vision of life, since it tends to hinder any effort toward progress and change, whether personal or social. In other words, fatalism is a self-fulfilling prophecy, for it brings about what it postulates, namely that it is impossible to change the direction of one's own life or for individuals to control the crucial circumstances of their lives. We must therefore inquire how fatalism comes about. Why is it that individuals, and especially groups, take up a fatalistic stance toward life? How are we to explain that the poor majority in Latin America accept as their conception of life a vision that keeps them locked where they are and without hope?

Most of the proposed explanations of Latin American fatalism tend to emphasize the decisive role played by psychological factors, either as traits of a presumed Latin American character or as personality characteristics that develop within Latin American culture. Let us examine both types of explanation.

Latin American Character

The Berkeley group named superstition as one of the traits of the Authoritarian Personality: "Superstition indicates a tendency to shift responsibility from within the individual onto outside forces beyond one's control; it indicates that the ego might already have 'given up,' that is to say, renounced the idea that it might determine the individual's fate by overcoming external forces" (Adorno et al., 1950, p. 236). This is a typically fatalistic trait, as indicated by the main item of the F Scale, which measures superstition: "Every person should have a deep faith in some supernatural force higher than himself to which he gives total allegiance and whose decisions he does not question."

The notion that the fatalistic conception of life is a character trait of Latin American peoples would explain the frequency with which it emerges in the many countries that make up the continent. This explanation has been proposed from a number of theoretical perspectives. Perhaps the most influential formulation and the one with the greatest claim to scientific rigor comes from the developmentalist vision presented by DESAL (the Center for Economic and Social Development of Latin America).

DESAL's primary concern is to explain the fact that there are dual societies in Latin America, and to find the best way to integrate marginalized populations into the social system by changing their fundamental values and attitudes (see Vekemans and Silva, 1970). Fatalism is regarded as one of the attitudes of the marginalized that prevents them from being integrated into the modern world and maintains their misery and social impotence (Silva, 1972).

Fernando Durán's work typifies this approach. According to Durán, most of the Latin American population presents the following character traits: (1) authoritarianism, "in the sense of tending to trust in authority as the basis for actions and judgments"; (2) "identification of the individual with a microcosm of social relations"; (3) conformity; and (4) an "inclination to regard the past and present as the temporal focus of human life, without paying sustained attention to the future." These character traits make it possible to understand phenomena such as *caciquismo* [deference to local *caciques* or strong-man leaders] (which is said to be based on the authoritarian conformity of the population) or the "lack of responsibility and initiative" (which is thought to be rooted in that dependence on authority and on the rural focus on the present) (Durán, 1978, pp. 100–105).

Along with these four character traits that Durán believes most Latin Americans share, one can find other differentiating traits, which give rise to five types of social character: (1) the urban resident, who has a modern, dynamic, and technological mindset; (2) the person of the provinces, tied to tradition and ritual; (3) the campesino, resigned and opposed to any change; (4) the Caribbean type, marked by a "tropical" spirit, that is, by flamboyant and irresponsible behavior; and (5) the Indian, who is generally isolated, passive, fatalistic, and inclined toward the realm of magic. In Durán's view, these five types of social character coexist side by side in every Latin American nation of the continent.

This approach to fatalism suffers from the same problems as DESAL's position on the underdevelopment of Latin American countries (see Sotelo, 1975; Martín-Baró, 1984f). The fact that broad segments of the Latin American population are "still" marginalized from the modern, capitalist, Anglo-Saxon world is said to be a legacy of colonial times. The fact that Hispanic culture is simply laid over indigenous cultures is regarded as being at the root of the cultural and normative breakdown of the personality of the marginalized person, who then lacks the attitudes necessary for adequately confronting the demands of a modern society. Social dichotomy is thus the result of this psycho-social deficiency of the marginalized sectors, who are submissive, centered on the present, and resistant to any change: the psychological becomes the basis for the structuring of society, rather than the other way around. Whether individuals become part of the established system or not thereby depends on their character traits, not on the nature of the social system.

A more subtle way of attributing fatalism to the character or personality of individuals is found in those who connect it to a low achievement motivation. For example, to say that Latin American workers or campesinos do not get ahead because they lack the ambition and drive found in North Americans is a seemingly more "technical," but no less psychologizing on that account, way of blaming the victims for their situation.

The experience of marginalized populations, however, very plainly shows how false this position is. Many marginalized people are not at all lacking in will, desire, drive, or even flexibility. In a series of studies on attitudes toward work, Leonard Goodwin (1972) found there was no difference between the "work ethic" or the life aspirations of people who were poor and those who were not. As regards the Salvadorans, their hardworking and tenacious character is so widely acknowledged that these virtues have become a folk stereotype. The war between El Salvador and Honduras in 1969 was very much related to the progress and socioeconomic power that Salvadoran emigrants had achieved in Honduras. Inside El Salvador, by contrast, the marginalized people who work hard make little or no progress: just like those who surrender "to fate," they can see no correlation whatsoever between effort and accomplishment. Perhaps in order to explain and even justify this lack of progress, the folk stereotype of Salvadorans embellishes their nickname as *"guanacos,"* that is, slow-witted birds who are easily cheated.

The fact that larger and larger proportions of the majority population in Latin America do not manage to become "integrated" into the dominant system and do not even enjoy its minimum benefits is not owing to lack of effort or insufficient motivation—at least not always or necessarily so. Rather, the social system itself is so structured that it cannot meet the basic needs of this majority population. The paradox lies in the fact that these "marginal" majorities are indeed integrated into the system, but as marginal; not because they either have or lack the required values and attitudes, and not because they are motivated or unmotivated to accomplish great things in their lives, but because they lack the minimum opportunity and the power to do so.

The Culture of Poverty

A different version of Latin American fatalism attributes this syndrome to the development of cultural patterns that are necessary for survival at a particular time, but that, as they are passed on, tend to perpetuate the very conditions which produce them, thus generating a vicious circle. This is the so-called culture of poverty.

The term was coined by Oscar Lewis, and social scientists eagerly seized upon it, since it reflected perfectly the fact that "the poor" lived in a different world with their own norms and values and their own characteristic behavior and customs. The characteristic features of the family in this subculture, according to Lewis (1969), are that couples are unwed; life is centered on the mother; there is no childhood in the sense of an extended sheltered period; fathers are often absent; there is a strong inclination toward authoritarianism; and the emphasis on family solidarity remains largely verbal. Individuals typically have strong feelings of being outcast, impotent, dependent, and inferior; they do not have enough impulse control, they are very focused on the present; they are resigned, fatalistic, and provincial; and they have not the slightest measure of class consciousness. According to Lewis, what causes these traits to constitute a subculture is not simply their presence but their functional conjunction. Hence, "the profiles of the subculture of poverty will probably differ in systematic ways with the difference in the national cultural contexts of which they are a part" (Lewis 1969, p. 193).

The culture of poverty is something more than poverty; it is a way of life that flourishes in a particular social context. "The culture of poverty is both an adaptation and a reaction of the poor to their marginal position in a class-stratified, highly individuated, capitalistic society. It represents an effort to cope with feelings of hopelessness and despair that develop from the realization of the improbability of achieving success in terms of the values and goals of the larger society" (Lewis, 1969, p. 188). Hence, fatalism becomes an adaptive response: to bend to the prevailing forces, to allow oneself to be led in the direction imposed by the established powers, constitutes the only survival strategy available to the vast majority of people within the marginalized sectors of Latin American societies. Historic inevitability becomes more acceptable when it is seen as natural fate; necessity becomes virtue, and thus even when life offers nothing but lemons, they come to taste sweet.

Although the culture of poverty arises as a mechanism for adapting to conditions of marginalization, once in place it seems harder to eliminate than poverty itself, for it is passed on through the family. Fatalism thus seems to turn into a self-fulfilling prophecy, since it discourages individuals from striving to escape from their poverty.

Some psychologists have recently identified the process of acquiring the culture of poverty with the development of "learned helplessness" (see Ardila, 1979). From a somewhat different psychoanalytic angle, Francisco Gonzalez Pineda (1971) holds that the extremes of submission on the part of the indigenous peoples of Mexico have helped them avoid annihilation. Likewise in psychoanalytic terms, Santiago Ramirez (1971, p. 76) states that the indigenous people "do not rebel against poverty, for it has enabled them to retain a degree of independence." We seem to have here proof that the secondary advantages obtained through fatalism tend to perpetuate it within the culture and as a psychological trait.

As in the case of the "Latin American character," the assertion that the culture of poverty explains the fatalistic syndrome falls into subtle psychologizing. It is claimed that, once established, such a trait or way of life takes on a functional autonomy that maintains and reproduces it. The implicit assumption is that even after social conditions have progressed, the individual will retain his or her fatalistic laziness. In other words, once "the culture of poverty" is in place, it will remain the cause of the fatalism of the population, independently of whether social conditions change or remain the same. Fatalism is regarded as sinking its roots more into the psychological functioning of persons than into the functioning of economic, political, and social structures.

That the traits of the culture of poverty are found in the marginalized populations of Latin America is a fact; the issue is whether once they are in place these features take on a functional autonomy. As it happens, the empirical data available do not confirm the existence of a subculture specific to the poor, perpetuating their situation as a functional mechanism independent of the overall social system. For example, in a study carried out among poor blacks in the United States, Coward, Feagin, and Williams (1974) found that the only aspects of the culture of poverty confirmed by their data were those which could be regarded simply as alternative indicators of the situation of poverty, and not as representations of a specific lifestyle or psychological orientation different from that of the rest of the population. The very evolution observed by Lewis in Cuba after the revolution seems to contradict the claim that the culture of poverty remains in place even after the occurrence of large-scale social changes that attack the systemic roots of poverty.

If the fatalistic syndrome continues to be perpetuated among the majority populations in Latin America, it is not because it is reproduced through cultural norms or as a poor people's way of life that is independent of changes in the broader social system. Fatalism is a way for people to make sense of a world they have found closed and beyond their control: it is an attitude caused and continually reinforced by the oppressive functioning of overall social structures. Marginalized children in *favelas*, or *champas*, or other shantytowns of Latin America internalize fatalism not so much because they inherit it from their parents as because it is the fruit of their own experience with society. Day by day they learn that their efforts in school get them nowhere; the street does not reward them well for their premature efforts at selling newspapers, taking care of cars, or shining shoes; and therefore it is better not to dream or set goals they will never be able to reach. They learn to be resigned and submissive, not so much as the result of the transmission of values through a closed subculture as through the everyday demonstration of how impossible and useless it is to strive to change their situation, when that environment itself forms part of an overall oppressive social system. Hence, just as marginalization is caused by a socioeconomic system to which the marginalized, as marginalized people, belong, the attitudes and values of a culture of poverty are being continually caused and reinforced by the normal functioning of this social system, which includes the poor as members. Even if it were true that "it is much more difficult to eliminate the culture of poverty than to eliminate poverty per se," as Lewis claims (1969, p. 197), it seems yet more difficult to eliminate the culture of poverty while maintaining poverty and the social and economic structures that produce and perpetuate it.

Political Utility of Fatalism

Fatalism's Truth: The Impossibility of Social Change

Just as there is something false about fatalism, there is also something true. It is false in attributing the failure to make progress to a fate predetermined by nature or even by God. Fatalism's truth lies in the verification that it is impossible for the poor majority in Latin America to change their social situation through their own efforts. Fatalism correctly picks out the symptom but errs in its diagnosis of the cause.

The history of any Latin American people can serve to corroborate fatalism's core of truth. The living standard of most Salvadorans is no better today than it was ten, thirty, or fifty years ago, even though the country's per capita income has risen steadily. Moreover, if Salvadorans are so hardworking, in accordance with what we have called the "folk stereotype," that lack of progress can hardly be blamed on their character or lack of effort. A study carried out in 1978 in a San Salvador *mesón* (a communal living space in which each family has one or two rooms and bathrooms are shared), found that the tenants were willing to live in such deplorable conditions because they regarded them as temporary and thought they would soon get more decent housing (Martín-Baró, 1978b). Nonetheless, a good number of them had already been putting up with this situation for several years, and all indications were that most if not all of these tenants would spend the rest of their lives in such housing, perhaps moving to other similar *mesones* or putting up a shack in some outlying shanty-town. In spite of what one would think from the perspective of the culture of poverty, psychologically almost all these tenants in the *mesón* yearned to improve their economic situation and their housing and were confident they would do so; what cut short their aspirations and dreams was the inexorable functioning of the social system, which kept the marginalized locked in that marginalized situation.

Politically, too, the majority in El Salvador have tried to open the way to social change, but their efforts have been no more successful than their efforts in the realm of work. A popular uprising in 1932 was drowned in a sea of blood (Anderson, 1971). In 1974 a significant part of the rural population was willing to participate in a proposal for "Agrarian Trans-formation" that the government offered as a route to social change. Not only was that project terminated two months after it was announced, but the campesinos who were involved suffered repression when they called for it to be implemented. Thus they paid with their own blood for having trusted in the word of the government and for having been so bold as to try to change their fate (see Ellacuría, 1976; Martín-Baró, 1977c). More recently, in 1980, the Salvadoran government set in motion a new agrarian reform plan, with the express purpose of "taking the banners out of the hands of the revolutionary movements" and eliminating some of the most explosive social conditions in the country. Although the program has con-tinued, primarily as a facade needed by the overall military enterprise of wiping out the revolutionary groups, its positive features have been blocked by the lack of genuine support and even by the constitution drawn up in 1982. Actually, the real conditions of its beneficiaries have remained as precarious as those of the rest of the campesinos, and in some instances they are even worse off (see Diskin, 1985; Olano and Orellana, 1985).

As dependency theory asserts, the situation produced internationally between rich and poor countries is reflected inside each country between rich or comfortable elites and the impoverished and marginalized majority. The growing impoverishment that makes the foreign debt of most Latin American countries unpayable seems to be reproduced in the growing impoverishment of the majority population in each country. Just as the impossibility of paying the debt is the result of international economic and financial arrangements favoring the industrialized countries, the impossi-bility of change in the situation of the majority populations in Latin America is the result of exploitative and marginalizing social structures.

Hence we can see that even though fatalism is a personal syndrome, it correlates psychologically with particular social structures. Once more we encounter the time-honored psychosocial assertion that there is a correlation between objective and subjective structures, between the demands of social systems and the character traits of individuals. We do not need to assume a mechanical cause-and-effect relationship or to postulate a "basic personality." We are simply noting the obvious fact that the organization and functioning of each social system favors some attitudes while impeding others and rewards some kinds of behavior while prohibiting and punishing others.

One of the errors of the classic conception of the relationship between social structures and personality structures lies in the implicit assumption that there is harmony and cultural unity among the sectors that make up a society. That assumption is characteristic of the functionalist vision of society, in which belonging to a social system entails embracing a community of values and norms. If, however, we establish that Latin American societies are based on the oppressive domination of some classes over others, we may then expect that the structures will affect people differently in accordance with their location in class terms. Thus, just as students of social learning have demonstrated that there are behaviors typical of each sex (that is, that men and women respond differently; see Mischel, 1966), we may safely assume that there are also class-based behavioral patterns (that is, patterns that are stimulated and reinforced differently according to the social class to which one belongs).

The implication—as obvious as it may be—is by no means trivial: fatalism is a behavioral pattern that the social order prevailing in Latin America encourages and reinforces in certain strata of the population. The rationality of the established system denies the people of these strata the satisfaction of their most basic needs, while at the same time permitting the dominant elites to wallow in luxury.

Knowledge of reality follows social praxis. From their alienated perspective, social classes take possession of their historical destiny and interpret it ideologically. Hence while the ruling classes develop a high degree of "achievement motivation" and attain "internal control" over reinforcements, the subjugated classes prove passive, fatalistically assuming that the place where their fate is decided is under "external control." The process by which the members of the ruling and subject classes are distinctively formed is of course not mechanical and uniform, but historical. That is to say, it is determined by what is specific to each situation and to each particular circumstance. We should not expect to find a homogeneous or total fatalism throughout all groups and persons of the subject classes, but rather many types and gradations of fatalism. Hence we must ask what form fatalism takes in each case, as well as the specific processes through which the behaviors embodying it have arisen and have been transmitted. As Lewis's studies indicate, in some cases the patterns of childrearing and education are the main mechanisms for socializing fatalism, while in others the educational work of the school or the churches may have an influence. In many other cases, especially for rural people, who are still a very high percentage of the Latin American population, the most productive breeding ground for fatalism is the experience of worker-boss relations in the countryside. In any case, fatalism can be transmitted in any number of diverse institutional settings, for what really counts as the final determinant of people's fate is the very way Latin American countries are structured. From the outset the structure condemns to failure whatever efforts people make to get ahead; members of the subject classes continually learn "their place" in society as the poor, the unlettered, the campesinos, or the indigenous.

Fatalism as Internalization of Social Domination

A society's structural reality is not a fact of nature, but of history. Its construction and functioning lie in the intersubjectivity of the groups and persons who make it up. Ideology, therefore, is not simply a superstructure added onto already constituted societies, but is itself an important element in the shaping of society. What brings about domination is not ideas, but rather power in social relations, acquired through the appropriation of the resources most necessary for human life. This is what enables one group to impose its will and interests over the rest. But such domination is not firmly established until individuals accept it psychologically, until it becomes a conception of life, and indeed *common sense*. Social colonization puts down roots only when it is ideologically articulated in the mindset of persons and groups, and is thus justified with the seal of what seems to be natural rather than historical. The myth of the "lazy native" is an important part of such ideological colonization (Alatas, 1977).

Frantz Fanon, who participated as a psychiatrist in the Algerian liberation process, was able to grasp the depths to which colonization reached into the very psychosomatic structure of the colonized. The violence imposed by the colonizer is introjected by the colonized. It remains anchored in their musculature as repressed tension, and in their minds as guilt. The colonized experience their subjection as a state of inhibition, which leads them, in a kind of psychological compensation, to dream dreams "of muscular prowess . . . of action and of aggression" (Fanon, 1963, p. 41) or to periodic explosions of violence toward their fellow colonized. The natives' guilt is never one they accept, but "rather a kind of curse, a sort of sword of Damocles" (p. 42) ever hanging over their heads blocking their liberating impulses.

Fanon's studies show how domination makes its way into the one who is dominated, but they also show that if this introjected control is to be maintained, external control must be exercised by the dominant power. Ultimately what prevents the colonized from appropriating the colonizing structures in toto is that to do so would be to negate their very reality as persons. Nevertheless, as long as they do not acquire reflex awareness of the contradiction in their life, bodily inhibition and psychic guilt will keep their behavior within the limits of what the colonial order requires.

In Latin America social relations are structured in such a way that they deprive most people of the minimal resources necessary for shaping their lives. As one of the supreme principles of life in society, private property enshrines the continuing plunder of the majority, who have no real chance to control their own destiny. One's birthplace becomes one's destination. Hence fatalism is a social, external, and objective reality before it becomes an internal and subjective personal attitude. The dominated classes have no real possibility of controlling their own future, of defining the horizon of their existence and shaping their life in accordance with that definition. Fatalism gives a meaning—regrettable though it may be—to the inevitability of conditions that offer people no other alternative in life but to submit to their fate.

Paulo Freire (1971) has shown the role of fatalism in the ideology of the oppressed. The oppressed are immersed in a condition in which they are robbed and rendered helpless; they seem to be in an insuperable "limit situation." Unable to get to the source of their condition, their consciousness takes refuge in a fatalistic attitude, transforming history into nature. Indeed, as they confront this predetermined destiny, the oppressed interpret their impotence as proof that they themselves are worthless, in contrast to the powerful figure of the oppressor, who seems to be able to do anything. That is why the oppressed experience an irresistible attraction toward the oppressor, who becomes the model with whom they identify and to whose orders they are almost completely docile. This process not only enshrines history as fate but is assured of being reproduced and maintained: through their fatalistic attitude and their submissive behavior, the oppressed contribute to maintaining the conditions of oppression. The expression "the lot of the poor . . ." with which until recently campesinos or shantytown dwellers tended to explain their situation or justify the modesty of their life aspirations, demonstrates this tendency to view things as "natural," thus fostering the very system out of which it emerges.

The Ideological Nature of Fatalism

If fatalism helps people in the oppressed classes find meaning in their lives, it also serves the ruling classes as a very valuable ideological instrument. In practice, ideological acceptance of fatalism amounts to acceptance of the oppressive social order. Fatalism is a powerful ally of the established system in at least two crucial respects: (1) In justifying the posture of resignation and acceptance toward the social conditions imposed, as if by nature, on each individual, fatalism facilitates social control by saving the ruling classes from having to resort to repressive coercion. (2) By inducing a docile reaction to the demands of those who wield power, it helps reinforce and reproduce the existing order. Thus, by facilitating oppression and reproducing the conditions of social control, the fatalism of the poor majority serves the interests of the ruling classes; that is, it installs in their psyche the very interests that keep them alienated and impede their human development.

In keeping with fatalism, historical forces are rendered mythical, so that they seem to resemble nature, or God. As Freire (1971, p. 48) points out, "under the sway of magic and myth, the oppressed (especially the peasants, who are almost submerged in nature) see their suffering, the fruit of exploitation, as the will of God—as if God were the creator of this 'organized disorder.' " The connection to symbols that are absolute, unattainable, and unchangeable serves to perpetuate alienated consciousness. Even Christian symbols are manipulated ideologically.

Perhaps here lies at least part of the reason for the current success of fundamentalists among the oppressed in Central America. Convinced once more that their destiny cannot be changed, frightened of the consequences of efforts to change their situation, many are finding meaning in millenarian beliefs, consolation in cathartic worship services, and serenity in their individualistic pietism. The quasi-Christian millenarianism of these sects leaves up to God the immediate salvation of the world, and sees no other role for human beings than to pray that the ultimate divine plan may soon come to fulfillment. The fixed destiny of one's own life is subsumed into the perhaps equally predetermined action with which God will bring human society to an end. What is important, therefore, is not changing the social order, but preparing the individual to receive God's salvation.

Given Latin American religiosity, the confluence of fatalism and religious beliefs is one of the elements that contributes most to safeguarding the stability of the oppressive order. When people accept almost as an article of faith that their destiny is already set, they regard their submission to the conditions of life as obedience to God's will; social docility becomes a religious virtue, and anything that might have an impact on the basic way society is organized is simply ruled out. Thus fatalism provides the ruling classes with an effective spearhead for defending their class interests.

Breaking Away from Fatalism

According to Fanon (1963, p. 42), psychological domination over the colonized is never complete: in their innermost spirit, the natives admit no accusation. They are "overpowered but not tamed," treated as inferior but not convinced of their inferiority. The guilt hanging over them like the sword of Damocles can turn its blade against the colonizer; physical violence deep in their musculature is ready to be channeled into liberating violence. There is no need to sow the seed of rebellion to throw off an unjust fate; it is already there in the spirit of the colonized and can sprout forth when circumstances are right.

Fanon's observation suggests that, rather than being a matter of all or nothing, the fatalistic stance appears in different degrees and with many nuances. The background to the belief that one's destiny is predetermined and unchangeable is always the mixed and uneven degree of control that each person actually has over his or her own life. Hence we may speculate that the greater the control persons and groups actually have over their present situation, the less convinced will be their fatalism, even if they continue to use the same framework to account for the way their life unfolds. Of course, ultimately the root of fatalism lies not in the psychological rigidity of individuals but in the unchangeable character of the social conditions in which people and groups live and are formed.

Hence we cannot propose getting rid of fatalism by either changing the individual or changing his or her social conditions; what has to change is the relationship between the person and his or her world, and that assumes both personal and social change. In order for the Latin American masses to do away with their fatalism, not only must they change their beliefs about the nature of the world and life, they must also have a real experience of changing their world and determining their own future. This is a dialectical process in which change in social conditions and change in personal attitudes go hand in hand.

Events in El Salvador since the 1970s, which have become especially dramatic since 1981 with the civil war, have enabled a significant proportion of the population to break away from fatalistic cognitive frameworks. If there are still campesinos today who prefer to bow down to a situation of oppression and exploitation it is not so much because they see it as their predetermined fate or God's will as because they fear the consequences (and how right they are!) that may befall them if they reject these conditions. They are afraid of being branded as "subversives," or they simply do not see any realistic alternatives. In any case, the expression "the lot of the poor. . . ," their traditional expression of fatalistic submission, has now disappeared from their speech and most probably from their psychology as well.

The dialectical process that might enable the bulk of the people of Latin America to abandon their fatalistic attitude entails three important changes: the process of recovering their historical memory, popular organization, and class practice.

Recovery of memory. The first element for putting fatalism aside is *overcoming the exclusive focus on the present,* not only by opening people's minds to the future, but also by *recovering the memory* of their personal and collective past. Only insofar as people and groups become aware of their historical roots, especially those events and conditions which have shaped their situation, can they gain the perspective they need to take the measure of their own identity. Knowing who you are means knowing where you come from and on whom you depend. There is no true self-knowledge that is not an acknowledgment of one's origins, one's community identity, and one's own history. Latin American peoples need a clear historical memory in order to trace the workings of their history, and to know where to seek the causes of their longstanding oppression and their present situation. As Fals Borda (1988, p. 95) says, they need "to discover selectively, through collective memory, those elements of the past which have proved useful in the defense of the interests of exploited classes and which may be applied to the present struggles to increase [concientización]." Such memory is especially important in the present circumstances when the ruling groups are carrying out a vast propaganda effort to blame the problems of Latin America on East-West conflict, and more specifically on "communist subversion," as though the ills of Latin America derived from Soviet expansionism or first began when Fidel Castro rose to power. If they attain a clearsighted historical consciousness, Latin Americans will be able to use events and facts to evaluate the ideological proposals now being put forward, and in so doing they will also be able to unmask the Orwellian quality of the dominant language.

Popular organization. A crucial element for doing away with fatalism lies in the poor majority pursuing its own interests through *social organization.* Only through this will it be possible to overcome individualism, that is, the notion that each individual must confront his or her life situation in isolation, and that success or failure is up to each individual alone, with the fate of one being unrelated to the fate of everyone else. Popular organization assumes that all members of the oppressed classes have a consciousness of their common interests and an understanding that if their world does not change it is largely because of their division and individualistic isolation. In El Salvador we have come to appreciate the important role of popular organizations for energizing the initiative of the oppressed, and even as an alternative to what has been traditionally offered by political parties. As a result, the oppressed can emerge from being on the sidelines of history and represent their own interests vis-à-vis other groups in society (see Ellacuría, 1983).

Class practice. The most important element for overcoming the fatalism of the majorities in Latin America is their own *class practice.* There would be no point to historic consciousness if it did not become effective in the search for a new social identity, nor would becoming organized serve a purpose unless it became embodied in activities to benefit the poor sectors so as to break the vicious cycle that keeps them passive and marginalized. Furthermore, it is difficult to conceive of a true historical consciousness developing or popular organizing taking place outside of the context of a popular practice, which must inevitably be a class praxis, that is, one organized around popular interests. Ultimately, overcoming the fatalism of the poor majorities in Latin America demands a revolutionary change, a change in political and economic structures—including those of social psychology—for they serve as a basis for organizing society in such a way as to cast people aside and destroy their initiative. Only revolutionary practice will enable Latin American peoples to break the inflexibility of social structures that rigidly serve the interests of the few; only then will it be possible to overcome the "one hundred years of solitude" that keeps them on the sidelines of history, yoked to a predetermined fate.

Bibliography

Works by Ignacio Martín-Baró

1966a. "La Muerte como Problema Filosófico." *ECA* 21, no. 212: 7–12.

1966b. "Miguel A. Sholojov, Premio Nobel de Literatura." *ECA* 21, no. 212: 15–16.

1966c. "Un Extraño Remedio para la Homosexualidad: Su Legalización." *ECA* 21, no. 213: 54.

1966d. "Pablo Antonio Cuadra, Tierra y Luz Nicaragüense." *ECA* 21, no. 215: 93–95.

1966e."La Forja de Rebeldes." *ECA* 21, no. 221: 287–288.

1967a. "La Figura del Año." *ECA* 22, no. 224: 369–370.

1967b. "Rubén Darío Entrevisto." *ECA* 22, no. 226: 444–445.

1967c. "¿Quién le Teme a James Bond?" *ECA* 22, no. 227: 511–512.

1968a. "El Pulso del Tiempo; Guerrilleros y Hippies, Blow Up." *ECA* 23, no. 234: 25–26.

1968b. "El Complejo de Macho, o el 'Machismo.' " *ECA* 23, no. 235: 38–42. Rpt. 1970: *ECA* 25, no. 267: 677–683.

1968c. "Propaganda: Deseducación Social." *ECA 23*, no. 243: 367–373.

1970a. "Psicología de la Caricia." *ECA* 25, no. 264: 496–498.

1971. "Problemas Actuales en Psicopedagogía Escolar." *ECA* 26, no. 273: 401–413.

1972a. "Una Nueva Pedagogía para una Universidad Nueva." *ECA* 27, no. 281–282: 129–145.

1972b. "Del Alcohol a la Marihuana." *ECA* 27, no. 283: 225–242.

1972c. "Peluqueros Institucionales." *ECA* 27, no. 283: 297–301.

1972d. "Munich 72: el Ocaso de una Mitología." *ECA* 27, no. 288–289: 697–701.

1972e. "Presupuestos Psicosociales de una Caracterología para nuestros Paises." *ECA* 27, no. 290: 763–786.

1972f. "Del Futuro, la Técnica y el Planeta de los Simios." *ECA* 27, no. 290: 795–799.

1972g. "Hacia una Docencia Liberadora." *Universidades* (Mexico) no. 50: 9–26.

1972h. *Psicodiagnóstico de América Latina.* San Salvador: UCA Editores.

1972i. "La Desatención Social del Poder Opresor." In 1972h, pp. 121–140. Rpt. 1976a, pp. 98–109.

1973a. "Algunas Repercusiones Psico-sociales de la Densidad Demográfica en El Salvador." *ECA* 28, no. 293–294: 123–132. Rpt. 1977a, pp. 429–442.

1973b. "Antipsiquiatría y Antipsicoanálisis." *ECA* 28, no. 293–294: 203–206.

1973c. "Cartas al Presidente: Reflexiones Psicosociales sobre un Caso del Personalismo Político en El Salvador." *ECA* 28, no. 296: 345–357.

1973d. "Psicología del Campesino Salvadoreño." *ECA* 28, no. 297–298: 476–495. Rpt. 1977a, pp. 479–506.

1974a. "¿Quién es Pueblo?: Reflexiones para una Definición del Concepto de Pueblo." *ECA* 29, no. 303–304: 11–20. English trans.: Chapter 10, this book.

1974b. "Elementos de Conscientización Socio-política en los Currícula de las Universidades." *ECA* 29, no. 313–314: 765–783. Rpt. 1990l, pp. 83–108. English trans.: 1991a, pp. 138–140.

1974c. "De la Evasión a la Invasión." *ABRA* (El Salvador), no. 0: 19–24.

1975a. "Cinco Tesis sobre la Paternidad Aplicadas a El Salvador." *ECA* 30, no. 319–320: 265–282.

1975b. "El Estudiantado y la Estructura Universitaria." *ECA* 30, no. 324–325: 638–651. Rpt. 1990l, pp. 109–130.

1975c. "El Valor Psicológico de la Represión Política mediante la Violencia." *ECA* 30, no. 326: 742–752. Rpt. 1976a, pp. 310–327. English trans.: Chapter 9, this book.

1975d. *Elementos de Conscientización en los Curricula Universitarios.* I. Martín-Baró et al. Guatamala: FUPAC.

1976a. *Problemas de Psicología Social en América Latina.* Ed. with introductory commentaries by I. Martín-Baró. San Salvador: UCA Editores.

1977a. *Psicología, Ciencia y Conciencia.* Ed. with introductory commentaries by I. Martín-Baró. San Salvador: UCA Editores.

1977b. "Del Cociente Intelectual al Cociente Radical." *ECA* 32, no. 345: 485–494.

1977c. "Social Attitudes and Group Conflict in El Salvador." Master's Thesis, University of Chicago.

1978a. " 'Vivienda Mínima': Obra Máxima." *ECA* 33, no. 359: 732–733.

1978b. "Ley y Orden en la Vida del Mesón." Co-author, M. Herrera. *ECA* 33, no. 360: 803–828.

1979a. "Cien Años de Psicología." *ECA* 34, no. 368: 432–433.

1979b. "Household Density and Crowding in Lower Class Salvadorans." Ph.D. diss., University of Chicago.

1979c. *Haciendo la Universidad.* Guatamala: FUPAC.

1980a. *La Voz de los Sin Voz: La Palabra Viva del Monseñor Oscar Arnulfo Romero.* Ed. R. Cardenal, I. Martín-Baró, and J. Sobrino. San Salvador: UCA Editores. English trans.: *Voice of the Voiceless,* trans. M. J. Walsh. Maryknoll: Orbis.

1980b. "Monseñor: Una Voz para un Pueblo Pisoteado." In 1980a, pp. 13–34. Rpt. 1990, *Christus* 55, no. 632: 28–38.

1980c. "Fantasmas sobre un Gobierno Popular en El Salvador." *ECA* 35, no. 377–378: 277–290.

1980d. "Ocupación Juvenil: Reflexiones Psicosociales de un Rehén por 24 Horas." *ECA* 35, no. 379: 463–474.

1980e. "Desde Cuba y Sin Amor." *ECA* 35, no. 379: 485–486.

1980f. "La Imagen de la Mujer en El Salvador." *ECA* 35, no. 380: 557–568.

1980g. "A la Muerte de Piaget." *ECA* 35, no. 383: 869–871.

1981a. "La Guerra Civil en El Salvador." *ECA* 36, no. 387–388: 17–32.

1981b. "El Liderazgo del Monseñor Romero: Un Análisis Psicosocial." *ECA* 36, no. 389: 151–172.

1981c. "Actitudes en El Salvador ante una Solución Política a la Guerra Civil." *ECA* 36, no. 390–391: 325–348.

1981d. "Aspiraciones del Pequeño Burgués Salvadoreño." *ECA* 36, no. 394: 773–788.

1982a. "Una Juventud sin Liderazgo Político." *Boletín de Psicología* 1, no. 5: 8–10.

1982b. "El Llamado de la Extrema Derecha." *ECA* 37, no. 403–404: 453–466. English trans.: 1991a, pp. 293–305.

1982c. "Un Psicólogo Social ante la Guerra Civil en El Salvador." *Revista de la Asociación Latinoamericana de Psicología Social* 2: 91–111.

1982d. "Escuela o Prisión? La Organización Social de un Centro de Orientación en El Salvador." Coauthors, V. Iraheta and A. Lemus de Vides. *ECA* 37, no. 401: 179–192.

1983a. *Acción e Ideología: Psicología Social desde Centroamérica*. San Salvador: UCA Editores.

1983b. "Los Rasgos Femeninos Según la Cultura Dominante en El Salvador." *Boletín de Psicología* 2, no. 8: 3–7.

1983c. "Polarización Social en El Salvador." *ECA* 38, no. 412: 129–142.

1983d. "Los Sectores Medios ante el Plan Reagan: Una Perspectiva Sombría." *ECA* 38, no. 415–416: 517–522.

1983e. "Estacazo Imperial: Abuso y Mentira en Grenada." *ECA* 38, no. 421–422: 1018–1021.

1984a. "La Necesidad de Votar: Actitudes del Pueblo Salvadoreño ante el Proceso Electoral de 1984." Co-author, V. A. Orellana. *ECA* 39, no. 426–427: 253–264.

1984b. "El Ultimo Discurso de Alvaro Magaña." *ECA* 39, no. 428: 425–427.

1984c. "Guerra y Salud Mental." *ECA* 39, no. 429–430: 503–514. Rpt. 1990a, pp. 71–88; 1990c, pp. 23–40. English trans.: Chapter 6, this book.

1984d. "El Terrorismo del Estado Norteamericano." *ECA* 39, no. 433: 813–816.

1984e. "La Sumisión a la Autoridad como Valor Social en El Salvador." *Boletín de Psicología* 3, no. 11: 19–26.

1984f. *Psicología Social V: Sistema y Poder*. San Salvador: UCA Editores.

1985a. "La Desideologización como Aporte de la Psicología Social al Desarrollo de la Democracia en Latinoamérica." *Boletín de la AVESPO* (Asociación Venezolana de Psicología Social) 8, no. 3: 3–9.

1985b. "Valores del Universitario Salvadoreño de Primer Ingreso." *Boletín de Psicología* 4, no. 15: 5–12.

1985c. "De la Conciencia Religiosa a la Conciencia Política." *Boletín de Psicología* 4, no. 16: 72–82.

1985d. "El Papel del Psicólogo en el Contexto Centroamericano." *Boletín de Psicología* 4, no. 17: 99–112. Rpt. 1990a, pp. 53–70. English trans.: Chapter 2, this book.

1985e. "La Encuesta de Opinión Pública como Instrumento Desideologizador." *Cuadernos de Psicología* (Universidad del Valle, Cali) 7, no. 1–2: 93–108. Rpt. 1990a, pp. 9–22. English trans.: Chapter 11, this book.

1985f. "El Trabajador Social Salvadoreño: Situación y Actitudes." *ECA* 40, no. 438: 229–240.

1985g. "La Oferta Política de Duarte." *ECA* 40, no. 439–440: 345–356.

1985h. "La Hacinamiento Residencial: Ideologización y Verdad de un Problema Real." *Revista de Psicología Social* (Mexico): 31–50. Rpt. 1990a, pp. 23–51.

1985i. "Los Niños Desplazados en El Salvador: Problemas y Tratamiento." Presented at Taller de Intercambio de Experiencias Sobre el Trabajo Psicosocial y Psicoterapéutico con los Niños y la Población Desplazada, sponsored by Rädda Barnen, Mexico, Feb. 18–22.

1985j. "Conflicto Social e Ideología Científica: De Chile a El Salvador." Presented at 20th Interamerican Congress of Psychology, Caracas.

1985k. "Psicología Latinoamericana." Editorial. *Boletín de Psicología* 4, no. 21: 39–41.

1986a. "La Ideología Familiar en El Salvador." *ECA* 41, no. 450: 291–304.

1986b. "El Pueblo Salvadoreño ante el Diálogo." *ECA* 41, no. 454–455: 755–768.

1986c. "Socialización Política: Dos Temas Críticos." *Boletín de Psicología* 5, no. 19: 5–20. English trans.: Chapter 4, this book.

1986d. "Hacia una Psicología de la Liberación." *Boletín de Psicología* 5, no. 22: 219–231. English trans.: 1991a, pp. 310–332; rpt. Chapter 1, this book.

1986e. "La Ideología de los Sectores Medios Salvadoreños." *Revista Mexicana de Psicología* 3, no. 1: 59–65.

1987a. *Así Piensan los Salvadoreños Urbanos (1986–1987).* San Salvador: UCA Editores.

1987b. "Del Opio Religioso a la Fe Liberadora." In Montero, 1987, pp. 229–268. English trans.: 1991a, pp. 347–370.

1987c. "El Latino Indolente: Carácter Ideológico del Fatalismo Latinoamericano." In Montero, 1987, pp. 135–162. English trans.: Chapter 12, this book.

1987d. "Votar en El Salvador: Psicología Social del Desorden Político." *Boletín de la AVEPSO* 10, no. 2: 28–36.

1987e. "¿Es Machista el Salvadoreño?" *Boletín de Psicología* 6, no. 24: 101–122.

1987f. "El Reto Popular a la Psicología Social en América Latina." *Boletín de Psicología* 6, no. 26: 251–270.

1987g. "Psicología Social Desde Centroamérica: Retos y Perspectivas." Interview. *Revista Costarricense de Psicología* 5: 71–76.

1987h. "Procesos Psíquicos y Poder." Manuscript. English trans.: Chapter 3, this book.

1988a. "From Dirty War to Psychological War: The Case of El Salvador." In *Flight,*

Exile, and Return: Mental Health and the Refugee, ed. A. Aron, pp. 2–22. San Francisco: CHRICA. Rpt. in Spanish: 1990a, pp. 109–122; 1990c, pp. 159–173; in English: 1991a, pp. 306–316.

1988b. "La Violencia Política y la Guerra como Causas del Trauma Psicosocial en El Salvador." *Revista de Psicología de El Salvador,* 7, no. 28: 123–141. Rpt. 1990a, pp. 89–107; 1990c, pp. 65–84. English trans.: *International Journal of Mental Health* 18, no. 1 (1989): 3–20; *Journal of La Raza Studies* [San Francisco State University] 2, no. 1 (1990): 5–13; *Manchester Guardian Weekly* (Jan. 14., 1990): 23–35; in J. Sobrino et al., eds., *Companions of Jesus* (Maryknoll: Orbis, 1990), pp. 79–97.

1988c. "La Mujer Salvadoreña y los Medios de Comunicación Masiva." *Revista de Psicología de El Salvador* 7, no. 29: 253–266.

1988d. "La Violencia en Centroamérica: Una Visión Psicosocial." *Revista Costarricense de Psicología* 12, no. 13: 21–34. Rpt. 1990a, pp. 123–146. English trans.: 1991a, pp. 333–346.

1988e. "El Salvador 1987." *ECA* 43, no. 471–472: 21–45.

1988f. "Opinión Preelectoral y Sentido del Voto en El Salvador." *ECA* 43, no. 473–474: 213–223.

1988g. "Los Grupos con Historia: Un Modelo Psicosocial." *Boletín de AVESPO* 11, no. 1: 3–18.

1988h. "Guerra y Trauma Psicosocial del Niño Salvadoreño." Presented at ACISAM conference, Sept. 12. Rpt. 1990c, pp. 233–249. English trans.: Chapter 7, this book.

1988i. "¿Trabajador Alegre o Trabajador Explotado? La Identidad Nacional del Salvadoreño." In 1990a, pp. 147–172.

1989a. *La Opinión Pública Salvadoreña (1987–1988).* San Salvador: UCA Editores.

1989b. "La Opinión Pública ante los Primeros Cien Días del Gobierno de Cristiani." *ECA* 44, no. 490–491: 715–726.

1989c. "Psicología Política del Trabajo en América Latina." *Revista de Psicología de El Salvador* 8, no. 31: 5–25. English trans.: Chapter 5, this book.

1989d. "Los Medios de Comunicación Masiva y la Opinión Pública en El Salvador de 1979 a 1989." *ECA* 44, no. 493–494: 1081–1093.

1989e. Review of F. J. Hinkelammert, *La Fe de Abraham y el Edipo Occidental. Revista Latinoamericana de Teología* 6, no. 17: 241–243.

1989f. *Sistema, Groupo y Poder: Psicología Social desde Centroamérica II.* San Salvador: UCA Editores.

1989g. "Asking Questions in El Salvador: As Dangerous as Expressing Them." Interview by M. Brinton Lykes. *Links* 6, no. 2: 10.

1989h. "Encuestas Pre-electorales en El Salvador." *ECA* 44, no. 485: 229–232.

1989i. Introduction to *Todo es Según el Dolor con que se Mira,* ed. E. Lira. Santiago: ILAS. English trans.: *Commonweal* (March 23, 1990): 184–186; rpt. in 1991a, pp. 138–140.

1989j. "La Institucionalización de la Guerra." *Revista de Psicología de El Salvador* 8, no. 33: 223–245.

1989k. "The Psychological Consequences of Political Terrorism." Video and transcription of presentation in symposium sponsored by CHRICA, Committee for Health Rights in Central America (347 Dolores Street, #210, San Francisco, CA 94110), Berkeley, Calif., Jan. 17.

1989l. "Solo Dios Salva: Sentido Político de la Conversión Religiosa." *Revista Chilena de Psicología* 10, no. 1: 13–20.

1990a. *Revista de Psicología de El Salvador* 9, no. 35. Memorial issue entirely devoted to works by Ignacio Martín-Baró.

1990b. Several articles in H. Cerutti Guldberg, ed., *Universidad y Cambio Social: Los Jesuitas en El Salvador.* Mexico: Magna Terra Editores.

1990c. *Psicología Social de la Guerra: Trauma y Terapia.* Ed. I. Martín-Baró. San Salvador: UCA Editores.

1990d. "The Writings of Ellacuría, Martín-Baró and Segundo Montes." (Brief extracts.) In Instituto de Estudios Centroamericanos and El Rescate, *The Jesuit Assassinations,* pp. 1–26. Kansas City: Sheed and Ward.

1990e. "Religion as an Instrument of Psychological Warfare." *Journal of Social Issues* 46: 93–107. Rpt. Chapter 8, this book.

1990f. "Interview with Fr. Ignacio Martín-Baró." By William Cadbury. *Northwest Review* 28: 9–13.

1990g. "La Familia, Puerta y Carcel para la Mujer Salvadoreña." *Revista de Psicología de El Salvador* 9, no. 37: 265–277.

1990h. "Una Entrevista con Ignacio Martín-Baró." Interview by Erick Cabrera. *Revista de Psicología de El Salvador* 9, no. 37: 299–308.

1990i. "A Psychologist in El Salvador: An Interview with Ignacio Martín-Baró Two Years before His Murder." By Alison Harris. *The Psychologist* 3: 264–266.

1990j. *Psicología de la Liberación para América Latina,* ed. G. Pacheco and B. Jimenez. Guadalajara: Instituto Tecnológico y de Estudios Superiores de Occidente, Depto. de Extensión Universitaria, Universidad de Guadalajara.

1990k. "Mass Media and Public Opinion in El Salvador." *Interamerican Public Opinion Report* (Jan.): 2, 12–14. Memorial issue.

1991a. Several articles in J. Hassett and H. Lacey, eds., *Towards a Society that Serves Its People: The Intellectual Contribution of El Salvador's Murdered Jesuits.* Washington, D.C.: Georgetown University Press.

No date. "Etica Psicológica." Mimeo. San Salvador: UCA José Simeón Cañas.

Works by Other Authors

Where Martín-Baró referred to works published in or translated into Spanish, we have substituted English-language references when available.

Achaerandio, L. 1983. "Introducción al Problema de los Desplazados en El Salvador (1980–1983)." *Boletín de Psicología* (UCA, San Salvador) 9: 4–10.

Adler de Lomnitz, L. 1978. *Como Sobreviven los Marginados.* Mexico: Siglo XXI.

Adorno, T. W., E. Frenkel-Brunswik, D. J. Levinson, and R. N. Sanford. 1950. *The Authoritarian Personality.* New York: Harper and Row.

"Agonía de un Pueblo: Urgencia de Soluciones." 1984. *Estudios Centroamericanos* 423–424: 1–12.

Aguilera, G., et al. 1981. *Dialéctica del Terror en Guatemala.* San José, Costa Rica: EDUCA.

Alatas, S. H. 1977. *The Myth of the Lazy Native.* London: Frank Cass.

Almond, G. 1960. "A Functional Approach to Comparative Politics." In G. A. Almond and J. S. Coleman, eds., *The Politics of the Developing Areas.* Princeton: Princeton University Press.

Althusser, L. 1969. *For Marx.* Trans. Ben Brewster. New York: Pantheon.

American Psychiatric Association. 1980. *DSM-III: Diagnostic and Statistical Manual of Mental Disorders,* 3rd ed. Washington, D.C.: APA.

Anderson, T. P. 1971. *Matanza: El Salvador's Communist Revolt of 1932.* Lincoln: University of Nebraska Press.

Ardila, R. 1979. "Psicología Social de la Pobreza." In J. O. Whittaker, ed., *Psicología Social en el Mundo de Hoy.* Mexico: Trillas.

——— 1982. "International Psychology." *American Psychologist* 37: 323–329.

——— 1983. *La Psicología en América Latina: Pasado, Presente y Futuro.* Mexico: Trillas.

Arendt, H. 1958. *The Human Condition.* Chicago: University of Chicago Press.

Argueta, L. 1985. "La Economía de El Salvador en 1984–1985: Algunos Elementos de Análisis." *Boletín de Ciencias Económicas y Sociales* (UCA, San Salvador) 8: 7–29.

Argueta, M. 1983. *One Day of Life.* New York: Vintage.

Aronson, E. 1969. "The Theory of Cognitive Dissonance: A Current Perspective." In L. Berkowitz, ed., *Advances in Experimental Social Psychology,* vol. 4. New York: Academic Press.

Bacevich, A. J., J. D. Hallums, R. H. White, and T. F. Young. 1988. "American Military Policy in Small Wars: The Case of El Salvador." Paper presented at the John F. Kennedy School of Government, March 22.

Banchs, M. A. 1982. "Las Representaciones Sociales: Un Enfoque Europeo para el Estudio de las Cogniciones Sociales." *Boletín de la AVEPSO* 5: 23–25.

Bandura, A. 1969. *Principles of Behavior Modification.* New York: Holt, Rinehart, and Winston.

——— 1971. *Social Learning Theory.* New York: General Learning Press.

——— 1972. *Aggression: A Social Learning Analysis.* Englewood Cliffs, N.J.: Prentice Hall.

Bandura, A., and R. H. Walters. 1959. *Adolescent Aggression.* New York: Ronald Press.

——— 1963. *Social Learning and Personality Development.* New York: Holt, Rinehart and Winston.

Baron, R. M. 1980. "Contrasting Approaches to Social Knowing: An Ecological Perspective." *Personality and Social Psychology Bulletin* 6: 591–600.

Barry, D., R. Castro, and R. Vergara. 1987. *La Guerra Total: La Nueva Ideología Contrainsurgente en Centroamérica.* Managua: CRIES.

Basaglia, F. 1972. *La Institución Negada: Informe de un Hospital Psiquiátrico*. Barcelona: Barral Editores.

Benítez Manuat, R. 1988. *La Teoría Militar y la Guerra Civil en El Salvador*. San Salvador: UCA Editores.

Berger, P. L., and T. Luckman. 1966. *The Social Construction of Reality*. New York: Doubleday.

Berkowitz, L. 1965. "The Concept of Aggressive Drive: Some Additional Considerations." In Berkowitz, ed., *Advances in Experimental Social Psychology*, vol. 2, pp. 301–329. New York: Academic Press.

——— 1975. *A Survey of Social Psychology*. Hinsdale, Ill.: Dryden.

Bermúdez, L. 1985. "Centroamérica: La Militarización en Cifras." *Cuaderno de Trabajo del CINAS* 4: 35–51.

——— 1987. *Guerra de Baja Intensidad: Reagan Contra Centroamérica*. Mexico: Siglo XXI.

Bermúdez, L., and R. Córdova. 1985. "Estados Unidos: Centroamérica, Cuatro Años de Intervención Militar (1981–1984)." *Cuaderno de Trabajo del CINAS* 4: 5–34.

Berryman, P. 1987. *Liberation Theology*. New York: Pantheon.

Binswanger, L. 1956. *Tres Formas de la Existencia Frustrada. Exaltación, Excentricidad, Manerismo*. Trans. E. Albizu. Buenos Aires: Amorrortu, 1972.

Bouchey, L. F., et al. 1981. " Las Relaciones Interamericanas: Escudo de la Seguridad del Nuevo Mundo y Espada de la Proyección del Poder Global de Estados Unidos." *Cuadernos Semenstrales* (Mexico) 9: 181–214.

Braunstein, N. A. 1979. "El Encargo Social y las Premisas Operantes en la Psicología Clínica." In Braunstein et al., 1979.

Braunstein, N. A., et al., eds. 1979. *Psicología: Ideología y Ciencia*. Mexico: Siglo XXI.

Bricht, S., et al. 1973. *El Rol del Psicólogo*. Buenos Aires: Nueva Visión.

Bronfenbrenner, U. 1961. "The Mirror Image in Soviet-American Relations: A Social Psychologist's Report." *Journal of Social Issues* 17: 45–56.

Bustos. *See* Gissi.

Cabarrús, C. R. 1979. "La Conversión Política, Camino de Conversión Cristiana." *Christus* (Mexico) 522: 13–21.

——— 1983. *Genesis de una Revolución*. Mexico: Ediciones de la Casa Chata.

Cable, S. 1988. "Attributional Processes and Alienation: A Typology of Worker Responses to Unequal Power Relationships." *Political Psychology* 9: 109–127.

Carrasco, P. E. 1988. "¿Convertir para Transformar? La Noción de Conversión en los Protestantes de América Central: Estudio de una Muestra de Relatos de Conversión." *Cristianismo y Sociedad* 95: 7–49.

CEPAL (Comisión Económica para América Latina y el Caribe). 1987. *Anuario Estadístico de América Latina y el Caribe*. United Nations.

Chomsky, N., and E. S. Herman. 1985. *Bains de Sang: Constructifs dans le Faits et la Propaganda*. Paris: Seghers.

Christlieb. *See* Fernández.

Codo, W. 1987. "Acción de los Psicólogos en los Sindicatos: Trabajo, Alienación y Transformación Social." In Montero, 1987.

Cohon, J. D. 1981. "Psychological Adaptation and Dysfunction among Refugees." *International Migration Review* 15: 255–275.

COLAT (Colectivo Latinoamericano). 1982. *Psicopatología de la Tortura y el Exilio.* Madrid: Fundamentos.

Comblin, J. 1978. *El Poder Militar en América Latina.* Salamanca, Spain: Sigueme.

Cooper, D. 1967. *Psychiatry and Anti-psychiatry.* London: Tavistock.

Coward, B. E., J. R. Feagin, and J. Williams. 1974. "The Culture of Poverty Debate: Some Additional Data." *Social Problems* 21: 621–634.

CRIES (Centro Regional de Investigaciones y Estudios Sociales). 1986. *Centroamérica: La Guerra de Baja Intensidad: ¿Hacia la Prolongación del Conflicto o Preparación para la Invasion?* Managua: CRIES.

Csikszentmihalyi, M., and O. Beattie. 1979. "Life Themes: A Theoretical and Empirical Exploration of Their Origins and Effects." *Journal of Humanistic Psychology* 19: 45–63.

Danner, M. 1994. *The Massacre at El Mozote: A Parable of the Cold War.* New York: Vintage.

Davis, K., and W. E. Moore. 1945. "Some Principles of Stratification." *American Sociological Review* 10: 242–249.

Dawson, R. E., and K. Prewitt. 1969. *Political Socialization.* Boston: Little, Brown.

Deconchy, J. P. 1984. "Systèmes de Croyances et Représentations Ideologiques." In Moscovici, 1984.

Deleule, D. 1972. *La Psicología, Mito Científico.* Trans. N. Perez and R. Garcia. Barcelona: Anagrama.

Delgado, E. M., et al. 1987a. "El Fenómeno de la Conversión Religiosa y su Incidencia en el Cambio de Actitudes Hacia lo no Religioso." Thesis for licensure in psychology, Universidad Centroamericana José Simeón Cañas, San Salvador.

——— 1987b. "Enfoque Psicosocial de la Conversión Religiosa." *Boletín de Psicología* (El Salvador) 26: 317–330.

Diamond, S. 1989. *Spiritual Warfare: The Politics of the Christian Right.* Boston: South End Press.

Díaz-Guerrero, R. 1973. "Interpreting Coping Styles across Nations from Sex and Social Class Differences." *International Journal of Psychology* 8: 193–203.

——— 1975. *Psychology of the Mexican: Culture and Personality.* Austin: University of Texas Press.

——— 1984. "Contemporary Psychology in Mexico." *Annual Review of Psychology* 35: 83–112.

Diego Ferrat, V. 1975. "Las Armas Secretas de la Junta Chilena: El Atentado a la Integridad Psíquica." *Diorama: Excelsior* (Mexico) (June 29): 10–11.

Diskin, M. 1985. "Agrarian Reform in El Salvador: An Evaluation." Mimeo. San Francisco: Institute for Food and Development Policy.

Dollard, J., et al. 1939. *Frustration and Aggression.* New Haven, Conn.: Yale University.

Dominguez, E., and D. Huntington. 1984. "The Salvation Brokers: Conservative Evangelicals in Central America." *NACLA Report on the Americas* 18: 2–36.

Durán, F. 1978. *Cambio de Mentalidad: Requísito del Desarrollo Integral de América Latina.* Barcelona: DESAL-Herder.

Durkheim, E. 1895. *The Rules of Sociological Method.* Glencoe, Ill.: Free Press, 1950.

Easton, D., and J. Dennis. 1969. *Children in the Political System: Origins of Political Legitimacy.* New York: McGraw-Hill.

"El Exterminio de 'Las Masas.'" 1984. *Carta a las Iglesias* (Centro Pastoral de la UCA, San Salvador) 69: 10–12.

Ellacuría, I. 1969. "Fundamental Human Rights and the Legal and Political Restrictions Placed on Them." In Hassett and Lacey, 1991.

———— 1976. "A sus Ordenes, mi Capital." *Estudios Centroamericana* 337: 637–643.

———— 1983. "Los Modos Sociales de Participación Política." Manuscript. San Salvador.

El Salvador, Ministerio de Planificación y Coordinación del Desarrollo Económico y Social. 1984. "Diagnóstico Económico Social 1978–1984." Mimeo. San Salvador.

Engestrom, Y. 1983. "The Image of War in the Minds of Children." Presented at the Seminar on Children and War, Siuntio Baths, Finland, March 24–27.

Eysenck, H. J., J. A. Wakefield, and A. F. Friedman. 1983. "Diagnosis and Clinical Assessment: The DSM-III." *Annual Review of Psychology* 34: 167–193.

Fals Borda, O. 1988. *Knowledge and People's Power: Lessons with Peasants in Nicaragua, Mexico and Colombia.* New Delhi: Indian Social Institute.

Fanon, F. 1963. *The Wretched of the Earth.* New York: Grove Press.

Farr, R. M. 1984. "Les Représentations Sociales." In Moscovici, 1984.

Fernández Christlieb, P. 1987. "Consideraciones Teórico-metodólogicas sobre la Psicología Política." In Montero, 1987.

Festinger, L. 1957. *A Theory of Cognitive Dissonance.* Stanford: Stanford University Press.

Flores, I. G., and E. A. Hernández. 1988. "Desde la Cotidianidad: Dimensión Política de la Socialización Religiosa." Thesis for licensure in psychology, Universidad Centroamericana José Simeón Cañas, San Salvador.

Frankl, V. E. 1950. *Psychotherapy and Existentialism.* New York: Washington Square Press, 1967.

———— 1955. *The Doctor and the Soul: An Introduction to Logotherapy.* New York: Knopf.

———— 1946. *Man's Search for Meaning.* New York: Simon and Schuster, 1962.

Fraser, M. 1983. "Childhood and War in Northern Ireland: A Therapeutic Response." Presented at the Seminar on Children and War, Siuntio Baths, Finland, March 24–27.

Freedman, A. E., and P. E. Freedman. 1985. *The Psychology of Political Control.* New York: St. Martin's Press.

Freire, P. 1971. *Pedagogy of the Oppressed.* New York: Herder and Herder.

———— 1973. *¿Extensión o Comunicación? La Concientización en el Medio Rural.* Buenos Aires: Siglo XXI.

———— 1978. *Education for a Critical Consciousness.* New York: Seabury Press.

French, J. R. P., and B. Raven. 1960. "The Bases of Social Power." In D. Cartwright and A. Zander, eds., *Group Dynanmics: Research and Theory.* Evanston, Ill.: Row, Peterson.

Freud, S. 1921. *Group Psychology and the Analysis of the Ego.* Trans. and ed. J. Strachey. *The Standard Edition of the Complete Psychological Works of Sigmund Freud,* vol. 18. London: Hogarth, 1961.

———— 1927. *The Future of an Illusion.* Vol. 21.

———— 1928. *Beyond the Pleasure Principle.* Vol. 18.

———— 1930. *Civilization and Its Discontents.* Vol. 21.

Freud, A., and D. Burlingham. 1942. *Young Children in Wartime.* London: George Allen and Unwin.

———— 1943. *War and Children.* New York: Medical War Books.

Frey, F. W. 1964. "Political Socialization in Developing Nations." Presented at a Political Research Development Conference at the Interuniversity Consortium for Political Research, Ann Arbor, July-Aug.

Fromm, E. 1941. *Escape from Freedom.* New York: Holt, Rinehart, and Winston.

———— 1947. *Man for Himself: An Inquiry into the Psychology of Ethics.* Greenwich, Conn.: Fawcett.

Fromm, E., and M. Maccoby. 1970. *Social Character in a Mexican Village: A Socio-psychoanalytic Study.* Englewood Cliffs, N.J.: Prentice Hall.

Geen, R. G., and D. Stonner. 1971. "Effects of Aggressive Habit Strength on Behavior in the Presence of Aggression-Related Stimuli." *Journal of Personality and Social Psychology* 17: 149–153.

Geertz, C. 1973. *The Interpretation of Cultures.* New York: Basic Books.

Gibbs, D. R., S. A. Mueller, and J. R. Wood. 1973. "Doctrinal Orthodoxy, Salience, and the Consequential Dimension." *Journal for the Scientific Study of Religion* 12: 33–52.

Gibson, J. J. 1966. *The Senses Considered as Perceptual Systems.* Boston: Houghton Mifflin.

Gissi Bustos, J. 1976. "Feminidad, Machismo: Mitos Culturales." In Martín-Baró, 1976a.

Glenn, N. D., and W. P. Frisbie. 1977. "Trend Studies with Survey Sample and Census Data." *Annual Review of Sociology* 3: 79–104.

Gonzalez Pineda, F. 1971. *El Mexicano: Su Dinámica Psicosocial.* Mexico: Ed. Pax-México.

Goodwin, L. 1972. *Do the Poor Want to Work? A Social-Psychological Study of Work Orientations.* Washington, D.C.: Brookings Institution.

Grimson, W. R. 1972. *Sociedad de Locos: Experiencia y Violencia en un Hospital Psquiátrico.* Buenos Aires: Nueva Vision.

Guinsberg, E. 1983. "Salud Mental en América Latina." *Salud Problema* (Universidad Autónoma Metropolitana, Xochimilco, Mexico) 9: 10–16.

Guion, R. M., and W. M. Gibson. 1988. "Personnel Selection and Placement." *Annual Review of Psychology* 39: 349–374.

Guiton, M., et al. 1973. *Psicología del Tortuador.* Buenos Aires: Rodolfo Alonso.

Hacker, F. 1973. *Agresión.* Trans. F. Formosa. Barcelona: Grijalbo.

Hassett, J., and H. Lacey. 1991. *Towards a Society that Serves its People: The Intellectual Contribution of El Salvador's Murdered Jesuits.* Washington, D.C.: Georgetown University Press.

Hess, R. D., and J. V. Torney. 1967. *The Development of Political Attitudes in Children.* Chicago: Aldine.

Heyward, H., and M. Varigas. 1973. *Antipsiquiatría.* Madrid: Fundamentos.

Hietanen, A. 1983. "The Militarization of Children: Some Trends." Presented at the Seminar on Children and War, Siuntio Baths, Finland, March 24–27.

Hoge, D. R., and R. De Zulueta. 1985. "Salience as a Condition for Various Social Consequences of Religious Commitment." *Journal for the Scientific Study of Religion* 24: 21–38.

Holmberg, M. 1984. "Children in Lebanon." In Rädda Barnen, 1984, pp. 27–28.

Hoppe, C. 1985. "Los Niños y la Guerra: Resumen de Investigaciones que Estudian Diferentes Aspectos sobre este Tema." Presented at Taller de Intercambio de Experiencias Sobre el Trabajo Psicosocial y Psicoterapéutico con los Niños y la Población Desplazada, sponsored by Rädda Barnen, Mexico, Feb. 18–22.

House, R. J., and J. V. Singh. 1987. "Organizational Behavior: Some New Directions for I/O Psychology." *Annual Review of Psychology* 39: 669–718.

Hurtado, T. M. 1986. "Organización: Necesidad y Experiencia de un Pueblo que Camina." *Estudios Ecuménicos* (Mexico) 6.

Ibisate, F. J. 1985. "Características y Resultados de la Gestión Económica." *Estudios Centroamericana* 43–44: 357–379.

Illich, I. 1971. *Deschooling Society.* Harmondsworth, Middlesex: Penguin.

INODEP. 1973. *El Mensaje de Paulo Freire: Teoría y Práctica de la Liberación.* Madrid: Marsiega.

Instituto de Investigaciones de la Universidad Centroamericana José Simeón Cañas. 1985. *Investigación: Desplazados y Refugiados Salvadoreños.* San Salvador: UCA.

Instituto de Investigaciones Económicas. 1983. "Hacia una Economía de Guerra: El Salvador 1982–1983." *Estudios Centroamericana* 415–416: 439–458.

Instituto de Estudios Centroamericanos and El Rescate. 1990. *The Jesuit Assassinations.* Kansas City: Sheed and Ward.

Insulza, J. M. 1982. "La Crisis en Centroamérica y el Caribe y la Seguridad de Estados Unidos." In CECADE and CIDE, *Centroamérica: Crisis y Política Internacional.* Mexico: Siglo XXI.

IUDOP (Instituto Universitario de Opinión Pública). 1988. "Debate Nacional 1988 (Anexo): Opinión del Pueblo sobre la Paz en El Salvador. Encuesta de Opinión Pública para el Debate Nacional." Convened by the Archbishop of San Salvador, San Salvador, June 17-Sept. 4.

Jaspers, K. 1913. *General Psychopathology.* Manchester, England: Manchester University Press, 1962. ,

Jervis, G. 1979. *Manual Crítico de Psiquiatría.* Trans. J. Jordá, N. Pérez de Lara, and R. García. Barcelona: Anagrama.

———— 1981. *Psiquiatría y Sociedad.* Madrid: Fundamentos.

Jodelet, D. 1984. "Représentation Sociale: Phenomènes, Concept et Thèorie." In Moscovici, 1984.

Kilham, W., and L. Mann. 1974. "Level of Destructive Obediance as a Function of Transmitter and Executant Roles in Milgram Obediance Paradigm." *Journal of Personality and Social Psychology* 5: 696–702.

Knutson, J. N. 1973. "Personality in the Study of Politics." In J. N. Knutson, ed., *Handbook of Political Psychology.* San Francisco: Jossey-Bass.

Kohn, M. L. 1963. "Social Class and Parent-Child Relationship: An Interpretation." *American Journal of Sociology* 68: 471–480.

———— 1969. *Class and Conformity: A Study in Values.* Homewood, Ill.: Dorsey Press.

La Fe de un Pueblo: Historia de una Comunidad Cristiana en El Salvador (1970–1980). 1983. San Salvador: UCA Editores.

Lane, S. T. M. 1985. "Linguagem, Pensamento e Representacoes Sociais." In S. T. M. Lane and W. Codo, eds., *Psicologia Social: O Homem em Movimento.* São Paulo: Ed. Brasiliense.

Langton, K. 1969. *Political Socialization.* New York: Oxford University Press.

Lasswell, H. D. 1949. "The Language of Power." In H. D. Lasswell and N. Leites, eds., *Language of Politics.* New York: G. W. Stewart.

———— 1948. *Power and Personality.* New York: Norton.

Latham, G. P. 1988. "Human Resources Training and Development." *Annual Review of Psychology* 39: 545–558.

Lawyers' Committee for International Human Rights. 1984. *El Salvador's Other Victims: The War on the Displaced.* New York: Americas Watch.

Lerner, M. J., and C. H. Simmons. 1966. "Observer's Reaction to the 'Innocent Victim': Compassion or Rejection?" *Journal of Personality and Social Psychology* 4: 203–210.

Le Vine, R. A. 1963. "Political Socialization and Culture Change." In C. Geertz, ed., *Old Societies and New States.* New York: Free Press.

Lewis, O. 1961. *The Children of Sanchez.* New York: Random House.

———— 1965. *La Vida: A Puerto Rican Family in the Culture of Poverty: San Juan and New York.* New York: Random House.

———— 1969. "The Culture of Poverty." In Daniel P. Moynihan, ed., *On Understanding Poverty.* New York: Basic Books.

Lewis, O., R. M. Lewis, and S. Rigdon. 1977a. *Four Men—Living the Revolution: An Oral History of Contemporary Cuba.* Urbana: University of Illinois Press.

———— 1977b. *Four Women—Living the Revolution: An Oral History of Contemporary Cuba.* Urbana: University of Illinois Press.

———— 1978. *Neighbors—Living the Revolution: An Oral History of Contemporary Cuba.* Urbana: University of Illinois Press.

Liem, R. 1987. "The Psychological Cost of Unemployment: A Comparison of Findings and Definitions." *Social Research* 54: 321–353.

———— 1988. "Unemployed Workers and Their Families: Social Victims or Social Critics?" In P. Voydanoff and L. Majka, eds., *Families and Economic Distress: Coping Strategies and Social Policy.* Newbury Park, Calif.: Sage.

Lindqvist, A. 1984. "Children in Lebanon." In Rädda Barnen, 1984, p. 29.

Lira, E. 1988. "Consecuencias Psicosociales de la Represión Política en Chile." *Revista de Psicología de El Salvador* 28: 143–159.

Lira, E., et al. 1984. *Psicoterapia y Represión Política.* Mexico: Siglo XXI.

Lira, E., E. Weinstein, and S. Salamovich. 1985–1986. "El Miedo: Un Enfoque Psicosocial." *Revista Chilena de Psicología* 8: 51–56.

Lofland, J., and N. Skonovd. 1981. "Conversion Motifs." *Journal for the Scientific Study of Religion* 20: 373–383.

Lomnitz. *See* Adler.

Lona, A. 1986. "Las CEBs y los Movimientos Populares en el Istmo." *Christus* (Mexico) 593.

Los Textos de Medellín y el Proceso de Cambio en América Latina. 1977. San Salvador: UCA Editores.

Madruga, J. M. 1987. "Comunidades Eclesiales de Base—Organizaciones Populares." *Estudios Sociales* (Dominican Republic) 69: 63–81.

Maira, L. 1982. "Fracaso y Reacómodo de la Política de Estados Unidos hacia Centroamérica." In L. Maira, ed., *La Política de Reagan y la Crisis en Centroamérica.* San José: EDUCA.

Marx, K. 1845. "Theses on Feuerbach." In K. Marx and F. Engels, *The German Ideology,* ed. C. J. Arthur. New York: International Publishers, 1969.

Mattelart, A. 1973. *La Comunicación Masiva en el Proceso de Liberación.* Buenos Aires: Siglo XXI.

———— 1978. "Ideología, Información, y Estado Militar." In Mattelart and Mattelart, 1978.

Mattelart, M., and A. Mattelart, eds. 1978. *Comunicación e Ideologias de la Seguridad.* Barcelona: Anagrama.

McClelland, D. 1961. *The Achieving Society.* Princeton, N.J.: Van Nostrand.

———— 1975. *Power: The Inner Experience.* New York: Irvington.

———— 1985. *Human Motivation.* Glenview, Ill.: Scott, Foreman.

McGuire, M. B. 1982. *Pentecostal Catholics: Power, Charisma, and Order in a Religious Movement.* Philadelphia: Temple University Press.

McLemore, C. W., and L. S. Benjamin. 1979. "Whatever Happened to Interpersonal Diagnosis? A Psychosocial Alternative to DSM-III." *American Psychologist* 34: 17–34.

McWhirter, L. 1983. "The Northern Ireland Conflict: Adjusting to Continuing Violence." Paper presented at the Seminar on Children and War, Siuntio Baths, Finland, March 24–27.

Millon, T. 1983. "The DSM-III: An Insider's Perspective." *American Psychologist* 38: 804–814.

Mischel, W. 1966. "A Social-Learning View of Sex Differences in Behavior." In E. E. Maccoby, ed., *The Development of Sex Differences.* Stanford: Stanford University Press.

Moffat, A. 1974. *Psicoterapia del Oprimido. Ideología y Técnica de la Psiquiatría Popular.* Buenos Aires: ECRO.

Montaner, C. A. 1988. "Por Que Fracasa Hispanoamérica." *El Nuevo Día* (Puerto Rico) (May 26): 73.

Montero, M. 1984. *Ideología, Alienación e Identidad Nacional: Una Aproximación Psicosocial al Ser Venezolano.* Caracas: Universidad Central de Venezuela, Ediciones de la Biblioteca Central (EBUC).

———— 1985. "La Psicología Política en América Latina. Una Revisión Bibliográfica: 1956–1985." Manuscript. Caracas: Departamento de Psicología Social, Escuela de Psicología, Universidad Central de Venezuela.

———— ed. 1987. *Psicología Política Latinoamericana.* Caracas: Panapo.

Montes, S. 1986. "El Problema de los Desplazados y Refugiados Salvadoreños." *Estudios Centroamericanos* 447–448: 37–53.

Morales, O. A. 1983. "Los Desplazados: Una Manifestación de la Crisis Actual." *Boletín de Ciencias Económicas y Sociales* (UCA, San Salvador) 4: 278–291.

Morán, M. C. 1983. "Un Centro de Desplazados." *Boletín de Psicología* (UCA, San Salvador) 9: 11–16.

Moscovici, S. 1972. "Society and Theory in Social Psychology." In J. Israel and H. Tajfel, eds., *The Context of Social Psychology: A Critical Assessment.* London: Academic Press.

———— ed. 1984. *Psychologie Sociale.* Paris: Presses Universitaires de France.

Neal, M. A. 1965. *Values and Interests in Social Change.* Englewood Cliffs, N.J.: Prentice Hall.

Niemi, R. G. 1973. "Political Socialization." In J. N. Knutson, ed., *Handbook of Political Psychology.* San Francisco: Jossey-Bass.

Olano, G. and M. Orellana. 1985. "Consideraciones sobre la Situación Financiera de las Cooperativas de la Fase I de la Reforma Agraria." *Boletín de Ciencias Económicas y Sociales* (UCA, San Salvador) 8: 77–94.

Peña, J. O. 1984. "Necesidades Familiares en un Grupo de Desplazados." *Boletín de Psicología* (UCA, San Salvador) 13: 18–20.

Piazza, T., and C. Y. Glock. 1979. "Images of God and Their Social Meanings." In R. Wuthnow, ed., *The Religious Dimension: New Directions in Quantative Research.* New York: Academic Press.

Pineda. *See* Gonzalez.

Poirier, J. 1970. "Formas de Impugnación, de Compensación y de Transposición de lo Real en las Sociedades en Vías de Desarrollo." In J. Lacroix, ed., *Los Hombres Ante el Fracaso.* Trans. J. Pombo. Barcelona: Herder.

Punamäki, R. 1982. "Conflict in the Shadow of War: A Psychological Study on the Attitudes and Emotional Life of Israeli and Palestinian Children." *Current Research on Peace and Violence* 1: 26–41.

———— 1987. "Psychological Stress Responses of Palestinian Mothers and Their Children in Conditions of Military Occupation and Political Violence." *Quarterly Newsletter of the Laboratory of Comparative Human Cognition* 9: 76–84.

Rädda Barnen, ed. 1984. *Child Victims of Armed Conflict.* Report on the Forum of Non-Governmental Organizations, Rome, April 28.

Ramirez, S. 1971. *El Mexicano: Psicología de sus Motivaciones.* Mexico: Pax-México.

Ray, J. J. 1988. "Cognitive Style as a Predictor of Authoritarianism, Conservatism, and Racism: A Fantasy in Many Movements." *Political Psychology* 9: 303–308.

Reich, W. 1933. *The Mass Psychology of Fascism.* New York: Farrar, Straus and Giroux, 1970.

Reimer, E. 1970. *An Essay on Alternatives in Education.* Cuernavaca: Centro Intercultural de Documentación (CIDOC).

Renshon, S. A. 1977. "Assumptive Frameworks in Political Socialization Theory." In Renshon, ed., *Handbook of Political Socialization: Theory and Research.* New York: Free Press.

Ressler, E. 1984. "Children in Lebanon." In Rädda Barnen, 1984, pp. 9–14.

Richard, P. 1983. "La Iglesia que Nace del Pueblo en América Latina: Su Historia, su Identidad y Misión en el Movimiento Popular." *Misiones Extranjeras* (Madrid) 78.

Richardson, J. T. 1985. "The Active Versus the Passive Convert: Paradigm Conflict in Conversion/Recruitment Research." *Journal for the Scientific Study of Religion* 24: 163–179.

Richelle, M. 1968. *Porquoi les Psychologues?* Brussels: Charles Dessart.

Rodriguez, M., L. Luzzi de Vidaurre, and O. E. Vidaurre. 1983. "La Participación de la Mujer en la Economía Salvadoreña." *Boletín de Ciencias Económicas y Sociales* (UCA, San Salvador) 6: 484–493.

Rolim, F. C. 1980. *Religiao e Classes Populares.* Petropolis, Brazil: Editora Vozes.

Rosenthal, G. 1982. "Principales Rasgos de la Evolución de las Economías Centroamericanas desde la Posguerra." In CECADE and CIDE, *Centroamérica: Crisis y Política Internacional.* Mexico: Siglo XXI.

Ross, C., J. Mirowsky, and W. Cockerham. 1983. "Social Class, Mexican Culture, and Fatalism: Their Effects on Psychological Distress." *American Journal of Community Psychology* 11: 383–399.

Rotter, J. B. 1966. *Generalized Expectancies for Internal Versus External Control of Reinforcement.* Psychological Monographs, 80.

Sabini, J. 1978. "Aggression in the Laboratory." In I. L. Kutash et al., eds., *Violence: Perspectives on Murder and Aggression.* San Francisco: Jossey-Bass.

Salazar, J. M. 1970. "Aspectos Políticos del Nacionalismo: Autoestereotipo del Venezolano." *Revista de Psicología* 1: 15–18.

——— 1983. *Bases Psicológicas del Nacionalismo.* Mexico: Trillas.

Salazar, J. M., and G. Marín. 1975. "El Fenómeno de la 'Imagen del Espejo' en las Percepciones Mutuas de Colombianos y Venezolanos." *Psicología* 4: 3–12.

Salazar, J. M., and C. P. Rodríguez. 1982. "Actitudes y Creencias en Relación con los Colombianos, Argentinos y Españoles entre los Venezolanos Residentes en Caracas." *Revista de la Asociación Latinoamericana de Psicología Social* 1: 3–20.

Salcedo, B. 1987. *Estudio del Crecimiento de la Iglesia Evangélica en El Salvador.* Presented at the Interdenominational Congress, San Salvador.

Santoro, E. 1975. "Estereotipos Nacionales en Habitantes de una Zona Marginal de Caracas." In G. Marín, ed., *La Psicología Social en Latinoamérica*. Mexico: Trillas.

Sayigh, R. 1977a. "The Palestinian Identity among Camp Residents." *Journal of Palestinian Studies* 4: 3–22.

—— 1977b. "Sources of Palestinian Nationalism: A Study of a Palestinian Camp in Lebanon." *Journal of Palestinian Studies* 5: 17–40.

Schacht, T., and P. E. Nathan. 1977. "But Is It Good for the Psychologists? Appraisal and Status of DSM-III." *American Psychologist* 32: 1017–1025.

Sears, D. O. 1974. "Political Socialization." In F. I. Greenstein and N. W. Polsby, eds., *Handbook of Political Science: Theoretical Aspects of Micropolitics*, vol. 3. Reading, Mass.: Addison-Wesley.

Segovia, R. 1977. *La Politización del Niño Mexicano*. Mexico: El Colegio de México.

Seminar on Children and War. 1983. Sponsored by the International Institute for Peace Studies of Geneva, the International Bureau for Peace, and the Peace Union of Finland, Siuntio Baths, Finland, March 24–27.

Sève, L. 1975. *Marxism and the Theory of Human Personality*. London: Lawrence and Wishart.

Sevilla, M. 1984. "Visión Global sobre la Concentración Económica en El Salvador." *Boletín de Ciencias Económicas y Sociales* 7: 155–190.

Sherif, M., and C. W. Sherif. 1964. *Reference Groups: Exploration into Conformity and Deviation of Adolescents*. Chicago: Henry Regnery.

Sidanius, J. 1985. "Cognitive Functioning and Sociopolitical Ideology Revisited." *Political Psychology* 6: 637–662.

—— 1988a. "Intolerance of Ambiguity, Conservatism and Racism—Whose Fantasy, Whose Reality?: A Reply to Ray." *Political Psychology* 9: 309–316.

—— 1988b. "Political Sophistication and Political Deviance: A Structural Equation Examination of Context Theory." *Journal of Personality and Social Psychology* 55: 37–51.

Silva Fuenzalida, I. 1972. *Marginalidad, Transición y Conflicto Social en América Latina*. Barcelona: Herder.

Sloan, T., and E. Salas. 1986. "El Papel de la Psicología Industrial en el Tercer Mundo: Analisís y Crítica." *Boletín de Psicología* (UCA, San Salvador) 26: 241–245.

Smith, D., and W. A. Kraft. 1983. "DSM-III: Do Psychologists Really Want an Alternative?" *American Psychologist* 38: 777–785.

Snow, D. A., and R. Machalek. 1984. "The Sociology of Conversion." *Annual Review of Sociology* 10: 167–190.

Sorin, M. 1985. *Humanismo, Patriotismo e Internacionalismo en Escolares Cubanos*. Havana: Ed. de Ciencias Sociales.

—— 1987. "América Latina: La Realidad Psicosocial del Cubano." *Boletín de Psicología* (UCA, San Salvador) 26: 301–305.

Sotelo, I. 1975. *Sociología de América Latina: Estructuras y Problemas*. Madrid: Tecnos.

Spielberger, C. D., I. G. Sarason, and N. A. Milgram, eds. 1982. *Stress and Anxiety,* vol. 8. Washington, D.C.: Hemisphere.

Stein, B. N. 1981. "The Refugee Experience: Defining the Parameters of a Field of Study." *International Migration Review* 15: 320–330.

Sudman, S. 1976. "Sample Surveys." *Annual Review of Sociology* 2: 107–120.

Szasz, T. S. 1961. *The Myth of Mental Illness.* New York: Delta.

Tajfel, H. 1981. *Human Groups and Social Categories.* New York: Cambridge University Press.

Tamney, J. 1984. "The Clergy and Public Issues in Middletown." Manuscript. Muncie, Ind.: Ball State University.

Téfel, R. A. 1976. *El Infierno de los Pobres: Diagnóstico Sociológico de los Barrios Marginales de Managua.* Managua: El Pez y la Serpiente.

Torres Rivas, E. 1981. *Crisis del Poder en Centroamérica.* Costa Rica: Cd. Universitaria Rodrigo Facio, EDUCA.

UNICEF. 1983. "Análisis Situacional de El Salvador." Mimeo.

Valverde, J. 1987. "Sectarismo Religioso y Conflicto." *Polemica* (Costa Rica) 3: 15–25.

Varela, J. 1971. *Psychological Solutions to Social Problems: An Introduction to Social Technology.* New York: Academic Press.

Vekemans, R., and I. Silva. 1970. *La Marginalidad en América Latina: Un Ensayo de Conceptualización.* Santiago: Centro para el Desarrollo Económico y Social de América Latina (DESAL).

Vidales, R. No date. "Crisis Capitalista e Iglesia en América Latina." Manuscript. Mexico: Centro Estudios Económicos.

Wallace, J., and E. Sadalla. 1966. "Behavioral Consequences of Transgression: The Effects of Social Recognition." *Journal of Experimental Research in Personality* 1: 187–194.

Walters, R. H. 1966. "Implications of Laboratory Studies of Aggression for the Control and Regulation of Violence." *Annals of the American Academy of Political and Social Science* 364: 60–72.

Walters, R. H., and M. Brown. 1963. "Studies of Reinforcement of Aggression: Transfer of Response to an Interpersonal Situation." *Child Development* 34: 563–571.

Watson, P. 1978. *War on the Mind: The Military Uses and Abuses of Psychology.* New York: Basic Books.

Weber, M. 1925. "Class, Status, Party." In H. H. Gerth and C. W. Mills, eds., *From Max Weber: Essays in Sociology.* New York: Oxford University Press, 1946.

——— 1904–1905. *The Protestant Ethic and the Spirit of Capitalism.* Trans. Talcott Parsons. New York: Scribner, 1958.

Weinstein, E. 1987. "Problemática Psicológica del Exilio en Chile. Algunas Orientaciones Psicoterapéuticas." *Boletín de Psicología* (UCA, San Salvador) 23: 21–38.

Weinstein, E., et al. 1987. *Trauma, Duelo y Reparación: Una Experiencia de Trabajo Psicosocial en Chile.* Santiago: Fasic/Interamericana.

Wells, J. 1987. *Empleo en América Latina: Una Búsqueda de Opciones.* Santiago: PREALC, Oficina Internacional del Trabajo.

White, R. K. 1966. "Misperception and the Vietnam War." *Journal of Social Issues* 22: 1–156.

Whitford, D. J. 1985. *Apuntes de Algunos Aspectos de la Historia de la Psicología en Nicaragua.* Managua: Universidad Centroamericana.

Zúñiga, R. 1975. "The Experimenting Society and Radical Social Reform: The Role of the Social Scientist in Chile's Unidad Popular Experience." *American Psychologist* 30: 99–115.

Acknowledgments

This book is a testimony to the international solidarity that Marín-Baró promoted, celebrated, and lived. In granting permission for the translations and publication, Fr. Rodolfo Cardenal, S.J., of the University of Central America, showed a confidence in our project and a trust in our judgment that we appreciate enormously, especially considering that he has never met us. Thanks to Charles Beirne, S.J., of the UCA, we were "introduced" to Fr. Cardenal. The Faculty Seminar on Central America at Swarthmore College, and particularly Hugh Lacey and John Hassett, were compañeros at every step of the process, providing moral and financial support and much good advice, for which we are very grateful. All of our translators were a pleasure to work with, and we thank them for their commitment to the project.

Frances Cuneo of Swarthmore compiled the extensive bibliography of Martín-Baró's works, and Catherine Ward-Seitz of Oakland and Ruth Waldvolgel of Switzerland worked tirelessly to help decide which essays should be included in the book. Elizabeth Lira in Chile, and José Guillermo Mártir and José Luís Enriquez of El Salvador thoughtfully reviewed the proposed table of contents and provided suggestions, as did members of the Boston chapter of the Committee for Health Rights in Central America, particularly M. Brinton Lykes and Ramsay Liem. The conscientiousness and solidarity of all these compañeros were much appreciated, and their contributions assured us that our selections were representative of Martín-Baró's prodigious output.

Andrea Soler, Carol Kessler, Eleanor Levine, Richard Bloom, Bobbie Baron, Bob Lassalle, Jeanie Morrow, Jan Austerlitz, and Rose Hauer all reviewed parts of the manuscript, while Caridad Alaco gave invaluable technical support, and Jeffrey Miller, Jeanette Sarmiento, Jerry Mandel, and Stewart Poritsky helped with details. To all of them, too, we are very grateful.

We also wish to thank Georgetown University Press and the Society for the Psychological Study of Social Issues for permission to reprint Chapters 1 and 8, respectively, and Blackwell Publishers for permission to reprint the table in Chapter 5.

In the spirit of the life and work of Ignacio Martín-Baró, we express our thanks to the University of Central America José Simeón Cañas and the Faculty Seminar on Central America at Swarthmore College, for carrying forward with their mission to support education and truth in El Salvador, and to CHRICA, the Committee for Health Rights in Central America, for its solidarity with the people of Central America in their struggle for justice. All proceeds from this book are being donated to these institutions, to further their excellent work.